Education
in Evolution

John Hurt

Education
in Evolution

Church, State, Society
and Popular Education
1800–1870

Rupert Hart-Davis   London

Granada Publishing Limited
First published in Great Britain 1971 by Rupert Hart-Davis Ltd
3 Upper James Street London W1R 4BP

ISBN 0 246 64041 3
Printed in Great Britain by Cox and Wyman
Fakenham

To Peter and Antony

Contents

Preface

By 1870, the year of the first Elementary Education Act, England and Wales already possessed a well-established elementary educational system. The bulk of the credit for this achievement must go, not to the voluntary societies, as is commonly supposed, but to that much-maligned figure, the Victorian civil servant. The officials of the Education Department performed their duties with such success that, when the decision was made to provide a school place for every child, they were able to take this enormous job in their stride. In this book the Revised Code is seen, not as a narrow-minded device that set English elementary education back for a generation, but as an important prelude to the 1870 Act. By simplifying the administrative process and making the school syllabus a predominantly secular one, Robert Lowe made future expansion possible and enabled the schools to meet the demands of a dynamic society and economy. The requirement that children should be able to read newspapers and books, with both profit and pleasure, write coherent letters to distant relatives, and know enough arithmetic to conduct everyday commercial transactions was far removed from the attitudes prevailing at the beginning of the nineteenth century. Then, it had been thought that universal education, far from benefiting the economy, would only disrupt it. If children were to be taught at all, their education was to be limited to the 'rudiments of letters and of morality and Religion'.

The key figure in the day-to-day work of the schools was the schoolmaster whose training is discussed in Chapter 5. When the first training colleges were established, England still lacked an adequate police force. The workhouse master and the schoolmaster were seen as the main agents for controlling the social unrest of the day. Hence Dr James Kay, the newly appointed secretary of the Education Department, saw that the schoolmaster had to be given a training that would not only enable him to discipline the masses but would also keep him subservient to his social superiors. Consequently it can be seen that Dr Kay—later Sir James Kay-Shuttleworth—and Robert Lowe had much more in common than has been previously supposed.

I wish to thank the authorities of the National Society and the governors of Hockerill College, Bishop's Stortford, Hertford-shire, for the research facilities they have given me. During the past few years I have also been helped by many other people. I wish to take this opportunity of thanking Professor F. M. L. Thompson of Bedford College, University of London, for super-vising my postgraduate studies, on which this work is primarily based. I also wish to express my gratitude to my colleagues, Dr P. S. Bagwell, Miss G. M. Horne, and Mr A. S. Taylor of the Polytechnic, Regent Street—to use an older and more familiar name—who have given freely of their time and advice over the course of the last few years. Finally I wish to thank Professor T. C. Barker of the University of Kent at Canterbury, first for asking me to contribute to this series and secondly for the con-structive advice and criticism he has so liberally given.

The Polytechnic of Central London.   J. S. Hurt

1 Schism and Cohesion

Are you pleased with the opportunity of getting learning? Which will be best, to read when you have no work, or to go sauntering and running about and getting into mischief? Are you obliged to the ladies and gentlemen who have provided Sunday schools for you?
Is it not a sign that they wish to see you good and happy?

MRS SARAH TRIMMER [*][1]

To render simple, easy, pleasant, expeditious, and economical, the acquisition of the rudiments of letters, and of morality and religion, is the leading object of Elementary Education.

THE REVEREND ANDREW BELL [†][2]

I have observed, with pain, the persevering efforts which have been made, in some parts of the country, to excite my subjects to disobedience and resistance to the law, and to recommend dangerous and illegal practices.

QUEEN VICTORIA [3]

The contrast between the readiness of the House of Commons to vote £70,000 for the repair of the Windsor Castle stables in 1839 and their reluctance to sanction a vote of £30,000 for providing schools for the children of the labouring poor is part of the lore of history. It has led posterity to underestimate the rapidity with which the new department of state established that year—the Committee of the Privy Council on Education—developed the English elementary educational system. Twenty-one years later, and ten years before the first Elementary Education Act, 1870, this government office had one of the largest administrative and clerical staffs of the Home Civil Service. More money was being spent on popular education in Great

[*] Sarah Trimmer, née Kirby (1741–1810): was an early pioneer of the Sunday school movement, authoress of a series of tracts and lesson books for children, and editress of the *Guardian of Education* (1802–6).
[†] Andrew Bell (1753–1832) founded the Madras (monitorial) system of education while serving with the East India Company (1787–96) and organized the teaching of the Madras system on behalf of the National Society, 1812–32.

Britain than on any other single project administered by a civil department. In 1860, the year in which the Education Department—the name by which the new government office in Downing Street was usually known—attained its majority it was already employing sixty inspectors. In the course of that one year alone these dedicated men had visited 10,403 schools and departments of schools* where they had found 7,249 certificated teachers and 14,403 pupil-teachers. They also went to thirty-eight training colleges containing 2,826 students. In the previous December they had examined not only all the training college students but a further 8,826 candidates. Some of them were the pupil-teachers at various stages of their training, others had completed their five years' apprenticeship and were seeking admission to a training college. Last, the group included a number of older teachers who, although they were already employed in the schools, had never been to a training college. Among these candidates were former pupil-teachers and evening-school teachers, with at least three years' experience, and other serving teachers who were over the age of twenty-two. They were being examined for their teacher's certificate, a qualification which would not only enable them to earn a higher salary but also entitle the schools in which they served to an annual grant. Before being admitted to the examination they had had to obtain a favourable report on their teaching ability from an inspector.[4] Finally, the much-travelled inspectors had made 426 visits to schools for pauper children where they saw 27,728 pupils,† and seventy-two ragged or industrial schools attended by 6,172 pupils.[5]

Clearly such a volume of work as this could never have been performed by those sickly youths whom Sir Stafford Northcote and Sir Charles E. Trevelyan alleged in their report had entered the civil service 'simply on account of its being a profession in which their health was less likely to break down than in any

---

* Mixed schools under one certificated teacher counted as one unit. A school in which boys and girls were taught separately under a certificated master and a certificated mistress was counted as two units or departments. In a very large school the provision of separate accommodation for the teaching of infants under a certificated infants' mistress constituted a third department.
† This figure includes 2,720 children present in workhouse schools that were visited twice during the year. Some of these children are counted more than once in the total number.

other'[6] or because they had 'failed elsewhere'.[7] On the contrary the Department's inspectors, who travelled the length and breadth of Great Britain by its rapidly expanding railway system, were amongst the hardest worked of all mid-nineteenth-century government officials. Similarly, the administrative staff in London included some of the most scholarly and cultured men who have ever sat behind a civil servant's desk.

The educational system that was developed in the nineteenth century still affects the structure and practice of our educational system today. That is why, for instance, 'the head is the boss'. 'The law says nothing specific about what should be taught in schools apart from religious instruction: this has to be provided, though not by the headmaster himself, who can opt out of it on grounds of conscience. Legally he would be within his rights if he divided the curriculum between Esperanto and basketball. The education committee would object, but a man who could concoct a philosophy to support his eccentricity would be hard to shift.'[8] Schools, however, are concerned with more than mere 'instruction'. 'Education is the influence exercised by adult generations on those that are not yet ready for social life. Its object is to arouse and to develop in the child a certain number of physical, intellectual and moral states which are demanded of him by both the political society as a whole and the special *milieu* for which he is specifically destined.'[9] Moreover, if we are to understand why England has been described as 'the most highly stratified of all modern western societies', we must examine the circumstances in which the modern educational system was developed and analyse the values it was designed to transmit from one generation to another. In attempting this task we must remember: 'The structure of education in a society is determined by seven factors: social stratification, job opportunities, religion, theories of social control, demographic and family patterns, economic organization and resources, and finally political theory and institutions.'[10]

'In the years between 1780 and 1832', Dr E. P. Thompson has observed, 'most English working people came to feel an identity of interests as between themselves, and as against their rulers and employers.'[11] The former social order in which the labouring classes had deferred to their social superiors was gradually being undermined by the new forces of industrialization and urbanization. A society with its communities of interests, in which such social divisions as existed were drawn vertically, was replaced by one in which the social strata ran horizontally. The phrases, 'the lower orders' and 'the poor', with their connotation of a patient and uncomplaining acceptance of the *status quo* were replaced by the new term 'the working class'. The new nomenclature carried with it overtones of conflict and antagonism.

Early educational enthusiasts, however, were quick to see that the traditional social values might be safeguarded by giving the children of the labouring poor a godly and religious upbringing. The effect of building a school, Joseph Lancaster* reassured his readers in 1806, would be 'that in a town exposed to all the evils of dissipation and vice, usual in commercial towns, where the rising generation are training up in ignorance, wickedness, and forgetfulness of God, very large numbers will soon be training in his fear; in the knowledge of his ways; and in the daily remembrance of his *commandments*'.†[12]

Over this issue Nonconformist and Anglican alike were in agreement. 'In every instance...under my observation in this kingdom', the Reverend Andrew Bell wrote in 1813, 'and in every report with which my brethren have honoured me of the effect produced by the Madras system in their parishes, the improvement in the subordination, and orderly conduct, and general behaviour of the children, has been particularly noticed, and must be regarded as infinitely the most valuable part of its character.'[13]

At first it had seemed that the need to solve the social problems of the day was so pressing that the rival denominations would be prepared to sink their differences. The British and Foreign School Society was founded in 1808. Its object was to propagate the nonsectarian system of education that Lancaster was developing in his school in the Borough Road. By this time Lancaster

* Joseph Lancaster (1778–1838), the son of a shopkeeper, became a Quaker and developed a system of monitorial education which he practised in his school in the Borough Road, London, founded in 1803. Dispirited through ill-health, poverty and a quarrel with the British and Foreign School Society, he later emigrated to the New World, visiting the U.S.A., Venezuela and Canada. He died in New York in 1838.
† Lancaster's italics.

was already a national figure. Through the good offices of his friend William Corston, one of the founder members of the Society, Lancaster had met George III at Weymouth in 1805. At this interview the King had pledged the support of the royal family. The meeting had concluded with the well-known phrase: 'It is my wish that every poor child in my dominions should be taught to read the Bible.' Support for the royal policy of educating the children of the labouring poor, the dependent classes, in the one basic skill of reading was widespread. Thanks to the royal precept, subscriptions for the year 1805-6 came not only from members of the royal family but also from six bishops, the lesser ranks of the clergy, and members of both houses of Parliament.[14]

Pedagogically the plans of Lancaster and Bell, the leading Nonconformist and Anglican advocates of the monitorial system, had much in common. At a time when there were hardly any schoolmasters worthy of the name, they had provided a solution to the problem of bringing literacy to the masses as quickly and as cheaply as possible. By using young children as monitors, or assistants, and breaking the learning process down into the smallest possible steps, they hoped that one master would be able to teach a thousand children, at one and the same time. Bell also thought that the classics could be taught in this way. Since histories of education describe the method at length, one example will suffice. 'In the syllabic lessons', Bell instructed, 'the words, whatever be the number of syllables of which they consist, are read in the first instance, syllable by syllable, as if they were monosyllables, thus...mis-re-pre-sen-ta-ti-on...'[15] In the eyes of the schoolmaster the monitorial system had one great advantage: his role was a supervisory one only. 'The great advantage', Bell wrote, 'is that it is his chief business to see that others work, rather than work himself; and that he is most usefully employed in doing what men in general are most ready to do.' By the 1840s, however, the halcyon days were over. The schoolmaster was expected to do his daily stint of teaching by going round the classes and taking over from his monitors as occasion required.[16]

The rapid development of a system of education under the aegis of a Nonconformist soon alarmed the Anglican Church. The Church of England felt itself threatened by Lancaster's assertion that education ought to be a national concern. The Anglican claim to a monopoly of the country's education, medieval in origin, was based more immediately and substantially on the Act of Uniformity of 1662. From 1698 onwards, Anglicans had provided educational facilities at the charity school level through the Society for Promoting Christian Knowledge. Thus Nonconformists, as the name of their society – the *British and Foreign* School Society – implies, were challenging the Anglican Church's assertion that it was the rightful schoolmaster of the nation. Moreover, Lancaster provided a nonsectarian education. His policy of not allowing the teaching of any 'peculiar creed', the only one that Nonconformists could possibly pursue if they were to command wide support, posed yet another challenge to Anglican pretensions. The Anglican counter-attack was led by Mrs Trimmer who in 1805, the year of Lancaster's audience of the King, asserted that Dr Bell was 'the originator of the admirable plan which Mr Lancaster has adopted'. As for his abjuration of any specific doctrine she tartly observed: 'I know of no *peculiar creeds* but those which constitute an essential part of the *National Religion*.'*[17] The debate that Mrs Trimmer had initiated on the identity of the inventor of the monitorial system was both profitless and irrelevant. This method of teaching had been used in Paris as early as 1747.[18] In form the question at issue was which of the two men could claim credit for having originated the new method. In substance the issue at stake was whether or not the Established Church was going to retain its former control over the education of the people.

In a sermon preached at St Paul's Cathedral in 1811, the Reverend H. Marsh, successive Bishop of Llandaff and Peterborough, rallied the faithful to the cause. The danger facing Anglicans was that 'children educated in such seminaries [the Lancastrian or British schools] would acquire an indifference to the Established Church'. 'And not only indifference but secession would result.' Hence in his peroration he exhorted his congregation, 'If we cannot recall the thousands who have deserted the Church, let us redouble our efforts to retain the faithful band, which rallies round her standard...For this purpose we must

* Mrs Trimmer's italics.

associate among ourselves.'[19] Four months later, in October 1811, the National Society for Promoting the Education of the Poor in the Principles of the Established Church was founded. This society, with a committee consisting of the archbishops and bishops of England and Wales, was in effect the education committee of the Anglican Church.

Despite the early appearance of these differences, all hope of cooperation was not yet lost. In 1818 the Select Committee on the Education of the Lower Orders stated: 'They have the greatest satisfaction in observing, that in many schools where the national system is adopted, an increasing degree of liberty prevails, and the Church catechism is only taught, and attendance at the established place of public worship only required, of those whose parents belong to the establishment.' They thus felt able to recommend that the village schoolmaster should be appointed by the parish vestry. To safeguard the position of the dissenters they added that their children should not be forced to learn any catechism or attend any church other than that of their parents.[20] In making these suggestions the Select Committee had undoubtedly been influenced by the evidence given by William Allen, the secretary of the British and Foreign School Society, who claimed that, 'since no proselytising is made in any of our schools...the Church of England is peculiarly indebted to this institution; for while we hold it a duty not to attempt to proselytise any of their children, we collect them from the streets, and are the means of sending thousands of them to the places of worship belonging to the establishment, most of whom, in all probability, would rarely, if ever, have attended at any divine service.'[21] Two years earlier, the Reverend T. T. Walmsley, the secretary of the National Society, had professed an equal readiness to let children remain loyal to the faith of their parents. As a result they had, he said, children of all denominations, even Jews, in their schools.[22]

Over the course of the next twenty years religious antagonism increased. At the same time the need to combine for the sake of maintaining law and order became greater. The National Society, reflecting the changing attitude of its parent body, became more and more intransigent. The repeal of the Test and Corporation Acts in 1828, followed by the grant of Catholic emancipation in 1829, did much to deprive the Established

Church of its former pre-eminence. The publication of the *Extraordinary Black Book* in 1831, the reform of Parliament the following year, and the proposal made in 1833 to secularize part of the revenue of the Irish bishoprics showed that the Church of England, if it was to survive, had to put its own house in order. John Keble's sermon on 'National Apostasy' heralded the counter-attack of the Oxford Movement. Three years later, in 1836, the appointment of a board of ecclesiastical commissioners with powers to reallocate the wealth of the Church, removed its more indefensible anomalies and thereby cut the ground from beneath its radical critics' feet. Churchmen were thus able to speak with a new confidence and boldly assert that the 'Church was the recognized and authorized instrument of education in this country'.[23] By the late 1830s the religious differences had become irreconcilable and the suggestion, put forward in 1818, for the building of nondenominational schools had become an impracticability. The Select Committee on the Education of the Poorer Classes of 1838 were unable to find a way out of the impasse. 'Under [the] existing circumstances,' they reported, 'and under the difficulties which beset the question, your committee are not prepared to propose any means for meeting the deficiency [in school places] beyond the continuance and extension of the grants which are at present made by the Treasury for the promotion of education through the medium of the National and the British and Foreign School Societies.'*[24]

The strength of the religious controversy, coupled with the deep entrenchment of existing vested interests, delayed yet another much-needed reform in education. As a result of a recommendation made by the 1818 Select Committee, a body of 'commissioners to enquire concerning charities in England for the education of the poor' had been appointed.† Publication of its reports began to show how widespread was the misappropriation of funds originally intended for education. The condition of Berkhamsted Grammar School in the County of Hertfordshire, for example, attracted particular notoriety during the mid-1830s. The headmaster, Thomas Dupré, who had inherited

* Treasury grants to assist the building of new schools were paid between 1833 and 1839, see pp. 27–28.
† Other charities in England and Wales were brought within its competence the following year.

the post from his father, had enjoyed an income of £250 a year since 1805. For the greater part of this time he had resided neither at the school nor at Willoughby, Lincolnshire, where he held a living. At first the salary of the usher, £125 5s. 4d., had been drawn by his brother. This sinecure had then passed to an old friend and eventually to Dupré's fourth son. By adhering rigidly to the terms of the original endowment which only allowed for the teaching of Latin and Greek to the children of Berkhamsted, the staff were able for over thirty years to avoid the inconvenience of having pupils on the foundation of the school.[25]

The publication of the carefully documented reports of the Charity Commissioners suggested a way in which the educational problem might be solved without involving the state in any extra expenditure. The Poor Law Commissioners of 1834, for example, ended their report with this recommendation: 'We believe that if the funds now destined to the purpose of education, many of which are applied in a manner unsuited to the present wants of society, were wisely and economically employed, they would be sufficient to give all the assistance which can be prudently afforded by the State.'[26] Although contemporary estimates put the annual value of these funds somewhere between £1,500,000 and £3,000,000, nothing came of the suggestion.[27] Throughout the great debates of 1839, the idea that had been put forward only five years earlier was never seriously pursued.

A major objection to the plan was that it would have raised the religious issues in a particularly acute form. Although contemporaries almost unanimously agreed that education had to be both religious and moral, they could not agree either on the kind of religious education that was to be given, or on how it should be imparted. In some respects Nonconformists, despite the recent repeal of the Test and Corporation Acts, remained second-class citizens. Faced with the exclusivist demands of the Anglican Church, they feared that any system of general education would give insufficient protection to minority groups. At the height of the crisis of April 1839, for example, William Lucas, a Quaker of Hitchin, wrote in his diary: 'Great exertions are now being made by the Church to get the education of the poor throughout the kingdom into the hands of the clergy, and to introduce the catechism, thus establishing what has been called the National system.' He feared that if a Tory government came to power it would 'take the means of education from the liberal and dissenting portion of the community ... and confide them to the priesthood, who after opposing every obstruction to the progress of light and knowledge in vain, now want it in their own hands to render it as nugatory and illiberal as possible, professing a wonderful zeal and friendship all at once for the cause of education.'[28] The fears that Lucas expressed should not be lightly dismissed. When the downfall of Lord Melbourne's administration seemed imminent in November 1839, *The Times* hailed the prospect of the formation of a Tory government with enthusiasm: 'The day of retribution is at hand, and the church will regain her rights.'[29]

For their part Anglicans felt apprehensive about the long-term effects of a policy of providing a nonsectarian education. The teaching of other creeds, under the umbrella of the state, would undermine their own position still further. It would result in 'placing the blaspheming Jew, the idolatrous Romanist, the Unitarian denying his Christ, or the sensual Turk on the same level as the humble and adoring believer of the Son of God'.[30] A plan that allowed instruction in all creeds 'would afford little security for the teaching of religion at all, and would introduce so much discrepancy, and so many errors and contradictions'.[31] The doors of the schools, the Archbishop of Canterbury declared, 'would be thrown open to the installation of the principles of every sect, however wild or extravagant'.[32]

Special provision for dissenters would also have involved the separation of secular from religious education. This, the Bishop of London thought, 'would thrust religion into the bye-ways and corners, deprive religion of her due honour and degrade her from her just supremacy'.[33] Apart from Francis Place* who bluntly stated that 'teaching reading, writing and arithmetic with the plain-sailing parts of morality had no more to do with religion than shoe-making had',[34] there were few who were prepared, in public, to remain unmoved by such a dire prognosis.

More generally acceptable was the ultra Tory Sir Robert

---

* Francis Place (1771–1854) by means of a library made his tailor's shop in the Charing Cross Road a well-known centre for the dissemination of radical ideas in the London area.

Inglis's* assumption that 'knowledge unless sanctified by religion was an unmitigated evil' and that 'religion was the main object of education'. Less acceptable, though, was his conclusion that 'since the Church...was the source from which the people should derive instruction, it was only when education flowed from the national church, that the legislature was justified in diverting any portion of the national funds to this object'.[35] Furthermore, the Church of England, together with the Tory party, could act as the natural rallying point for all who wished to conserve the existing social order. The Church, Sir Robert Peel told the House of Commons in 1839, was 'now awakened to the absolute necessity of assuming that position which she ought to assume, in constant and cordial cooperation with the landed proprietors, and other influential classes of this country'.[36] What was good for Peelite conservatism, the forging of an alliance with the landed classes and the emergent *bourgeoisie*, was also good for the Church of England.

By the late 1830s the course of events outside the House of Commons had created a sense of urgency. 1830 had been the year of agrarian disturbances in the South and East of England. The rising of the rural proletariat had shown that 'a hitherto inert mass, active at best in a few scattered areas and villages, was capable of large-scale, coordinated or at least uniform action over a great part of England'.[37] Amongst the propertied classes the fear still remained that the countryside might rise again in conjunction with the urban proletariat whose increasing restlessness was manifested in growing trade union activity and Chartism. With these considerations in mind, R. A. Slaney, the M.P. for Shrewsbury who had been the chairman of the 1838 Select Committee, warned the House of Commons the following year that 'If they did not give the humbler classes of society the means of obtaining a good practical education, in a short time it would be found that those people were not to be ruled by any government which could be found either on this or the other side of the House.'[38] On one point at least, Anglican, dissenter and secularist

* Sir Robert Inglis (1786–1855) was M.P. for Dundalk (1824–6), for Ripon (1828) and for the University of Oxford (1829–54). The champion of the Protestant Church, he became known as 'the Member for Heaven' because of his opposition to such measures as the repeal of the Test and Corporation Acts, the grant of Catholic emancipation and the admission of Jews to Parliament. He also opposed the reform of Parliament in 1832.

alike could agree. The building of more schools would help to prevent the social unrest of the day from escalating into widespread revolution.

One of the leading advocates of a policy of controlling the lower orders of society by means of a suitable education was Dr James Kay who became the secretary of the Committee of the Privy Council on Education on its establishment in 1839. Sir James Kay-Shuttleworth's experiences (he assumed the additional name on his marriage in 1842 and was created a baronet in 1849) had given him a knowledge of the urban and rural working classes that few could rival. As a doctor to the Ardwick and Ancoats dispensary in Manchester he had seen some of the worst of the social conditions that uncontrolled industrialization could produce. He had then served as an assistant Poor Law Commissioner in East Anglia where he was given first-hand accounts of the recent disturbances. The parishes in one district, for example, before the implementation of the Poor Law Amendment Act, 1834, had 'accumulated within their limits a lawless population of paupers, disbanded smugglers and poachers, who extorted the scale allowance from the reluctant overseers by threats of violence'. In another parish 'the windows of the [workhouse] dining hall were so much broken by the practice of throwing stones at the governor as he passed through the hall, that the meals of the inmates could not be served except by daylight, as no candle could be kept lighted in the room'.[39]

As early as 1832, Dr Kay (as he then was) had warned the propertied classes of the danger of neglecting the social problems of the day. 'The operative population constitutes one of the most important elements of society,' he wrote, 'and when numerically considered, the magnitude of its interests and the extent of its power assumes such vast proportions, that the folly which neglects them is allied to madness. If the higher classes are unwilling to diffuse intelligence among the lower, those exist who are ever ready to take advantage of their ignorance; if they will not seek their confidence, others will excite their distrust; if they will not endeavour to promote domestic comfort, virtue, and knowledge among them, their misery, vice, and prejudice will prove volcanic elements, by whose explosive violence the structure of society may be destroyed.'[40]

In 1839 Dr Kay produced a semi-official apologia for the new government department created that year. In it he described the great change that he thought had taken place in the moral and intellectual state of the working classes during the previous half-century. 'Formerly, they considered their poverty and sufferings as inevitable...', he wrote, 'now, rightly or wrongly they attribute their sufferings to political causes; they think that by a change in their political institutions their condition can be enormously ameliorated.' After referring to the development of Luddism and trade unionism, he asserted that the anarchical spirit of the Chartist association which was developing would 'if left to the operation of the causes now in activity, become every year more formidable'. With his East Anglian experiences evidently much in mind, he thought that the condition of rural society gave a similar cause for concern. 'The abuses of the Poor Law, together with the almost universal neglect of instruction, have reduced this class to a state of mental and physical torpor.' This apathy, though, could not be taken for granted. He went on to warn that the labourers 'sought to extort by fear what they could no longer procure by virtuous exertion. Property seemed [to be] their enemy, therefore they wrapped in one indiscriminating flame the stacks and homesteads of the southern counties, seeking the improvement of their lot by the destruction of capital.' The remedy for these evils was to provide 'a good secular education to enable them to understand the true causes which determine their physical condition and regulate the distribution of wealth among the several classes of society'. This would secure to them 'useful knowledge and...guard them against pernicious opinions'.[41]

Kay-Shuttleworth also apparently shared the commonly accepted belief that any form of secular instruction had to be combined with careful moral and religious instruction. In his evidence to the Select Committee of 1838 he stated that pauper children should be given an education that would train them to habits of usefulness, industry and virtue. 'For this purpose,' he said, somewhat reservedly, 'the Bible, the Testament, the Book of Common Prayer, and the Church catechism are considered essential school books.'*[42] 'The great object to be kept in mind,' he wrote in a report to the Poor Law Commissioners, 'in

* The exact nature of Kay-Shuttleworth's religious beliefs is only one aspect of this man's life that requires much further research.

regulating any school for the instruction of the children of the labouring class is the rearing of hardy and intelligent working men, whose character and habits shall afford the greatest amount of security to the property and order of the community. In industrial training...it is chiefly intended that the practical lesson, that they are destined to earn their livelihood by the sweat of their brow, shall be inculcated.'[43]

The idea that instruction in a simple trade or craft could be used as a means of giving both vocational and social training was a widely shared one. 'You will find,' one pamphleteer wrote, 'no means more powerful of enlivening the sluggish and taming the stubborn tempers than digging and singing. Let a boy only dig heartily, and sing cheerfully, and we shall make something of him, without many hours of poring over books and slates, or without drawling out pages of reading.'[44] Similarly, training in knitting, straw-plaiting and coarse-needlework was thought to be particularly suitable for poor little boys under the age of ten. Such instruction, it was held, 'would be found useful as a means of early instilling the principle that manual work is honourable; and that children come to school not only to learn to read and cypher, but to get their living, in that state of life into which it has pleased God to call them'.[45]

By the late 1830s, though, it was no longer sufficient to teach children the traditional virtues of willing subjection to their social superiors, gratitude to them for their charity and meekness of spirit.[46] Although such teaching was appropriate to the calmer waters of the eighteenth century, it provided an unseaworthy craft for the turbulence of the nineteenth. Earlier men had demanded cheaper food, now they demanded higher wages and a redistribution of property. A growing working-class consciousness had to be fought on its own ground. If the labouring classes were to be reconciled to a nascent capitalist society, they had to be taught the principles of *laissez-faire* economics. An anonymous contributor to the *Quarterly Journal of Education*, a publication of the Society for the Diffusion of Useful Knowledge, accordingly pointed out that an education that was confined to the teaching of reading and writing 'is incomplete and may, indeed, be perverted to the very worst purposes. They [the labourers] should, first of all, be made acquainted with the motives which have induced every society emerging from bar-

barism to establish the rights of property; and the advantages resulting from its establishment, and the necessity of maintaining it inviolate, should be clearly set forth... The circumstances that give rise to those gradations of rank and fortune that actually exist ought also to be explained: it may be shown that they are as natural to society as differences of sex, of strength, or colour... and that equality...violently and unjustly brought about could not be maintained for a week.'[47]

The National Society also looked to the secular arm for assistance. The two spheres, the temporal and the sacerdotal, were neatly straddled by Richard Whateley, Archbishop of Dublin, whose *Introductory Lectures on Political Economy* were published by the Society for Promoting Christian Knowledge in a simplified version for schools as *Easy Lessons on Money Matters for the Use of Young People*.[48] Usually, though, the National Society relied on religious instruction as an antidote to social unrest. The possibility that reading the Scriptures might have as socially inflammatory an effect as perusing the *Poor Man's Guardian*, 'a mischievous penny publication, which was circulated with a very pernicious effect',[49] never seems to have been seriously considered.

So strong and unshaken was the belief in the efficacy of this well tried method of combating social unrest that the National Society argued that 'the [1842] disturbances were caused not so much by physical as by moral destitution; they arose not so much from the cravings of want as from the promptings of an undisciplined and disaffected spirit'[50]. The Society reported: 'In whatever districts Church principles predominated, no disorder took place, however grievous the privations of the people, except in cases where the rightly disposed inhabitants were overpowered by agitators from a distance.'[51] Accordingly a special appeal was launched for raising funds with which to build schools and train teachers for the mining and manufacturing districts. By 1845, £151,985 had been collected for fighting what the National Society described as 'the holiest war that has ever [been] waged— a war against ignorance, vice, and infidelity'.[52]

An uneasy ally of the National Society in this crusade was the state. The first tentative steps towards the assumption of responsibility for the education of the poor had been taken in

Ireland, that great experimental administrative laboratory of the nineteenth century. As early as 1813 the Dublin Education Society, later known as the Kildare Place Society, which had been founded with the help of Lancaster, had received a grant of £7,000. From 1813 onwards it obtained an annual subsidy that gradually rose from £10,000 to £30,000. A policy of supporting a voluntary agency eventually led, as it did in England, to the appointment of a specialist government agency. The Board of National Education in Ireland, formed in 1831, was the Hibernian precursor of the Committee of the Privy Council on Education.

Meanwhile in Great Britain, the only help either society received from the government came indirectly. The British and Foreign School Society had enjoyed the patronage of successive monarchs from the reign of George III onwards. On the other hand its attempts to obtain help from the government, despite its appeals in 1814 and 1823, were unsuccessful.[53] In contrast, the National Society fared better. On a number of occasions, when its funds were in danger of exhaustion, the Society appealed to the Crown, the titular head of the Church, for help. In response, a series of royal letters, in which the clergy were instructed to lubricate the generous impulses of their congregations by preaching special sermons, was issued. As the following table shows, royal exhortation gave a valuable boost to the Society's bank balance:

Table I YIELD OF THE ROYAL LETTERS

1823	£32,710
1832	£23,470
1837	£24,802
1840	£26,527
1842	£33,383
1846	£27,167

Source: *Reports of the National Society, 1830–49, passim.*

Of all the arguments that were used to persuade the propertied classes to subscribe to the building of schools, that of the need to avert revolution was the most effective. Chartist leaders, albeit unintentionally, were more successful in loosening the purse strings of the charitable than were the incumbents of the throne. The total yield of the six letters was only £16,000 more than the sum raised after the troubles of 1842. Furthermore, despite the remarkable success of that particular appeal, the royal letter of that same year was the most successful of the six.

The National Society also enjoyed, from time to time, the privilege of a free cover for the transit of its mail. This concession was first granted in June 1815 for the circulation of a subscription list. June 1815, however, was the month of the Battle of Waterloo. The National Society, anxious to avoid a clash with the appeals being made on behalf of the dependants of those killed in battle, prudently delayed sending out its requests for subscriptions until the following January.[54] In 1831 the Society carried out a statistical survey of the educational facilities offered by the Anglican Church, without having to pay any postal charges. Although the initial 12,000 or more questionnaires were circulated in this manner, the Society was not allowed to send reminders, free of charge, to the 2,013 places from which no reply had been received.[55] The rival society was less fortunate. In his evidence to the Select Committee of 1834, Henry Dunn, the secretary, took care to point out that the British and Foreign School Society had received no help at all. As a result, the expense of postage had been instrumental in preventing them from obtaining a correct list of all the schools conducted on their system.[56]

Further references to applications for free covers occur in the National Society's minute books for 1834, 1835 and 1836. The outcome of the first two requests is not recorded, that of 1836, however, was successful. The minutes show that after the concession was granted, the committee resolved to take on an extra clerk to handle the work involved in making a 'general inquiry into the state and progress of Sunday and all other Church of England schools'.[57] Lastly if the arrangements made for the circulation of the royal letter of 1832 provide a reliable guide,[58] the National Society enjoyed the further boon of being relieved of the considerable postal charges it would have incurred in sending out copies of the royal letters before the establishment of a uniform postal rate in 1840.

In 1833 the state, which so far had worked on a semi-official basis through the two societies, supplemented its previous policy of indirect help with the offer of a direct subsidy of £20,000 to assist them in building new schools. After the defeat of a number of measures to set up rate-aided schools, the government accepted the fact that it had no alternative but to work in cooperation with the existing voluntary organizations. Bills allowing the levying of a rate for education had been defeated in 1807 and 1820. A third attempt was made in 1833 when John Roebuck had introduced a bill to make provision for compulsory education. The debate that took place on his proposal produced one result. On Saturday 17 August a thinly attended House of Commons voted £20,000 for the building of school houses in England and Wales. Then on 29 August the Factory Act, shorn of a clause that would have allowed the raising of a penny rate to subsidize the building of schools for children working in the factories, received the Royal assent. The next day a Treasury minute was published that offered to meet half the cost of building new schools. Voluntary contributions were to cover the other half. So as to help the manufacturing districts as much as possible, the minute directed that 'a preference be given to such applications as come from the larger cities and towns, in which the necessity of assisting in the erection of schools is most pressing'.[59] This was the only provision that was made from public funds for meeting the cost of implementing the education clauses in the Factory Act of 1833.

When the grant was renewed the following year, the Treasury found that the outstanding applications of the two societies amounted to £44,238. It was accordingly decided to help those schools 'where the number of scholars proposed to be educated is in the proportion of two to every pound applied for' and to offer the balance on the same principle, i.e. £1 for every two scholars.[60] Four years later, the Treasury refused to give grants for what appeared to be Sunday schools only.[61] Such schools provided little if any secular instruction. In 1833 the Reverend J. C. Wigram, the secretary of the National Society, had condemned the practice of teaching writing on Sunday. In some schools, he stated, it was held out as a bait to attract those who did not value religious instruction for its own sake. 'It is vain to hope,' he added, 'that the purest doctrinal truths can counteract the evil which will arise from this habitual desecration of the Lord's Day.'[62] In these circumstances the Treasury quite rightly thought that the limited funds available could best be used by giving day schools priority over those that were open only on Sunday.

The grant was renewed annually until the end of 1838. By this time the shortcomings of the system had become manifest. 'The consequence of this loose administration was such as might have been foreseen,' wrote an official of the Education Department nearly fifty years later. 'The schools were constructed on no approved plan...There was no security for the efficiency of the instruction, or even for the maintenance of the fabric; and, as a fact, the buildings were often seen in a few years to be falling into ruin, or serving to house an admittedly inefficient school.'[63]

If the late 1830s posed a new problem, they also provided central government inspection, that great administrative device of the decade, as a means of tackling it. The first example of this came with the appointment in 1832 of two part-time inspectors of anatomy. They were quickly followed by others for factories in 1833, the relief of the poor in 1834, and prisons in 1835. Despite these precedents, however, the Treasury handed over the task of inspecting the new schools built with the help of public money to the societies. It also gave them £500 apiece to help to meet the cost.[64] The National Society, which, through its secretary, Wigram, had informed the Select Committee on Education in 1838 of its implacable opposition to any form of inspection not under its exclusive control, had won the first round in a fight that was to bedevil the early months of the life of the Committee of the Privy Council on Education.[65]

It is hard to blame the government for compromising at this stage. To some extent it had been playing the role of the sorcerer's apprentice since 1833. By making what were virtually unconditional grants, it had enabled the societies to expand their activities and thereby reinforce their claim to being regarded as the legitimate agencies for the education of the people. This helped to encourage not only their mutual intransigence but also their jointly shared uncompromising attitude towards the state. Consequently when Lord John Russell opened a debate on education in February 1839 he had to confess that the government's freedom of manœuvre was severely restricted. In other countries, he stated: 'The government had from the beginning undertaken the task of educating the people.' In England the ground was already occupied by the 'Established Church, and in other parts by the Wesleyans and other dissenting societies, which gave education according to their own religious principles'. It was thus impossible for the government to introduce its own scheme of education without 'doing violence to the habits and feelings of the people of this country'. Consequently Lord John Russell was forced to admit that once again the state had no alternative but to cooperate with the voluntary societies who were the 'recognized and established modes' for the promotion of popular education.[66]

The events of the next few months showed just how unsatisfactory was the arrangement that had been made. On 7 August, two days after the publication of the relevant minute, the National Society was asked to forward a report of the results of its inspection of the Society's new schools. In reply, the Society pointed out that their rivals, the British and Foreign School Society, were also receiving £500 for inspecting 117 completed schools and forty-three that were still under construction. The corresponding figures for the National Society were 427 and 265 respectively. Although its request for more money was turned down, it secured, probably for the last time, a free cover for the returns that had to be submitted by each school. 'My Lords will not object,' the Treasury's letter of 3 September stated, 'to such returns being directed to their Lordships' secretary at the Treasury, the letters being headed "School Return" on the outside. That by this course, the charge of postage will not be incurred; but the papers will be liable to be opened, in case it should be deemed necessary on account of any enclosures.' By the following January, T. Spring Rice, the Chancellor of the Exchequer, was becoming impatient for the report. 'I shall be questioned on the subject, I have no doubt,' he wrote, 'and papers will be moved for.' Despite the National Society's assurance that it would send the report by Easter, a further reminder had to be sent on 17 July. Five days later, the long-awaited document was dispatched.[67]

Meanwhile the Select Committee on the Education of the Poorer Classes in England and Wales had published its report. Its main findings were: (1) That in the Metropolis and the great towns of England and Wales, there exists a great want of education among the children of the Working Classes. (2) That it is desirable that there should be means of suitable daily Education (within the reach of the Working Classes) for a proportion of not less than one eighth part of the population.[68]

It was clear that the state needed to do more than just distribute grants to those areas that were fortunate enough to win a prize from the Treasury in the annual lottery. The unsuitability of this department as an instrument for implementing an expansionist education policy was commented on by Thomas Wyse, M.P. for Waterford City, who was also the secretary of the Central Society of Education. During a debate in the House of Commons that took place on 12 February 1839, Wyse pointed out that the Treasury had failed, despite its stated intention, to appoint any inspectors. 'As to other duties,' he added, 'they seem never to have been thought of.' £10,000 allocated for the building of a normal school remained unemployed. The composition of books had not even been contemplated—no report beyond the mere number of scholars, and other more material circumstances, had ever been laid upon the Table of the House. Of all bodies, the Treasury, from the nature and multiplicity of its duties, and the qualifications of its members, was in his opinion the least likely to be well fitted for the purpose of distributing the grant of £20,000 that the House 'in the abundance of their generosity' had voted.[69]

'Still much remains to be done,' Lord John Russell informed the Lord President of the Council in a letter he had laid before the House on the day of the debate in which Wyse took part, 'and among the chief defects yet subsisting may be reckoned the insufficient number of qualified schoolmasters, the imperfect mode of teaching which prevails in the greater number of schools, the absence of any sufficient inspection of the schools, and examination of the nature of the instruction given, the want of a Model School which might serve for the example of those societies and committees which anxiously seek to improve their own methods of teaching, and, finally, the neglect of this great subject among the enactments of our voluminous Legislation. Some of these defects,' the letter continued, 'appear to admit of an immediate remedy, and I am directed by Her Majesty to desire, in the first place, that your Lordship, with four other of the Queen's Servants, should form a Board or Committee, for the consideration of all matters affecting the Education of the People.'[70] Lord Lansdowne obeyed the Royal Command. On 10 April 1839, the Queen's Most Excellent Majesty in Council ordered 'that the Most Noble Henry Marquis of Lansdowne,

Lord President of the Council; the Right Honourable John William Viscount Duncannon, Lord Privy Seal; the Right Honourable Lord John Russell, one of Her Majesty's Principal Secretaries of State; and the Right Honourable Thomas Spring Rice, Chancellor of Her Majesty's Exchequer, be and they are hereby appointed a Committee to superintend the application of any Sums voted by Parliament for the purpose of promoting Public Education.'[71]

The new Committee set to work the next day. It displayed an extraordinary lack of political awareness by resolving 'not to adhere invariably to the rule which confines grants to the National Society and the British and Foreign School Society and not to give preference in all cases whatever to the school to which the largest proportion is subscribed'. This proposal, which was not repudiated until July 1840,* laid the way open for the creation of a state-sponsored system of education. Two other equally contentious plans were put forward. Firstly, it was decided that a model or normal school should be built for the training of teachers. Secondly, a decision was made 'to appoint inspectors, not exceeding at first two in number, to carry on an inspection of schools which have been or may be hereafter aided by grants of public money, and to convey to Conductors and Teachers of Private Schools in different parts of the country a knowledge of all improvements in the art of teaching, and likewise to report to this Committee the progress made in education from year to year'.[72] The project of building a normal school can be dismissed briefly. The suggestion was made that an Anglican chaplain should be appointed and that ministers of other sects should be allowed to visit the students. It will be readily appreciated that the objections of the religious societies proved insuperable and that the Committee deemed it politic to abandon the scheme less than two months later.[73]

After announcing a tactical withdrawal on one front the state determined to take a firm stand, the same day, at a point of strategic importance on another. 'The Committee recommend,' the Minute of 3 June 1839 continued, 'that no further grant be made, now or hereafter, for the establishment or support of Normal Schools, or of any other Schools, unless the right of

* See p. 35.

inspection be retained, in order to secure a conformity to the regulation and discipline established in the several Schools, with such improvements as may from time to time be suggested by the Committee.' The reiteration of the Committee's intention to appoint inspectors to secure conformity to a uniform system of education alarmed all those who distrusted the idea of state interference in education. Anglicans had an especial cause for alarm. It seemed as if the Education Committee, which was an exclusively lay body, was going to deprive them of what they regarded as their inalienable right of supervising the instruction of the nation in the doctrines of their Church. On 5 July, the Archbishop of Canterbury led the attack by persuading the House of Lords to approve a series of resolutions condemning the government's policy. He then headed a delegation of peers to the Queen.

A few days later, with the peers' address to the throne rejected, the Church swung into action through the agency of the National Society. At a meeting on 12 July, Lord Ashley successfully moved the motion 'that under the circumstances, and the constitution of the Board of the Privy Council, and the terms of the two minutes, it is inexpedient that the National Society should accept or transmit any application for a grant of money'. Three days later, further resolutions were adopted which showed that the National Society was prepared to cooperate with the state only on its own terms. They stated their readiness to make applications for grants not inconsistent with the principles of the National Society and to set up their own scheme of inspection 'as soon as their organization is complete, and they are furnished [by the government] with adequate pecuniary means'.[74]

These proposals were flatly rejected by Kay-Shuttleworth on the grounds that it would have been impossible for the Privy Council to present faithful reports to Parliament if they were based solely on the statements of the National Society's own inspectors. In an attempt to allay their fears he asked Dr Otter, who had been the principal of King's College, London before his elevation to the See of Chichester, to nominate an inspector 'solely for the purpose of visiting the National schools'. 'The high character of this prelate,' Kay-Shuttleworth hopefully wrote on 17 July, 'and the eminent place which he held at the head of a seat of learning founded and supported by the Primate and other distinguished members, both lay and clerical of the Established Church, will be a guarantee to the National Society of the friendly intentions of the Committee.'[75] Even this did not satisfy the National Society for as they pointed out in reply, although a particular bishop was making the nomination, the inspector was going to be designated 'Their Lordships' Inspector'. 'Furthermore the result of inspecting secular to [the] exclusion of religious instruction would be the encouragement of the former to the disparagement of the latter... Parents... and still more [the] children, will naturally undervalue lessons to which no attention is paid on the day of the examination.' Their letter then reached the crux of the argument. 'For the government to insist...that, because it has contributed one third or one fourth towards the erection of the mere building, it shall be entitled to inspect, *and perhaps eventually to control*,* the entire discipline and economy of the school, upon principles contrary to the wishes of the other subscribers, would be a pretension hardly to be justified.'[76]

Shortly afterwards the National Society broke off negotiations. Some idea of the atmosphere of these critical months can be derived from a consideration of two further incidents. Towards the end of September Harry Chester, the Assistant Secretary of the Education Office, sent a note by hand to the offices of the National Society asking for a copy of a circular, dated the previous day, that they were about to send to their subscribers. Although Chester added that the Committee of the Privy Council was due to meet on the day of his note, his request was refused. Not until four days later was he sent a copy of the circular together with a formal and stilted apology.[77] At the end of the next month the Society began to consider a problem raised by the Reverend J. Gratrix, the Rector of Halifax, who asked whether they were 'prepared to allow instruction in the catechism to be omitted in the case of factory children who were under compulsion to attend and whose parents object.' Consideration of the issue was deferred until a special meeting took place at the end of April with the two archbishops and nine bishops in attendance. Finally in mid-May an equivocal resolu-

* Author's italics.

34

tion that threw the responsibility back upon Gratrix was adopted.[78]

The deadlock between Church and state was broken by a meeting between the Marquis of Lansdowne and the Bishop of London at which the Lord President conceded the point that the Committee of the Privy Council 'would be happy to avail themselves of the assistance of the Archbishops and Bishops who are members of the Privy Council and are usually consulted as to ecclesiastical matters, in the appointment of any inspector'. The Marquis then evidently continued to sound out opinion for, in a letter written to the Archbishop of Canterbury describing the course of events, he added that 'since the meeting with the Bishop of London he had been led to believe that it might prove more satisfactory...if the appointment of an inspector...were submitted to the Archbishop for his separate approbation as the supreme ecclesiastical authority in such province'.[79]

The full extent of the state's surrender can be seen from a careful study of the Concordat reached with the Archbishop of Canterbury on 15 July 1840. No person was to be appointed as an inspector of Anglican schools save with the concurrence of the archbishop of the appropriate province. Inspectors were to be appointed during pleasure, each archbishop having the power to withdraw his concurrence upon which the authority of the inspector lapsed. What was to happen if the state wanted to dismiss an inspector who continued to enjoy the support of his Primate was left for posterity to decide. Instructions with regard to religious instruction were to be framed by the archbishops, and were to form part of the general instructions to the inspectors. In turn, the general instructions had to be communicated to the archbishops before they were finally sanctioned. Inspectors were to send copies of their reports to their masters, the Committee of the Privy Council, the Archbishop of the province and the bishop of the diocese. Lastly brakes were put on the pace of educational advance in the poorer areas. It was agreed 'that the grant of money be in proportion to the number of children educated, and the amount of money raised by private contribution, with the power of making exceptions in certain cases, the grounds of which will be stated in the annual Returns to Parliament'.[80] Thus those districts too impoverished to afford

35

Anglican schools were not going to be allowed to have non-sectarian ones built for them by the state.

Just as the Concordat preserved ecclesiastical control at the top, so did the terms of the instructions to inspectors preserve it at the bottom. In drafting them care was taken to see that the autonomy of the school managers, in effect the clergy of the parish, remained inviolate. Hence the duties of the inspectorate were so carefully defined that their role became an advisory but in no way a regulatory one. 'My Lords,' said the instructions issued in August 1840 for the guidance of new entrants, 'have in view the encouragement of local efforts for the improvement and extension of elementary education ... The employment of inspectors is therefore intended to advance this object, by affording to the promoters of schools an opportunity for ascertaining at the periodical visits of inspection, what improvements in the apparatus and internal organization of schools, in school management and discipline, and in the methods of teaching have been sanctioned by the most extensive experience. The inspection of schools aided by public grants is, in this respect, a means of cooperation between the Government and the committees and the superintendents of schools...; you are in no respect to interfere with the instruction, management, or discipline of the school, or to press upon them any suggestion that they may be disinclined to receive... It is of the utmost consequence that you should bear in mind that this inspection is not intended as a means of exercising control, but of affording assistance...the Inspector having no power to interfere, and not being instructed to offer any advice or information excepting where it is invited.' A similar repudiation of the intent expressed in the Minute of 3 June 1839 preceded the lengthy questionnaire that the inspector had to complete on each school he visited. 'These questions,' the inspector was warned, 'are not to be received as an indication, in any respect, of what the Committee of Council consider desirable, either as respects the method or the matter of instruction, but as a means of collecting the facts in each case... Neither is the inspector to receive those enquiries as an exposition of the extent to which, in the opinion of the Committee, intellectual instruction should proceed.'

The retreat did not stop here. In 1840 Kay-Shuttleworth, who only the previous year had stressed the importance of the part that a good secular education could play in the process of social regeneration, had to write, 'Their Lordships are strongly of opinion that no plan of education ought to be encouraged in which intellectual instruction is not subordinate to the regulation of the thoughts and habits of the children by the doctrine and precepts of revealed religion.' Anglican inspectors were accordingly given precise instructions about the inquiries they were to make. On the matter of church attendance alone, they were told: 'The inspector will inquire, with special care, how far the doctrines and principles of the church are instilled into the minds of the children. The inspectors will ascertain whether church accommodation, of sufficient extent, and in a proper situation, is provided for them; whether their attendance is regular, and proper means taken to ensure their suitable behaviour during the service; whether inquiry is made afterwards by their teachers how far they have profited by the public ordinances of religion which they have been attending.'[81] The detailed nature of the inquiries that had to be made into the teaching of religion made it the most searchingly examined of all school activities. When it is remembered that the Bible was often used as a reading book and that history and geography lessons frequently had a scriptural content, it will be realized that many Church schools were little more than state-subsidized extensions of the Established Church.

The magnitude of the concessions that the state had to make to secure acceptance of its system of inspection demonstrates the success and confidence with which the Church exploited its newly revived social and political strength. Fortunately for dissenters, the decision to make popular education the concern of the state was taken after they had secured full civil rights. By 1839, the principle of religious exclusiveness, under which the Church of England would have secured full control, was no longer the principle of the state. Unfortunately for the state, the decision to make popular education the concern of the state came a generation too late. Twenty-five years earlier, when religious tension was less, agreement between the various parties might have been secured more easily. But twenty-five years earlier, the necessary money would not have been forthcoming. In 1815 there had been concern about the dangers that would result from educating the labouring classes; in 1839 there was concern about the consequences of leaving them in ignorance. Yet even then the forces of obscurantism nearly prevailed. The House of Lords had approved the primates' motion by a majority of 111; the House of Commons which had decided, by a majority of five to go into committee of supply to consider the education vote, had voted supply by the even narrower majority of two.

2 'No man can serve two Masters'

I assert that it is an impossibility for any inspector to report on the individual qualifications of any considerable number of children...He knows nothing of the individuals in [a school]; and it would be an intolerable waste of time if he were even to endeavour to make himself acquainted with their names.

E. CARLETON TUFNELL[*1]

Mr Cook says that he should 'see the staple work of a school of 150 boys very easily in about an hour and a half', and that in that time 'he should hear every boy read, should see the writing of every boy, and try the arithmetic, and in fact go through all'.

THE NEWCASTLE COMMISSIONERS[2]

Consideration and indulgence, the virtues of the private man, may easily become the vices of the public servant; and...I think that in the inspection of schools there is a peculiar temptation to exercise these qualities unduly.

MATTHEW ARNOLD[†3]

Equal in political delicacy to the task of negotiating the terms of the Concordat with the Anglican Church was another, that of recruiting the first members of the school inspectorate. Since so much of the future success of the Department depended on the personality and integrity of these officials, they had to be chosen with great care. In an attempt to assuage the fears of the Established Church, the right of nominating the first Anglican

* E. Carleton Tufnell (1806–86), son of the M.P. for Colchester, was educated at Eton and Balliol College, Oxford (First in Maths, 1828). He was co-founder with Kay-Shuttleworth of the Normal School at Battersea, assistant Poor Law Commissioner and inspector of workhouse schools. He served on the Royal Commission on the Employment of Children (1862–7) and also on the Royal Commission for the Employment of Women in Agriculture (1867–71).
† Matthew Arnold (1822–88) was the first son of Thomas Arnold, headmaster of Rugby School (1828–42). He was educated at Winchester and Rugby Schools, Balliol College, Oxford (English Verse Prize, 1843, second class Lit. Hum., 1844) H.M.I. (Her Majesty's Inspector) (1851–83), Professor of Poetry at Oxford (1857–67), and he served on the Newcastle Commission (1861) the Taunton Commission (1865) and the Cross Commission (1886).

inspector had been given to Dr Otter, the Bishop of Chichester. His previous tenure of the principalship of King's College, London, made him a man of impeccable qualifications. This college had been opened in 1831 as the Anglican riposte to the foundation, three years earlier, of University College, London, 'that godless institution in Gower Street'. The Bishop chose John Allen, who had been placed in the *senior optime* class in the mathematical tripos at Cambridge in 1832. Allen had then become a lecturer in mathematics and chaplain at King's College. When Dr Otter had been elevated to the episcopate, he had shown his high regard for Allen by making him the examining chaplain for his diocese at the early age of twenty-six.[4]

Hugh Tremenheere, who was to be for a short time the first inspector of Nonconformist schools, seems to have had equally sound credentials. After taking his degree at New College, Oxford, in 1827, he had been called to the Bar. By 1838 he had become a revising barrister on the western circuit. Here he had met E. W. Pendarves and Sir Charles Lemon who were Members of Parliament for Cornwall. With William Erle, another barrister on the same circuit, the two M.P.s had supported Tremenheere's attempts to become an inspector with the new government department. By 1839, Tremenheere's reputation was more than a local one. He had established himself in the wider field of the political and literary circles of the day through his contributions to the Whig periodical, the *Edinburgh Review*.[5] He possessed also the added advantage that his interest in education was well enough known for that high Tory and Anglican newspaper, *The Times*, to announce the news of his eventual appointment with moderate approval: 'We understand that Mr Tremenheere has been selected on account of the attention which he has for a considerable time past most assiduously paid to the discipline and methods of teaching in the most approved schools which this country contains.'[6]

The two nominees were summoned for interview before an enlarged Committee of the Privy Council on 29 November 1839. Possibly because of the difficulties facing the government, the President of the Board of Trade, the Rt Hon. H. Labouchere, the Judge-Advocate-General, Sir George Grey, and Lord Monteagle had been appointed to the Committee three weeks earlier.[7] Lord Monteagle, formerly Thomas Spring Rice, while holding office as the Chancellor of the Exchequer, had been involved in extensive but unsuccessful negotiations with the National Society since 1835 when the Treasury had offered £10,000 for the building of a Normal or Model school. It is unlikely that his appointment gave the Committee's deliberations that infusion of political skill and sensitivity that its resolutions of the previous April showed it so badly needed. That same month he had shown his lack of sympathy with the issues at stake by informing the National Society: 'I have always thought, and still think, that more good, and above all, more rapid good, would have been done, if it had been practicable to bring the two Societies under one general rule; all that was wanting was, that your rule respecting catechism should not have been enforced in the case of dissenters.'[8]

When Allen and Tremenheere were interviewed on 29 November, negotiations between the Established Church and the Committee over the question of the inspection of Church schools had reached a state of deadlock. Hence it was only possible to offer them work on a part-time basis. Their Lordships 'having in view that the duties of the inspectors will not at present occupy the whole of their time, but will require that they hold themselves in readiness to obey the directions of this Committee' decided to employ them on a daily basis, as and when they were required. They were to be paid two guineas a day for inspecting schools in the London area and an extra guinea, together with travelling expenses, for any work they did outside London.[9]

Since only Allen and Tremenheere were called for interview, their appointment might seem to be yet another example of the way in which the patronage system traditionally operated. What is not known, however, is how many other applicants, if any, had already been eliminated by some earlier informal screening process. Moreover, the Education Department was established at a time when the civil service was undergoing reform. It was throwing off its eighteenth-century legacy of inefficiency and beginning to adapt itself to the demands imposed on it by the industrialization of the nineteenth. In 1836, Sir Henry Taylor, later an Assistant Secretary to the Colonial Office, had suggested that candidates for the public service should be recruited from the ranks of those who had distinguished themselves academically.

He proposed that nominations should be made by the heads of colleges and masters of the great schools. 'In addition,' he wrote, 'our periodical literature furnishes one great index; debating clubs are another field.'[10] Thus the appointment to the civil service of Allen and Tremenheere by the outward form of the methods of the eighteenth century did more than help to assuage Anglican suspicion and satisfy Whig reformist opinion. It met the needs of a more dynamic age for honest and efficient administration.

From the start the scope of the inspectors' duties was expanded to include the making of special reports. Less than a month after his appointment Tremenheere, for example, was instructed to make a visit to South Wales and report on the state of education in the Newport area where there had been an uprising at the beginning of November.[11] The making of the Concordat inevitably increased the amount of work required of the two inspectors. In February 1841 they were put on a full-time and permanent basis and given an annual salary of £600, as from the beginning of the year, plus their 'actual costs of locomotion'.[12] The subsequent growth of the inspectorate can be seen from the following table.

Table I THE GROWTH OF THE INSPECTORATE

Year	Inspectors	Assistant Inspectors	Inspector's Assistants
1840	2	—	—
1843	3	—	—
1846	8	—	—
1849	21	—	—
1852	23	2	—
1855	29	10	—
1858	30	16	—
1861	36	25	—
1864	62	—	14
1867	Figures not available		
1870	62	—	18
1871	73	—	28

Source: *Returns Relating to Inspectors and Assistant Inspectors*, P.P. 1861, XLVIII, p. 2 (338). *Reports of the Committee*, 1864–71, *passim*.

The first two inspectors had been particularly fortunate. In 1848 the Select Committee on Miscellaneous Expenditure observed:

'The salaries of the inspectors appear high; even if it should be thought necessary to give them to persons of collegiate education, they exceed the usual average of pay to curates in this country, the class of gentlemen with whom they would appear to be in a somewhat similar position. When the system is more fully developed, Your Committee think they might be reduced.'[13] The hint was soon taken. By 1850, newly appointed inspectors had been put on the lower annual salary of £450.[14] At the same time younger men from the universities were being recruited into the new grade of assistant inspector at £250 a year, a salary that still gave them roughly twice as much as they could normally have expected as curates. In addition they all received an allowance of 15s. a day for personal expenses for every day 'not taken as a holyday'. The Committee of Inquiry which investigated the organization of the Privy Council Office in 1853 thought that this system was unsatisfactory. 'The daily allowance,' they stated, 'occasioned scruples as to the employment of their time, which were a cause of disquiet to delicate minds, without, in fact, conducing to any advantage as regards the public service... [It] discourages them', the Committee added, 'from taking holydays even to the extent necessary for their health, and consequently for their efficiency as public servants.' They accordingly recommended that the daily allowance should be commuted to an annual one of £250. They also drew up an incremental salary scale that rose from £200 to £600 by triennial increases of £50. These increments, though, could be raised to £75 at the discretion of the Lord President.[15] There can be little doubt that the earlier salary level of £600 had been not so much the rate for the job as the rate designed to attract Allen and Tremenheere into the inspectorate. Once the Education Department had become established as a permanent institution, it was realized that school inspection could offer a young man in holy orders a career for life. Hence a graduated salary scale was introduced which, in financial terms, compared favourably enough with normal promotion prospects in the Established Church for the Department to be able to take its pick of young Oxford and Cambridge graduates.*

The introduction of the Revised Code in the early 1860s

See pp. 174-5.

which required the examination of every child in reading, writing and arithmetic brought the inspector more work. As compensation he was offered an extra £50 a year if he performed the herculean task of examining 12,000 children. To help him with his extra duties the new grade of inspector's assistant was created. The assistants, recruited from the ranks of certificated teachers, were strictly confined to routine examination work. The Department was at great pains to avoid the furore that would have arisen if ex-schoolmasters had been allowed to cross the demarcation line between examination of the children and inspection of the schools. Inspectors were told: 'It is only by your thoroughly comprehending the limited and subsidiary character of the assistant's duty that you will repel the imputation of setting a young man to judge his elders, and often his superiors, in the art of school keeping. The assistant has no such judgement to deliver; he has only to see certain exercises performed, and to mark them one by one for the inspector.'

The salary of the inspector's assistant rose from £100 a year by increments of £10 to £250. He could supplement this with a bonus of a penny for every child he examined up to a limit of £50. Since he had no other duties to perform, he did not become eligible for any extra money until he had already tested 12,000 pupils. When travelling he was expected to have less expensive tastes than his principal. His lodging allowance was limited to 12s. 6d. a week.[16]

The passing of the Elementary Education Act of 1870 necessitated an expansion and reorganization of the inspectorate. A new grade containing ten senior inspectors was created. Their salary was £700 a year plus an allowance of £50 for taking charge of a district. Meanwhile, inspectors stayed on their old scale of £200 to £600. Their assistants, profiting from the upward trend of schoolmasters' salaries that began after 1870, were given an extra £25 a year and the slightly more generous lodging allowance of 7s. 6d. a night.[17]

There can be no doubt that in many cases this money was well earned. The work load imposed on the individual inspector made him, in theory, one of the hardest worked of all Victorian civil servants. Faced with the virtually impossible task of reconciling the conflicting demands of all who were concerned with education, his daily round was often unenviable and frustrating. He was expected to safeguard the interests of his secular masters by ensuring that the money they offered was well spent. At the same time he had to respect the autonomy of the school manager. His instructions specifically stated that he was 'in no respect to interfere with the instruction, management, or discipline of the school, or to press upon them [the school managers] any suggestion that they may be disinclined to receive... the inspector having no power to interfere, and not being instructed to offer any advice or information except where it is invited'.[18]

Even then some clergy preferred to have nothing to do with the Education Department. As late as 1867 Lord Robert Montague, the Vice-President of the Department, quoted the following letter in the House of Commons. 'Reverend and dear Sir—Do not pronounce me discourteous for declining to receive you on the 23rd instant [July] in your capacity of government school inspector. I deprecate official visits, from any quarter, to clergymen's schools, deeming them inexpedient and intrusive; and, although pecuniary assistance would be most acceptable, I prefer the alternative of complete independence.'[19]

The strongest opposition to state intervention came from the two extremes of the religious spectrum. Within the Church of England the Tractarian party, inspired by the œcumenical claims of the Oxford Movement, made a stand for exclusive clerical control over education. If they accepted any help from the state it was to be on their terms only. Two of the leading personalities were Henry Manning, who later became a cardinal in the Roman Church, and Archdeacon Denison. G. A. Denison, Archdeacon of Taunton from 1851 onwards, was also the incumbent of East Brent in South Devon. His living he owed to the good offices of his brother, the Bishop of Salisbury. A vacancy had occurred while the brother was temporarily in charge of the neighbouring diocese of Bath and Wells which contained the parish of East Brent.

Shortly after his induction, Denison took objection to the way in which inspectors' reports were forwarded to the archbishop. The fact that he could make an issue such as this a matter of public controversy well illustrates the difficulties facing the

Committee and its inspectorate. The Concordat had stipulated that when the inspector presented any report to the Committee he was to send a duplicate to the appropriate bishop and archbishop. The letter of instructions to H.M.I.s (Her Majesty's Inspectors) of August 1840, however, stated that he was to send the duplicate through the Committee office to the archbishop. Denison argued that this arrangement meant that the Church and state were not being treated as concurrent authorities. He accordingly stated that he was not going to allow any inspector into his school in the future. Thereby he defied the Department, for his school had earlier received a building grant and was thus liable to inspection. He also withdrew his application for an annual grant under the recently published minutes of 1846 with what he described as the utmost thankfulness. To his dying day he held the Department at bay. No inspector was ever allowed into the parish school, and he remained steadfast in his belief that the grant was the bribe of a traitor.[20]

Another group that was not prepared to accept help from the government was the Congregational Board of Education. Up to the date of the foundation of this body, Congregationalists had worked with the British and Foreign School Society, but 'the introduction into Parliament of a bill for the furtherance of education in the manufacturing districts [Graham's Bill] led to the formation of a separate organization to promote popular education partaking of a religious character, and under no circumstances receiving aid from public money administered by Government'.[21]

Until their disbandment in 1867 they went it alone with such determination that the Reverend W. J. Unwin, the principal of their training college at Homerton, was able to tell the Newcastle Commission in 1861 that they had already sent out about 373 teachers. This they had done despite their belief that 'the receipt of public money raised by taxation, and granted by Government for sustaining the Christian religion' violated their principles. Their objection was that the grant 'equally aids all varieties of religious creed; thus setting aside the supremacy of truth, and creating a precedent for bringing all forms of religious teaching under state pay'.[22]

The clergy of the various denominations were not always the

worst culprits. One inspector, the Reverend F. C. Cook,* thought that it was frequently the opposition of the lay managers that was decisive in making it impossible for the clergy to have their schools inspected. Another inspector, the Reverend J. J. Blandford† suggested that the real reason for their opposition was not a fear that the state would eventually usurp the functions of the lay managers altogether, but that they were unwilling to make any improvement to their schools. One group of managers, he reported, had said to him of their old schoolmaster: 'He is very incompetent, but we like him for he gives us no trouble, and is very civil.' Blandford explained that 'he duly touched his cap when he met any of the managers, and never troubled them to get books or maps, or blackboard, or any other apparatus necessary to the efficient carrying on of the school.'[23]

Some of the clergy were daunted by the prospect of having to deal with an impersonal bureaucracy for the first time in their lives. Previously they had been able to settle their parochial affairs by informal social contact through their rural dean or the bishop of their diocese. If they were J.P.s, they had transacted their administrative duties through the chairman of the county Quarter Sessions. Now they had to write to the offices of the National Society and the Education Department in London. 'Correspondence with a public office is so novel a matter to the clergy and proprietors of these outlying parishes,' the Reverend J. P. Norris‡ stated in 1866, 'that they are more repelled by the formidableness of the correspondence than by any other reason.'[24]

Some of the difficulties were of their own making. They seldom realized that their first step was to write a short letter asking either the Department or the Society for an application

---

* F. C. Cook was educated at St John's College, Cambridge (fourth classic, 1828). He was inspector of schools for the London diocesan board (1842–4), H.M.I. (1844–64) and Canon of Exeter (1864–89). He was also an eminent Egyptologist and Hebrew scholar, contributed to numerous theological works, and was editor of the *Speaker's Commentary* (1871–88).

† J. J. Blandford was the son of a clergyman. He was educated at Rugby and Christ's College, Cambridge (B.A., 1839). He held various clerical posts, and was H.M.I. (1847–93).

‡ J. P. Norris, the son of a physician, was educated at Rugby and Trinity College, Cambridge (seventh classic, 1846, Latin essay prize, 1848, Fellow, 1848). He was H.M.I. (1849–64) and Canon and later Archdeacon of Bristol (1864–91).

form for a grant. They frequently wrote long letters setting out the history of their schools and followed them up with a visit to the offices. So frequent was this practice that Harry Chester, the Assistant Secretary, thought it advisable to point out that a short note would suffice: 'Sir, have the goodness to send me the forms for an application for a grant to build a school.' The public had little idea, he complained, of how much the time of public officers was wasted and their tempers tried by unnecessary interviews.[25]

Such was the inexperience of the clergy that, when they received a reply in the name of 'My Lords', they thought that it came direct from the Lord President and his colleagues and not from a clerk in the office. 'The majority of rural clergymen,' Robert Lowe* somewhat unkindly remarked on one occasion, 'think that there is always a Board sitting round a table with a green cloth, and wax candles burning.'[26]

It is inevitable that the vociferous minority who protested against government inspection have left more evidence of their views than have those who quietly accepted it and even welcomed the expertise the inspector had to offer. Correspondence between the Hertfordshire Diocesan Board and the Department suggests that there was a greater and much more widespread readiness to cooperate with the central government than is usually held to be the case. In turning down a request made by the Hertfordshire Board in 1850 for the appointment of more inspectors, R. R. W. Lingen,† Kay-Shuttleworth's successor, wrote, 'to visit each school at least once a year, another nine inspectors would be required, and a very much larger addition would be required to meet the proposals of the memorialists of

---

* Robert Lowe, 1st Viscount Sherbrooke (1811–92) held office under Aberdeen and Palmerston, in 1852 and 1855. He was Vice-President of the Committee of the Privy Council on Education (1859–64) introduced the Revised Code, led the Adullamites in opposition to the Reform Bill of 1866, was Chancellor of the Exchequer (1873–4) and Home Secretary (1880).

† R. R. W. Lingen (1819–1905), the son of a Birmingham manufacturer, was educated at Bridgnorth Grammar School, and Trinity College, Oxford (First class Lit. Hum., 1841). He was a Fellow of Balliol (1843), won the Latin essay prize (1846) and was an Eldon Scholar. He joined the staff of the Education Office after conducting an inquiry into Welsh education (1847), and became Secretary (1849). He was later Permanent Secretary to the Treasury (1869), was created K.C.B. (1878) and First Baron Lingen on retirement in 1885.

some of the other boards'.[27] A memorial signed by 609 laymen and 1,892 clergy in the same year, 1850, provides further evidence that the Tractarians did not speak for the whole of the Church of England. 'The minutes of the Privy Council,' the signatories affirmed, 'including the management clauses as at present existing, are upon the whole sound and judicious, and not calculated thereby to interfere with the legitimate authority of the clergy.'[28] Evangelical and Broad churchmen, ready and eager to cooperate with the government, not only welcomed inspection because of the benefits it would bring their schools but were also prepared to adopt a form of school management that was designed to give the laity some part in their running.[29]

The welcome, though, that was initially given to the inspector was always in danger of wearing thin, for he was a visitor who was accepted on sufferance for the sake of what he had to offer. All the schools with which the Department dealt were private property; over such schools the central government had no power of compulsory inspection until the Education Act of 1944 was passed. Furthermore, the Department gave notice of its intention to inspect. This remained the rule until 1871, when surprise visits were allowed.[30]

The speedy removal of H. S. Tremenheere, the first inspector to be sent out on circuit, is commonly held to have been the consequence of his failure to appreciate the delicacy of his position. Yet the report he made on the London schools he visited in 1842, which provided the immediate cause of the dispute between the British and Foreign School Society and the Education Department, was no more outspoken than others that were being made at this time by Allen. In fact Tremenheere, as his transfer to the more lucrative but politically less controversial task of inspecting mines — without at first being allowed underground—would suggest, had been the unfortunate pawn in a game of power politics. Nonconformists, who did not as yet share the safeguards that the Anglicans had secured, had been alarmed by a statement made by Lord John Russell. 'If the inspectors appointed for Church schools,' he told the House of Commons on 24 July 1840, 'should visit districts in which there shall be other schools, and if the managers of the schools shall not object,' he could see no reason 'why the inspectors should not inspect the others.'[31] To dissenters this seemed to be the thin end of the wedge. They feared that, under a Tory administration, the inspection of their schools and the training college at Borough Road, for which they were seeking a building grant of £5,000, would be carried out by men hostile to their beliefs. They accordingly took steps to forestall such an eventuality. They used the occasion of Tremenheere's removal to ensure that his successors would be appointed on terms comparable to those already obtained by the National Society.[32]

Tremenheere's departure to another government office has deprived the historian interested in the development of the English educational system in its social context of much valuable material. In writing his report on South Wales he had acted on the assumption that 'a mere enquiry into the state of education would leave untouched many subjects tending to illustrate the peculiarities most prominent in the condition of the society which has grown up in these remote valleys'.[33] Thus two years before the publication of a more famous report on the plight of women and children working in the coal-mines, Tremenheere had already drawn attention to the employment of young children of 'eight or nine years of age or even earlier... opening and shutting air doors'.[34] Similarly his report on East Anglia described the effects that the war-time rise in the price of corn had had on the working conditions of the farm labourer and the structure of the agricultural industry. In it he also drew attention to the moral and social effects of the agriculture gang system more than a generation before this problem was investigated by a commission.[35]

The long journeys made by the inspectorate at this time help to substantiate the thesis that the industrialization of Great Britain not only produced social problems of an unprecedented scale and intensity, but also provided the methods of tackling them with unprecedented assurance and success.[36] No inspector would have been able to travel as widely and rapidly as he did without the development of the railway. John Allen, for example, visited 150 schools in Northumberland and Durham in August and September 1840. In the course of this tour he left London on 10 August, and saw the Bishop of Durham two days later. He came back to London for ten days for family reasons at the end of the month, and finally returned home on 3 October.[37] The following year he relied even more on the rapidly expanding railway network and visited 119 schools in an area bounded by Cornwall, Kent and Yorkshire.[38]

The appointment of additional inspectors gradually eased the burden. By 1845 there were eight. Allen, for example, no longer had the whole of England and Wales as his parish. He now confined his travels to the counties of Berkshire, Buckinghamshire, Hampshire, Hertfordshire, Kent, Surrey and Sussex. On the other hand his work in one respect remained as burdensome as before. In that year alone he visited 340 schools.[39] Large though his district still was, the newly appointed Reverend Frederick Watkins* had an even greater task. He had to inspect the six northern counties of England. In his first report he stated that they contained more than a quarter of the population of England and that his district extended 180 miles from Berwick to Sheffield, and 130 miles from Flamborough Head to St Bees.[40] In these circumstances it is not surprising that the target set in the minute of 22 November 1843, of inspecting schools 'in the most populous and manufacturing districts, once, at least, in every half year' was never realized.[41] Within a short time it had been completely abandoned. The minute of 25 August 1846 spoke of the desirability of an annual inspection, but stated that it was only possible at that time to inspect once every two years. Their Lordships were unwilling to make sufficient appointments to allow for an annual inspection but announced their intention of appointing three more inspectors.[42]

Not only were the schools that had to be inspected increasing in numbers, but inspection soon became more complicated. The inauguration of the pupil-teacher scheme in December 1846 made fresh demands on the inspectorate who now had to examine the apprentices annually, approve new candidates, and make sure that the teacher was instructing them properly. The result was that schools that had only received a building grant were frequently neglected. Yet these, together with those that had received no state assistance at all, were the ones that most needed guidance and encouragement.

At first inspectors went to the schools without regard to their

---

* F. Watkins, the son of a clergyman, was educated at Shrewsbury, Westminster, and Emmanuel College, Cambridge (B.A. 1830, twenty-seventh senior optime). He taught at Haileybury, became Fellow of his college (1838–47) and was H.M.I. (1844–73).

geographical location but in the order in which school managers had applied for apprentices. To cut out unnecessary travelling, the inspectors were told, in July 1849, to divide their districts into six regions and to allocate two months to each. This reorganization had the further advantage that pupil teachers could be examined centrally.[43]

Theoretically the inspector was supposed to allocate his time as follows:

Table II THE INSPECTOR'S YEAR

7 weeks	Examining teachers and students in training colleges for certificates of merit.
2 weeks	The central examination of pupil-teachers.
4 weeks	Vacation.
4 weeks	Writing a general report and performing general duties.
35 weeks	Inspecting 175 schools at the rate of one a day.

Source: *Minute of the Committee of the Privy Council*, 25 July 1850. P.P. 1851, XLIV, p. 119 (523).

Unfortunately inspectors were seldom able to keep to this programme. Watkins, despite his loss of the three north-western counties in his original district in 1847, still had a larger area and more schools to supervise than anybody else. Between 1 November 1849 and 31 October 1850 he travelled 8,208 miles to visit 260 schools; he examined 168 uncertificated teachers, 572 apprentices, and a further 276 candidates for their indentures. His other duties, which included writing two reports covering fifty-eight pages of printed foolscap and the compilation of a further fifty-two pages of reports on the individual schools, left him no time for a holiday that year.[44] E. Douglas Tinling,* who visited 203 schools, had only one day off.[45] Joseph Fletcher,† who travelled 8,409 miles to see 253 schools in the thirteen months between the end of November 1849 and the end of the next year,

* E. D. Tinling, the son of an armiger, was educated at Christ Church College, Oxford (B.A., 1837). He was Rector of West Worlington, Devon (1844-7) H.M.I. (1847-87) and Canon of Gloucester (1867-97).
† J. Fletcher (1813-52), a barrister-at-law, served on the Handloom Inquiry (1841), the Children's Employment Commission (1841-3), was H.M.I. (1844-52) and edited the *Statistical Journal*.

was more fortunate. He managed to take twelve days' holiday together with Good Friday and the two Christmas Days.[46] When these achievements are remembered, it is remarkable that only one inspector, the Reverend H. W. Bellairs,* had to take time off that year as a result of ill health.[47]

The trouble was that even on Departmental calculations, there were not enough inspectors. With sixteen officials for 4,396 schools in 1850, each man had an average assignment of 275 schools a year to visit. This was a hundred more than the Department thought he could reasonably manage. To reduce the allocation to the desired level, another nine recruits to the inspectorate were needed. However, only one inspector and two assistants were appointed. One of the assistants, the Reverend G. R. Moncrieff,† was sent to help the hard-pressed Watkins, who was responsible for 565 schools. The second, the Reverend W. P. Warburton,‡ such were the exigencies of the service, had to give a hand to three inspectors. Although Moncrieff and Warburton were assistants, there was little difference between them and their seniors. They received the same travelling allowances and, after 1853, the same salary scale. The Education Department sent a list of schools to be visited to the principal who allocated some to his junior and compiled the annual report.[48]

Worst off of all were the non-Anglican inspectors, for although they might have roughly the same number of schools to inspect the area they had to cover was considerably larger. In his evidence to the Newcastle Commission T. W. M. Marshall,§ for

* H. W. Bellairs, the son of a clergyman, was educated at Christ Church College, Oxford (B.A., 1835), held various clerical posts, was H.M.I. (1844–72), Vicar of Nuneaton (1872–91) and assisted in foundation of the Ladies' College, Cheltenham, 1854.

† G. R. Moncrieff, the fourth son of J. W. Moncrieff, Bart, a Lord of the Session and Justiciary of Scotland (1828–51), was educated at Balliol College, Oxford (second class Lit. Hum., first class, Maths, 1838), held various clerical posts, and was H.M.I. (1850–84).

‡ W. P. Warburton, the son of an armiger, was educated at Balliol College, Oxford (first class Lit. Hum., 1849) was Fellow of All Souls (1849–53), H.M.I. (1851–85).

§ T. W. M. Marshall, the son of a government agent for the colonization of New South Wales, was educated at Trinity College, Cambridge (B.A., 1840) was a curate in Wiltshire (1841–5), was received into the Roman Catholic Church, 1845, was H.M.I. (1848–60) and was honoured by Pope Pius IX for his *Christian Missions, Their Agents, Their Method and Results* (3 vols, 1862).

example, stated that on his appointment in 1848 he had been the sole inspector of Roman Catholic schools for the whole of Great Britain. By 1859, however, two more inspectors had been appointed so that his area had become limited to London and all England south of a line between London and Bristol. Inspecting schools in the London area alone took up two-thirds of his time. Because of this for a number of years, he had felt unable to take on any more commitments in the London area for fear he should neglect his other responsibilities.[49]

Not all allegations of overwork can be taken at face value. One explanation of Marshall's reluctance to take on more schools, for example, may well be that he was too busy writing his three-volume work, *Christian Missions, Their Agents, Their Method and Results* (published in 1862). The late 1840s, though, were years of crisis for the inspectorate. The publication of the pupil-teacher minutes at the end of 1846 led to a rapid increase in the demand for their services. At first the inspectorate did not grow rapidly enough to enable its members to cope with the expanding volume of work. Yet by 1852 the increase of the establishment to twenty-three inspectors and two assistants had so eased the burden that the Committee of Inquiry of the following year commented: 'It should be impressed upon each inspector, at the time of his first appointment, that he is not only expected to give his whole time to the duties of his office, and to decline all other employment which would be inconsistent with their performance, but that he is to regard the visiting and inspection of schools as his chief function.' To drive the point well home, they added: 'We think it desirable with a view to encouraging the inspectors to exert themselves, that this advance [the triennial increment of £50 or £75] should not be in the ordinary way of an annual increase of salary [and]...that it should be made to depend upon the satisfactory character of the inspector's services during that period.'[50] By 1860, most of the inspectors had recovered much of their former diligence. Thirteen Anglicans and their assistants visited 4,084 schools for annual grants and a further 814 for simple inspection.*[51] There were three, however, who failed to mend their ways. They were dismissed.[52]

One of those who suffered this penalty was J. R. Morell, an

* Schools that had received a building grant only had a less thorough or 'simple' inspection.

inspector of Roman Catholic schools. In all he had three disputes with the Education Office. He had evidently given help to pupil-teachers taking their examination at a school in St Leonards and at a later date had conducted an inspection under the Revised Code irregularly at St Mary's School, Coventry. It was his unprofessional conduct at Cardiff in 1863 that finally gave the Lord President the chance to dismiss him.

Kelly, the schoolmaster, who received a bad report from Morell, complained that Morell had only spent twenty minutes in the school, and had not only failed to examine the pupil-teachers properly but had not even looked at the register. At a later stage this register was filled up so carelessly that the children were shown as present on religious holidays. The school managers, for their part, argued that the inspection had been correctly conducted, but had to admit that it had lasted forty minutes at the most. As for Kelly, he had 'imbibed too much drink', a common failing amongst schoolmasters at this time, and was actuated by malice.

Lingen pointed out to Morell that, in an inspection that had probably not exceeded forty minutes, he claimed to have tested a top class of fifteen in five subjects, a second class in four subjects, and the remaining six in seven subjects. Furthermore he had kept only sixty-four of his 153 engagements for the previous year. In addition he had falsified his diary. On the one hand he had justified rushing the inspection on the grounds that, after a full day's work (!), he had to catch the steamer to Bristol, yet according to his diary he had travelled the following day.[53]

Morell's subsequent attempts to justify his behaviour provide an interesting commentary on unofficial practices within the Department. 'There are various contingencies in which for regularity's sake the official statement and the actual fact cannot literally coincide... Thus a Sunday's journey must be entered on another day; and an inspector's assistant can charge for journeys which he never takes, in lieu of personal expenses, at a distance from home.'[54] In the course of fighting his case Morell enlisted the support of his fellow inspectors.[55] One commented, 'You might have gone to London and back in the meantime without prejudicing their service. I constantly go home at my own expense, without telling them a word about it.'[56] To this Morell added a footnote, 'The fact is that I was in London in the

55

course of the week, without showing it or charging it in my diary.' In other words he had spent twenty to forty minutes in a Cardiff school on Tuesday 17 September, gone to London, and had subsequently begun inspection in the Plymouth area on the Thursday.

The Education Office now had ample justification for demanding his resignation. 'The Lord President', Lingen wrote on 13 February 1864, 'considered that this account of your conduct established your unfitness to hold an office the sole function of which turns upon accuracy of statement. Had the false entry stood by itself; had you not justified the practice; had you never been officially censured for an instance of disingenuousness followed by detection; had the performance of your duties not exhibited unexampled irregularity; even so, the Lord President could not have allowed you to remain in the service, after such an act, without putting on record some emphatic censure.'[57]

Another inspector, the Reverend M. Mitchell,* was much more fortunate. At the end of January 1853 Lingen, the Secretary, complained: 'I am to inform you that complaints of your manner have reached Lord Granville† from several quarters, and that his Lordship on enquiry finds that previous complaints of a similar character have been made to the Council Office. The Lord President feels bound to state that it would be impossible for him to pass over such complaints if they continue to be made without taking measures which would be painful to him.'[58] A second letter written to Mitchell a few months later shows why the Lord President had taken such a firm line. 'There cannot be two opinions upon the indecorum of the practices which you describe of wiping your hands on the pinafores of the children and of kissing them. Their Lordships are obliged to remind you of the terms in which their secretary was instructed to characterize such practices in 1848 when the managers of the Tamworth Infant School complained of similar behaviour.'[59] Mitchell, despite his unfortunate propensities, remained an inspector until his death in 1876.

* M. Mitchell, was educated at University College, Oxford (B.A., 1832) and was H.M.I. (1847–76). His will was proved for £100,000.
† Granville George Leveson-Gower, 2nd Earl Granville, held various ministerial offices including that of the Lord Presidency of the Council (1852–5) under the Earl of Aberdeen, and (1855–8, 1859–65) under Viscount Palmerston.

The Department's greatest handicap was that it was still bound by the terms of the Concordat which had been negotiated when the public education service was in its infancy. An arrangement that may have been workable in 1840 when there were only two inspectors failed to meet the needs of the 1860s. The Newcastle Commissioners reached the heart of the problem when they commented: 'At present every inspector is independent, and practically almost uncontrolled by the central office. This state of things has grown up gradually and accidentally; it is in itself undesirable, and will become still more so when a greater number of schools are brought under inspection.'[60]

In these circumstances and in the light of some of the evidence they heard, it is hardly surprising that the Commissioners found grounds for criticizing the conduct of the inspectorate. Lingen, the Secretary, for example, had emphatically stated that his officials did not ensure that every child could read and write, or make proper progress in his education.[61] The evidence given by the Reverend F. C. Cook, one of the Department's most senior men, must have made a deep impression on the members of the Commission. He had not only claimed that he could see the staple work of a school of 150 boys in about ninety minutes but had admitted that he did not consider himself bound to examine every boy. His concern was the somewhat nebulous and limited one of seeing that every boy had sufficient means of acquiring information. He saw the inspector's duty as that of remaining in the school long enough to see that every part of the instruction was thoroughly carried out; that the organization was quite complete and that the qualifications of the teachers were sufficient.[62] Thus the Commissioners had ample justification for concluding that inspection was, at times, hurried, that the standards of the inspectors differed, and that they tended to judge a school too much by concentrating on the performance of the oldest children.[63]

It is possible that inspections carried out by other government departments were also superficial. Certainly the school inspectors were not the only ones who had grounds for thinking that at times they were being asked to do the impossible. David Roberts has drawn attention to the tasks facing the mid-Victorian inspectorate. In 1839, for example, four chief and fourteen assistant inspectors had to cover 4,654 factories between them.

At the Poor Law Board twelve inspectors were responsible for nearly 600 unions by the early 1850s. It is easy to see why Henry Parker was unaware of the conditions in Andover workhouse where the paupers fought over the bones they were supposed to grind. He had seventy-nine unions consisting of 1,653 parishes to look after.[64] Even as late as the mid-1870s, conditions were little better. One inspector at the Home Office was responsible for 1,658 factories and 6,307 workshops. During the financial year 1873-4 he and his assistant had visited 501 factories and 4,511 workshops. Similarly, six of the twelve coal mine inspectors had more than 400 collieries each.[65] As the following table shows, more than half the inspectors visited a minimum of 200 schools each that same year.

Table III NUMBER OF VISITS MADE BY SCHOOL INSPECTORS DURING THE FINANCIAL YEAR 1873-4

Number of visits made	Number of inspectors who performed this task
400+	1*
351–400	—
326–350	2
301–325	1
276–300	5
251–275	4
226–250	14
201–225	17
176–200	9
151–175	8
126–150	2
101–125	1†
−25	1‡

Source: *Return of Number, Names and Salaries of Inspectors*, P.P. 1875, XLII, pp. 30–33 (214-7).

* This inspector made 452 visits.
† A newly appointed inspector who made 119 visits in six months.
‡ An examiner on temporary transfer from the Education Office.

In one particular respect the work of school inspectors was probably more onerous. Workhouses and factories were usually in easily accessible market towns or other centres of population. It is unlikely that these visits required as much cross-country travelling as did those to the rural schools.

It must always be remembered that factory and colliery inspectors, with their powers of prosecution, had an authority that school inspectors lacked. Affronted school managers could complain to the Privy Council Office, as at times they did even after 1870; ignore the inspector's advice altogether and, if necessary, forgo the state's grants. 'Such a situation,' wrote Matthew Arnold, 'made state supervision useless if it could be rejected the moment it became a reality... The counsels of inspection,' he pointed out, 'to be of any worth, had to be in some way or other authoritative.' He accused the English squire of wishing to have the stimulus of inspection, but at the same time wanting to keep his school entirely independent. He liked to have an inspector down from London occasionally, as he might call in a landscape gardener or an architect, to talk to him about his school, to hear his advice, and to be free to dismiss him, as he might dismiss the landscape gardener or the architect, the moment his advice became unpalatable. He wished to have, concluded Arnold, a public functionary to act as a showman to his school once a year.[66] The result was, Cook told the Newcastle Commissioners, that the inspector was perfectly aware that he was being inspected all the time that he was examining the school quite as much as was the school itself.[67]

Ex-H.M.I. John Allen, by now vicar of Prees and poacher turned gamekeeper, thought that even the questions put by the inspector to the children could threaten the independence of the school managers. In a letter to *The Times* he complained that H.M.I. the Reverend J. P. Norris had refused to test the children in his school on the passages of Scripture they had learnt by heart; instead he had tested them on passages with which they were unfamiliar. At another school the examination in secular subjects had taken up so much time that scarcely any attention was given to the children's religious instruction. 'The question was,' he argued, 'whether or not the H.M.I. ought, except where he thought that the current of teaching ran altogether in a wrong direction, to abstain from examining the scholars in such a way as must directly interfere with the instruction and management of the school. The inspector should elicit what was done according to the views of the managers, rather than needlessly direct and control according to his particular opinions and sympathies.'[68]

Thus the readiness of clergy and laity alike to defend their autonomy frequently prevented inspection from becoming 'a means of cooperation between the government and the committees and the superintendents of the schools', let alone an instrument of financial control. The outspoken inspector was soon brought to heel. When, for instance, the Reverend W. Birley,* who was W. J. Kennedy's† assistant, protested with misplaced enthusiasm at the start of his career about conditions in two Manchester schools, Kennedy was told 'to confer with him in a friendly manner'. He was to remind his junior that 'H.M.I.s cannot too carefully bear in mind that in the local schools they have to deal with persons who are voluntarily imposing upon themselves a great deal of trouble and expense for a public object...The direct power of H.M.I.s is limited to that of entering schools and reporting upon them... An inspector therefore who assumes to prescribe or dictate...beyond what the minutes require, is exceeding his powers.'[69]

The delicacy of the relationship that existed between inspector and school manager, together with the absence of any objective test, such as that later provided by the Revised Code, made it virtually impossible for officials to administer the minutes with any rigour. The less diligent had every excuse for turning a blind eye. The heavy work load imposed on each inspector, the absence of any need to examine each class, let alone each child, gave the less conscientious inspector every incentive to cut the corners and skimp his work. Naturally, school managers, schoolmasters and pupil-teachers did not complain. They had a vested interest in the maintenance of an easygoing system. Too much was at stake. One great weakness of the grants offered before the introduction of the Revised Code was their inflexibility. The Department paid all or nothing.‡ The strength of the opposition that was generated by the decision to introduce the Revised Code shows the apprehension with which the passing of the old order

---

* W. Birley, the son of an armiger, was educated at Trinity College, Oxford (B.A., 1835), held various clerical posts, was H.M.I. (1852–65), and was incumbent of Charlton-cum-Hardy, Manchester (1843–65).

† W. J. Kennedy, the son of a clergyman, was educated at King Edward VI's Grammar School, Birmingham, and St John's College, Cambridge (Porson Prize for Greek iambics, 1835, B.A., 1837). He was Curate of St Martin-in-the-Fields, London (1842–3), Secretary to the National Society (1844–8), H.M.I. (1848–78) and Vicar of Barnwood, Glos. (1878–91).

‡ The terms on which the grants were offered are described in Chapter III.

was viewed. School managers had every reason to be fearful of the future. The report of the Newcastle Commission had revealed a wide gap between the inspectors' assessments of the schools and the performance of the pupils.

One of the hardest tasks facing the Commission had been that of establishing the standards used by the inspectors in assessing the performance of the schools they visited. In making the attempt they were guided by the criteria laid down by the Reverend W. H. Brookfield* a few years earlier.[70] In a school rated 'excellent', he expected to find a top class of fifteen children aged twelve and a half to thirteen who would fill a slate with an extemporaneous account of flax, or sugar, or a river, or a brewery, or a flour mill, or a zoological garden, showing good observation, memory, reflection, faultless spelling, rarely deficient grammar, and writing that might awaken, not the envy, but the approbation of a government department.

One example of these essays has survived. 'The race horse,' wrote one boy, 'is a noble animal used very cruel by gentlemen. Races are very bad places. None but wicked people know anything about races. The last Derby was won by Mr I'Anson's Blinkbonny, a beautiful filly, rising four. The odds were twenty to one against her; thirty started, and she won only by a neck.' Although the school manager apologized profusely and expressed grave doubts about the author's future, Brookfield possessed a sense of humour. No harm had been done, the boy would 'stay clear of the treadmill'.[71]

In a fair school, that is one of the average creditable kind, but with nothing to boast of, Brookfield expected a top class, perhaps a little younger than in the 'excellent' school, who could read a page of natural history, about an elephant, a cotton tree, or a crocodile with tolerable fluency and scarcely a mistake. Most of them would be able to name the counties on an unlettered map of England, and the kingdoms on a map of Europe, write a short account of an object such as an animal, a tree, or a flower with trifling errors of grammar and spelling, and reach similar

* W. H. Brookfield, the second son of a solicitor, was educated at Rugby and Trinity College, Cambridge (B.A., 1833, President of the Union, 1831 and 1833). He was Curate of St James's, Piccadilly (1840), perpetual Curate of St Luke's, Soho (1841–8), H.M.I. (1848–65), Chaplain-in-Ordinary to Queen Victoria (1862–74), Rector of Somerby, Lincs. (1861–74) and moved in the leading literary circles of his day.

standards in other subjects. The bad school he defined as one with a cold, ill-ventilated and unfurnished room containing a crowd of boys who learnt nothing but what boys are prone to teach one another. The only books in such a school would be a few torn Testaments; the writing of the boys, if legible, would be rendered unintelligible by their spelling.[72] F. C. Cook, in the same year, also told the Newcastle Commission how he judged a school. He expected a 'boy of fair average attainments, at the age of 12 years in a good school to have learned: (1) To read fluently, and with intelligence, not merely the school books, but any work of general information likely to come his way. (2) To write very neatly and correctly from dictation, and from memory, and to express himself in tolerably correct language. (3) To write all elementary rules of arithmetic with accuracy and rapidity... (8) The principles of political economy, with especial reference to questions which touch on the employment and remuneration of labour...[as the] effects of strikes on wages and etc., are taught with great clearness and admirable adaptation to the *wants** and capacities of artisans, in the reading books generally used in the metropolitan schools.'[73] The Commissioners, who were duly impressed, commented: 'The standards adopted in this description by Mr Brookfield appear to us just and sensible; they appear to be also those of Mr Cook, and it may fairly be supposed that the general estimate of the inspectors corresponds with the two whom we have selected.'[74]

It is clear that children in 'good' schools would have had no difficulty in passing Standard VI of the Revised Code. To pass this test, a child had to be able to read a paragraph from a newspaper, write a paragraph dictated from the same paper, and complete a sum in practice or bills of parcels successfully. If we accept the criteria laid down by Brookfield as our norm, school managers, eager to enhance the reputation of their schools, would have had little difficulty in securing nearly 100,000 passes in each subject. Yet in the first full year of the operation of the Revised Code, the passes in Standard VI for England and Wales were 3,523 in reading, 3,284 in writing, and 3,103 in arithmetic.[75]

As Table IV overleaf shows, the standards adopted by the inspectors of the various denominations differed. As Watkins

* Author's italics.

pointed out, some of the claims made were beyond all belief. 'The Roman Catholic Northern and Western district [H.M.I. S. N. Stokes*], which is nineteenth in its number of certificated teachers, is eighth in attainments of children. Indeed this district is a perfect marvel. Excepting the Episcopal schools in Scotland...it is lowest in the number of certificated teachers, it is lowest in the age of children at school, it is the lowest in the outlay for their education...; and yet if the returns made are to be considered as showing the real state of the case, it is eighth in the attainments of its school children, under all these disadvantages.[76] Furthermore, even within a denomination standards varied. The 310 assessments of teaching in Anglican schools as 'Bad or Imperfect' were made by sixteen inspectors in the year ending 31 August 1860. No less than 187 were made by three of them (H. W. Bellairs, eighty-eight; W. H. Brookfield, fifty-six, of which thirty were for grammar; J. G. C. Fussell, forty-three). A fourth, E. D. Tinling, contributed a further forty-one. Thus a quarter of the officials made over two-thirds of the adverse reports. Similarly, a further three at the other end of the scale made only four adverse reports between them (W. P. Warburton, three; G. R. Moncrieff, one, and D. J. Stewart, nil).†

Despite the manifest inadequacies of the system that these figures reveal, it does not necessarily follow that inspectors were either culpably negligent or wilfully dishonest. Given the political context within which the English elementary education system had developed, they could do little more than acquiesce in all but the grossest breaches of the regulations. The state had to work within the strait-jacket of the voluntary system. There was a woeful lack of the means of providing education for the children of the labouring poor. Yet at the same time, the belief that government intervention endangered local and personal self-reliance and initiative was almost universally held. It was better to have bad schools than to have none at all. Anglican inspectors, however, could afford to be more critical of the shortcomings of

---

* S. N. Stokes, the son of a solicitor was educated at St Paul's School and Trinity College, Cambridge (B.A., 1844). He was called to the Bar (1852), was H.M.I. (1853–91) and served on the Royal Commission on Primary Education in Ireland (1868–76).
† The remaining scores are J. P. Norris thirty; M. Mitchell, nineteen; F. Watkins, thirteen; W. J. Kennedy, eight; J. J. Blandford and H. L. Jones (four each).

Table IV

Number of schools

Denomination	Scripture	a	Catechism	a	Reading	a	Writing	a	Arithmetic	a
Church of England	4,893	13	4,662	18	5,095	16	5,091	12	5,070	107
Protestant schools not connected with the Church of England					1,002		997		990	1
Roman Catholic					283		281	2	283	1
Established Church of Scotland	646		651		655		644		644	
Free Church of Scotland	335		334		473		473		472	
Totals	5,874	13	5,647	18	7,508	16	7,486	14	7,459	109

The figures in columns (a) give the numbers of schools in which the subject was badly or imperfectly taught.

their schools than could the officials of other denominations. The minority groups were in too weak a position, socially and financially, to admit that all was not well with their schools. The Anglican Church, with its greater financial resources, was less dependent on the state for assistance than were the other denominations. In the early 1860s, the Department provided 4s. 6½d. in every £1 of the revenue received by Anglican schools that were open to annual inspection. To the British schools it gave 5s. 2¼d. and, to those of other denominations, (mainly the Wesleyans and the Congregationalists), it gave 5s. 3½d.[77]

The introduction of the supposedly objective procedure of examining each child in reading, writing, and arithmetic for the purposes of the Revised Code failed to eliminate the subjective element. Denominational differences remained.

assessed in:

Geography	a	Grammar	a	History	a	Music from notes	a	Drawing	a	Total number of assessments	Total	a	Percentage of bad assessments
4,223	36	3,540	89	1,434	17	311	1	394	1	34,713	310	0·9
963	4	939	9	532	4	22		199		5,644	18	0·3
256		270	4	119	1	23		15		1,530	8	0·5
619		610		131		97		36		473	—	—
468		467		239		40		15		3,316	—	—
6,529	40	5,826	102	2,455	22	493	1	659	1	49,936	336	0·7

Source: *Report of the Committee*, P.P. 1861, XLIX Table 2 (Summarized), p. 7 (35).

In the same way, the child who was examined by the Reverend E. P. Arnold* in Cornwall or Devon stood less chance of passing his annual test than did a child from Yorkshire who appeared before the Reverend F. Watkins. Arnold's pass-rates in reading, writing, and arithmetic, were 81·21 per cent, 78·57 per cent and 60·53 per cent respectively, while those of Watkins were 91·5 per cent, 86·5 per cent, and 81 per cent.[78]

In addition, the results of the tests in reading were usually better than those in the other subjects. One reason for this was that the schools often only had one book which the class learnt

---

* E. P. Arnold, the third son of Thomas Arnold, headmaster of Rugby School (1828–42), was educated at Rugby and Balliol College, Oxford (third class Lit. Hum., 1848). He was a Fellow of All Souls (1851) and H.M.I. (1854–77).

Table V PERCENTAGE PASSES FOR THE YEAR ENDING
31 AUGUST 1869

England	Reading	Writing	Arithmetic
Church of England	89·41	87·39	76·58
British Schools etc.	90·89	89·92	77·69
Roman Catholic	93·66	92·81	84·13
Scotland			
Church of Scotland	97·37	90·78	85·90
Free Church	98·46	93·38	90·34
Episcopalian	91·45	92·59	89·13
Roman Catholic	96·93	89·13	77·16

Source: *Report of the Committee*, P.P. 1870, XXII, p. 14.

off by heart. After 1870, however, the inspector was allowed to choose a book not in general use in the school when testing reading above Standard II.[79] In reading more than in any other subject the children had the benefit of the doubt. As H.M.I. the Reverend D. J. Stewart* pointed out: 'If scholars can fairly pronounce the words in the books which they use it is hardly possible to say that they cannot read.' On one such occasion, he examined the top class without looking at the text. Not until a third of them had read did he have any idea of what they were reading.[80]

In conclusion, it is worth considering why this inspectorate, the largest possessed by any department of the state in the 1860s, had so little influence on the making of policy. The outstanding feature of departmental organization was the lack of personal contact between the central office and the worker in the field. In the early days there had been an annual conference for the inspectors in London. The first check came in 1859 when inspectors were prevented from putting matters concerning departmental policy to the vote. This was probably the last meeting of all. Shortly afterwards Robert Lowe stopped them altogether.[81] After the cessation of these conferences, it was apparently possible for an inspector to go for years without seeing anybody from the

* D. J. Stewart, educated at Trinity College, Cambridge (B.A., 1839, junior optime), held various clerical posts (1843–50), was H.M.I. (1851–91), and honorary Canon of Ely Cathedral (1893–8).

central office. One inspector, for example, who was appointed after 1870, thought that he only saw three members of the office staff during the course of thirty-five years.[82]

Of all the changes that were made in policy, the one on which we would most have expected the inspectors to have been consulted was the introduction of the Revised Code. Yet the evidence of those who appeared before the Select Committee on the Constitution of the Committee of Council on Education in 1865 and 1866 shows that little attempt was made to consult them. At the most, the advice of Cook and one or two others was sought.[83] It was not until Vice-President A. J. Mundella* introduced a new code in 1883 that machinery was set up by which departmental officials were able to make use of the expertise possessed by the inspectors.[84] Thus the Revised Code had been introduced by officials who had never inspected a school in their lives and who had kept their inspectorate at arm's length.

Education, it must be remembered, was an issue that aroused violent political and religious passion. For this reason the reports of the school inspectorate did not make an immediate impact on policy making. They were never more than one of a series of factors that slowly helped to create a climate of opinion conducive to change. As the perusal of almost any parliamentary debate shows, minds often remained obstinately closed to reality. In both Houses of Parliament religious and political issues were uppermost in men's minds; purely educational matters received scant attention. For this reason it seems that few who spoke in either House, apart from the main speakers, had ever read the departmental reports at all, let alone with profit. Where prejudice was at a premium, hard fact which the reports provided in abundance was at a discount.

* A. J. Mundella (1825–97), Liberal M.P. for Sheffield (1868–85) and Sheffield, Brightside Division (1885–97) was Vice-President of the Committee of Council on Education (1880–5), President of the Board of Trade (1886, 1892–4), and sometime President of the British and Foreign School Society. He wrote extensively on labour, social, economic and educational issues.

3 In the classroom

A barn furnishes no bad model; and a good one may be easily converted into a school.

THE REVEREND T. T. WALMSLEY[1]

The place is squalid, unthrifty-looking and wretched, and so is the school. The master has lost one arm and does not wear a coat, very seldom changes his shirt, and, I should think, never combs his hair.

H.M.I. THE REVEREND H. MOSELEY*[2]

In the centre of one of the richest districts of the metropolis, St George's Hanover Square, I have inspected a set of schools for many years...
It [the infants' school-room] was dark, and could not be properly lighted; so dark, in fact, that not one-half of the children could see to read even on a fine day.

H.M.I. THE REVEREND F. C. COOK[3]

The means by which the Education Department was created, an Order in Council, has often been cited as evidence of governmental weakness. Although it is true that the Melbourne administration used this constitutional device at a time when its ability to command a majority in the House of Commons was failing, the decision to tackle the educational issue was, in the circumstances, an act of considerable political courage. No government before 1870, whatever the strength of its standing in the House of Commons, was able to pilot a substantial measure for the improvement of elementary education through the legislature. The only act passed before the introduction of the Elementary Education Act, 1870 was a purely technical measure to create the office of Vice-President in 1856. Hence, the Education Department, unlike any other major government office, lacked any statutory authority during its formative years. To implement its

* H. Moseley, the son of a schoolmaster, was educated at Newcastle, Abbeville and St John's College, Cambridge (B.A., 1826, seventh wrangler). He was Professor of Astronomy at King's College, London (1831–44), F.R.S. (1839), H.M.I. (1844–63), Canon of Bristol Cathedral (1854–72), and author of works on the natural sciences.

policy it had to rely exclusively on a series of grants payable on receipt of satisfactory reports from its inspectorate.

When the Department was formed in 1839, there were neither sufficient schools, teachers, desks, nor even books to allow anything approaching an adequate education to be given to the children of the labouring poor. Consequently the first phase of its activities was devoted to encouraging the patrons of education to expand the resources available by offering grants to supplement local effort. So great, though, was the fear of governmental interference that the Department could never take the initiative; it could do no more than create the conditions that would foster the charitable work of the propertied classes. Furthermore it was an axiomatic belief that, while local effort could be supplemented by the superior resources of the government, it was never to be superseded. As had been realized in 1839, only by these means could the societies preserve their controlling interest. Up to 1870 the price of keeping their autonomy inviolate was paid by the countless children who were denied any opportunity of going to school. In the wealthy areas, where funds could be raised easily, school places were readily provided, at times in excess of requirements, whereas in the poorer areas, where the civilizing influence of the classroom was needed the most, the children had to await the advent of the nonsectarian school board.

The religious monopoly, though, was breached by the state not in 1870, as is commonly supposed, but in 1862 when the Revised Code was introduced. By emphasizing the secular element in education at the expense of the religious, it forced Anglican schools to subordinate the paramountcy of their former function to the needs of a modern industrial society. This code, in turn, was the outcome of a closer and more detailed control that had been growing since 1839. To understand this development, the terms of the minutes under which the grants were paid to the schools must be examined in some detail and an assessment made of their impact on the life of the schools.

By 1860, the year in which the terms of the original grants were consolidated into a code, there were four main types of grant available to a school, three of which had as their primary objective the expansion of the means of education. They were the building grant — the Department's administrative legacy of the 1830s from the Treasury — the pupil-teacher grants of 1846 and

1847, and the grants for the purchase of books and educational apparatus that also began in 1847. The fourth, the capitation grant, offered to rural areas in 1853 and then extended to urban ones in 1856, had the aim not only of subsidizing the provision of improved means of education but also of raising the quality of the education provided. For a school to qualify for aid, children had to satisfy certain attendance requirements and pass an examination conducted by the inspector. Thus the years 1853–63* were ones of transition, in which the activities of the schools were regulated partly by criteria laid down by Kay-Shuttleworth and partly by those that anticipated the terms of the Revised Code.

As can be seen from the following table, more than a half of the total of £6,710,862 14s. 10d. spent on education between 1839 and 1862 was paid out under these grants.[4]

Table I GRANTS PAID TO SCHOOLS, 1839–62

	£	s.	d.
Building grants	1,332,249	1	6
Books, maps and scientific apparatus	52,520	11	2
Teachers' salaries, stipends of pupil-teachers etc.	3,206,383	16	2
Capitation grants	409,895	2	5

Source: *Report of the Committee.* P.P. 1863, XLVII, p. 50.

Of all these grants, the first, the building grant, was naturally the most important. At first limited to the erection of a new school or the extension of an existing one, its scope was widened in 1843 to include the provision of school furniture and other necessary apparatus.[5] At the same time a grant was made available for the building of a schoolmaster's house. In a speech Lord Wharncliffe, Lord President of the Council, made at Barnsley in October 1844, a description was given of the kind of house that befitted a schoolmaster. 'The schoolmaster,' Lord Wharncliffe explained, 'ought to be provided with…a house, by no means too large, so as to exalt him too much in the scale of society; but

---

* The code was introduced in two stages. Schools applying for a grant for the first time came under its provisions after 1 July 1862, those schools in England and Wales already under inspection came within its scope after 1 July 1863.

he should be taken out of a cottage and put into a decent residence, which would be calculated to make those persons lower than himself, inclined to show a proper feeling of respect for the schoolmaster who teaches their children.' Later, under a minute of 20 January 1859, it became possible to obtain help in building rooms designed and equipped for the teaching of drawing, mechanics, physics, chemistry, and natural history. Up to 1853, the rate of the grant was 2s. 6d. a square foot for a school with a teacher's residence and 1s. 8d. for one without. The Department had inherited the rate of 1s. 8d. a square foot from the Treasury who had limited their grant to 10s. for each child for whom an allowance of six square feet of floor space was made. Then, to assist the poorer parishes, the rates were increased to 6s. and 4s. for rural areas. In addition, to help Nonconformists who lacked any form of parochial organization, the definition of 'locally raised funds' was widened to include all moneys raised within a radius of four miles of the site of the school. In 1855 these concessions were extended to urban areas. The upshot of these changes was that the Department had committed itself to finding half the total cost, estimated in 1852 at between 11s. and 12s. a square foot, of building new schools.

Within four years, however, the Department had found that schoolrooms were often built on a much larger scale than was necessary for the purpose of daily instruction. In effect the government was subsidizing the building of church halls and assembly rooms. To avoid this misappropriation of public money, their Lordships decided that they 'would agree with the promoters...upon the maximum number of children for whom accommodation in the proposed new schools was to be provided'. To discourage the more unscrupulous school managers still further, but at the same time to encourage those who needed help the most—the builders of small schools—the grant was changed to 4s. a square foot plus £100 for a teacher's residence. This happy solution was a short-lived one. A year later, the grant was cut to 2s. 6d. a square foot and £65 for the teacher's house. It remained at this level until the withdrawal of the offer of assistance towards the building of schools at the end of 1870.[7] Unfortunately for potential school managers, the reduction in the grant came at a time of increasing building costs. After 1860, the wages of carpenters and masons began to rise.

Through the offer of this grant the Department aspired to play a positive role both by encouraging the establishment of new schools and by ensuring that they conformed to certain architectural standards. In this respect the lead had been taken by Kay-Shuttleworth's former department, the Poor Law Commission, who had used their power to authorize loans to ensure that work-houses were built to approved specifications. Kempthorne,* their architect, as well as building some of the first workhouses in the country, had also designed a district school for workhouse children. His plan, published together with Kay-Shuttleworth's report on the training of pauper children in 1838, by including a needle room, a laundry, scullery and kitchen for the girls, and shops for training shoemakers, tailors and carpenters, made, by contemporary standards, lavish provision for their education.[8] In return for a fee of £500, which at first he 'demurred to accept' as he thought it inadequate, Kempthorne produced building specifications and plans for twenty-three different types and sizes of schools for the Education Department.[9]

In contrast to the Poor Law Commissioners, who were able to exercise a close control over the building of workhouses, the Education Department, dependent on the goodwill of private individuals, could do no more than require 'every building to be of substantial erection and that in the plans thereof, not less than six square feet be provided for every child'. Since the school managers merely had to divide the area of their floor space by six when applying for a grant, without making any allowance for either the teacher or the blackboard, this requirement was of little or no consequence.

When Harry Chester, the assistant secretary, gave evidence to the Newcastle Commission, he claimed that the grants had 'absolutely revolutionized the whole system of building schools'. At first, he stated, the village bricklayer and carpenter had built by rule of thumb.[10] Typical 'school buildings', he said elsewhere, 'had been low, thin, dingy, ill-ventilated, often without means of warming, often without proper conveniences, with no furniture but a teacher's desk, a few rickety forms, a rod, a cane, and a

---

* S. Kempthorne, who built workhouses at Abingdon (the first completed under the 1834 Poor Law Amendment Act), Bishop's Stortford etc., was one of the first associates of the Institute of British Architects. He emigrated to New Zealand in 1841.

fool's-cap; the floors were invariably of brick—the worst kind of floor, as it is tenacious of moisture, cold to the feet, easily abraded into red dust, and soon worn into holes.'[11]

By 1860, the days when the school manager had no more guidance than that 'a barn furnished no bad model' had gone for ever. He now sent up, Chester informed the Commission, elaborate plans, working drawings, and specifications, based on the copies of the model plans supplied to each applicant. The Department had an architect, Major M. R. Hawkins,* 'a very quick intelligent man', who made any necessary alterations. While modifications were being made the plans could travel to and fro up to four times before the office reached agreement with the managers concerned.[12] Even then the grant was not paid until a builder or architect who was not a party to the contract had certified that the work had been completed according to specification. Moreover, the school manager was normally expected to have a freehold tenure. To obtain this, recourse could be made to the School Sites Acts, if the original tenure was copyhold or leasehold. Help could also be sought from the Department's counsel, W. G. Lumley.† Finally the school had to open free from debt.

Although Chester had claimed that a revolution had taken place, Lingen could only specify one requirement that was absolutely insisted upon. Floors, in new schools, had to be wooden.[13] Despite the Department's offer of help to meet the cost of replacing stone floors, school managers were reluctant to make the change. In January 1854, the Department asked the inspectorate if they thought the Department would be justified in compelling managers to install wooden floors in existing schools. They also obtained the support of the Board of Health who stated: 'Wooden plank flooring for schoolrooms is most desirable.' The Board of

* M. R. Hawkins, educated at Charterhouse School, worked under Cubitt, was adviser to the Privy Council Office (1841–72), and built the Royal Patriotic Asylum at Wandsworth Common, the Church of St Michael and All Angels, Praed Street, Paddington, and others.
† W. G. Lumley, educated at Christ's Hospital and Trinity College Cambridge, was called to the Bar in 1827. He was a revising barrister under the 1832 Reform Act, Professor of English Law, University College, London (1834–8), Secretary to the Poor Law Board (1839–47), Assistant Secretary, Local Government Board (1847–71) Q.C., (1868) and author of various works on local government law, including *The Public Health Acts* (various editions, 1876–1950).

Health, in turn, quoted the opinion of the proprietor of a manu-factory employing a large female labour force. He had found that 'the substitution of wooden flooring...increased the working ability of the female operative force by one hour per day.'[14] Since school managers were not the children's employers, this argu-ment did not impress them. Although the Department failed to compel those school managers already in receipt of annual grants to make the change, a tougher line was taken with a school that applied for a grant for the first time. On 13 May 1856 it was decided that if such a school did not possess a wooden floor and the inspector gave an unfavourable report on the warmth, dryness, and ventilation of the room, 'My Lords will require it [the floor] to be changed'.[15] By this time the Department, offer-ing a capitation grant as well as others for the training of teachers and the purchase of books, was in a strong position to exploit the attractiveness of its terms by making managers accede to its regulations.

Although the Department eventually had some success in its dealings with new applicants, the condition of many of those schools that had received aid from an early date remained unsatis-factory. As local expenditure could only be encouraged, never compelled, there was no way by which managers of existing schools could be forced to meet the gradually rising standards imposed by the Department. As Chester pointed out, although the inspector reported on the more obvious defects, such as cracks in the walls, it was virtually impossible to make managers put them right. This was, he explained, because the current school managers were not necessarily the people who had originally received the grant. Consequently there was no way, except by appealing to their better nature, of ensuring the execution of repairs.[16] Finally the Committee's powers were circumscribed by their inability to impose standards that were more rigorous than those of the religious societies on whose cooperation they had at all times to depend. The National Society, for example, also stipulated that there should be six square feet of floor space for each child, that the site should be freehold, and that the school should open free from debt.

Hence even in inspected schools there was often much that was left to be desired. 'The school room is sometimes converted,' wrote H.M.I. the Reverend C. J. Robinson,* 'into a kind of store for superannuated organs, chandeliers, and other ecclesiastical furniture now released from...the unrestored church.'[17] Not only were the children distracted by their surroundings, but they cannot have found the atmosphere conducive to study. H.M.I. the Reverend D. J. Stewart thought: 'The arrangements which are often tolerated in school playgrounds would, in other circumstances, be condemned as inconsistent with health or decency... It is the whole business of the school to reclaim children from the barbarities forced on them in their ill-built, ill-regulated houses. I have been in school rooms,' he added, 'where the atmosphere was poisoned by the effluvium from the offices. The teachers have complained that in hot weather the dwelling houses and school rooms alike are unbearable.'[18] In making criticisms such as these, the inspectorate was reflecting a new regard for human dignity that was both a cause and a result of nineteenth-century reform. Some people, though, thought that the working classes had no desire to share its benefits. 'The builder of a new school house,' one assistant commissioner to the Newcastle Commission stated, in 1861, 'smiles at any fastidious suggestion about necessary outhouses, and says, "They will never be used; no one understands the sense of them".'[19]

In this struggle for better classroom conditions, inspectors often found that their greatest enemy was the schoolmaster who not only kept all the windows shut even on the hottest day but stuffed up all the air bricks as well. 'I have sometimes seen,' wrote the Reverend F. Watkins, 'the steam covering the windows, and perspiration streaming down the children's faces; without (apparently) a suspicion on the part of the teacher that the room was unsufferably and unhealthily hot and close. In several cases,' he added, 'I have seen the air grates, recommended in Your Lordships' minutes, stopped up—"because they let in too much air".'[20] The Reverend H. Moseley was impressed by the determination shown by schoolmasters in defeating every expedient by which the architect had provided for the due ventilation of their rooms. 'I have with my own hands,' he wrote, 'broken open the aperture for ventilation in the ceiling of one, which the

* C. J. Robinson, educated at Rugby School and Christ Church Oxford (B.A., 1854), was Curate at West Ham (1855-6), at Hatfield (1856-9) and was H.M.I. (1859-81).

schoolmaster had nailed down to prevent the cold air, as he said, from entering.'[21] The Reverend M. Mitchell, another inspector who was concerned about the stuffiness of the classroom, also carried on a personal campaign against latticed windows. Although they did not let in much light, school managers often preferred them, as the builder could use up odd pieces of glass instead of fixing plain glass. The latter was expensive. Mitchell, for instance, records that in one school, where his wishes prevailed, the installation of two skylights cost under £1 but the glass cost £2 10s.[22]

The problem of securing adequate ventilation was peculiar neither to the schools of the poor nor to the middle of the nineteenth century. The Reverend E. P. Arnold, for instance, thought that some of his colleagues were making an unnecessary fuss. The closeness of the schoolroom in the afternoon, in his opinion, compared very favourably with that of a crowded church or drawing-room.[23] Where schoolchildren had to endure 'the effluvium of the offices', church congregations suffered in another way. One correspondent to *The Times* thought that: 'Conditions in church [were] aggravated by the presence of vaults with their decaying contents beneath.'[24] Moreover there was considerable discussion of this question in the early issues of the *Educational Times*, the journal of the College of Preceptors, an organization that was concerned with schools attended by children of middle-class parents. 'To Clergymen and Preceptors,' one typical advertisement ran, 'headaches, dizziness, lassitude and numerous similar ills are continually borne by Preceptors and their pupils. In nineteen out of twenty cases these evils will arise through breathing an impure atmosphere.'[25] The remedy required, though, was not necessarily the advertiser's ventilation apparatus but the willingness to open a few windows. So long-lived was the belief that disease was carried in the air that as late as 1904 the Hon. Mrs Lyttleton, in her evidence to the Interdepartmental Committee on Physical Deterioration, complained that teachers did not care enough about fresh air. They were often afraid of it, she averred, and children were brought up in a bad atmosphere.[26] Two years later, in a memorandum to the Interdepartmental Committee on Medical Inspection, Dr James Kerr, the Medical Officer (Education) for the London County Council, stated that the bad atmosphere of most school rooms had much to do with infantile debility and was the most pressing problem in school hygiene. When the whole school was assembled in the hall, at the beginning of the day, the atmosphere became excessively foul within ten or fifteen minutes—it was invariably the younger children who fainted or vomited.[27]

It is clear that few schools, by 1860, had reached the ideal portrayed by Harry Chester in which the 'school rooms were as comfortable and as pleasing to the eye as possible, [with] a few good maps, a few good diagrams, a few good prints, and a very few well chosen texts'. Instead, he found, perhaps on the walls of an infants' school, 'the most awful texts [such as], "Our God is a consuming fire", "All liars shall have their part in the lake that burneth with fire and brimstone", or "The wicked shall be turned into hell."' He also advocated the provision of washing facilities, 'but not on a large scale', for 'the children should come to school with clean hands'. Schools, he thought, should contain libraries, and possess gardens that had facilities for raising pigs, rabbits, and poultry. In addition there should be bee-hives. For the girls he wanted a wash house and a laundry.[28] The short-comings of the schools, that undoubtedly existed, were not the result of administrative apathy—indeed civil servants were the pace-makers—but of the failure of local persons to respond to the challenge thrown down by an innovating and dynamic bureaucracy.

It has to be remembered that what was achieved was done, at times, despite the ignorance and prejudice of the school manager. In its attempts to provide a decent and healthy environment for children, the Committee was trying to secure better living conditions than many of them enjoyed at home. Unfortunately some subscribers did not see why such munificence should be offered at their expense. Similarly the Committee's desire to raise the living standard of the schoolmaster was not always shared by his employers. Complaints about the condition of teachers' houses appeared in the professional journals, the *School and the Teacher* in 1855, and the *Educational Guardian* in 1859.[29] So frequently was the master badly housed that the Department had to remind H.M.I.s in 1859 that it did not make grants 'for the erection of residences which are not sufficient to accommodate, with decency, a married teacher, with a family of both sexes.'[30] Shortly afterwards, Chester thought it necessary to advise school managers, 'in opposition to the ordinary opinion and practice', to provide a larder and pantry—small ones would suffice—for the teacher's house.[31] On yet another occasion, Lingen had to point out that a house built for a teacher with the aid of public money was not to be let out to another person to supplement the parochial funds.[32]

In 1846 the Department took an important step in extending its control over education by offering annual grants for the training of pupil-teachers and monitors. This innovation, however, was so far-reaching, both in its effects on the schools and as an agent of social change, that it is treated separately in the next two chapters. One important consequence it had, though, can be discussed here. If the pupil-teachers were to receive an initial training in the schools, those schools undertaking the work had to possess books. Hence the Department found it had to expand its activities in yet another field, by remedying the inadequate supply of books.

As is well known, school managers were able to obtain Bibles, Testaments, religious formularies, and other books of religious instruction through the voluntary societies. Thanks to the Society for Promoting Christian Knowledge, Bibles were cheap. A well-bound copy of the New Testament cost 6d. whilst their fourth reader, a secular book, of the same size and similar binding, cost 1s. 6d. Hence, if children learnt to read at all, they did so mainly from the Bible. The general opinion of the inspectorate was that, regardless of the number of years the children spent in this way, they remained utterly unacquainted with the subject matter of the simplest narratives or the outlines of the fundamental doctrines. Despite this failure to understand what they read, one inspector thought that the Bible had certain advantages for children over secular books that were not specially adapted to their needs. 'Its diction is associated with every effort they have ever made to read. Its forms of expression are, perhaps, more readily seized by the poor than those of other books, because more remains amongst them, than amongst the educated classes, of the language of that period in our history when it was first translated.'[33]

Even when secular instruction was given, the opportunity was taken to combine it with religious teaching. An arithmetic book written by the Reverend J. C. Wigram, a secretary to the

National Society, posed the following problem for a child in the 1830s. 'When Moses dedicated the tabernacle, each of the twelve princes of Israel made an offering to God of two oxen, five rams, five he-goats, and five lambs. How many of each did they offer? How many animals in all?'[34] Moreover, a mixture of the sacred and the profane existed in the reading books. Thus a child learnt from the *Second Reading Book*, published by the Irish Commissioners of Education, that 'It is God that teaches the little birds to act so skilfully in building their nests and so tenderly in rearing up their young.'[35]

To enable the Department to bring more books of a suitable quality into the classroom, a letter was sent to all H.M.I.s asking them to submit a list of books they were prepared to recommend.[36] Then a few months later, in December 1847, the new grant, under which the Department offered to meet a third of the cost of providing books, in the first instance, and a fifth of the cost of renewal, after three years, was announced. Moreover, bulk purchasing made it possible to offer the books, even if no grant were paid, at a reduction of between 32 per cent and 55 per cent of the price the public normally paid.

The offer was a generous one. School managers could have up to two shillings' worth of books a pupil, or half-a-crown's worth if the school contained pupil-teachers. An outlay of 2s. 6d. equipped a child in the top class with what, in the 1850s, were regarded as his basic necessities.

	Published price	Concession price
A Treatise on Arithmetic	2s. 6d.	11d.
Rural Spelling Book	1s. 6d.	8d.
The Fifth Reading Book	1s. 8d.	11d.
	5s. 8d.	2s. 6d.

Thus for an outlay of 1s. 8d. plus a grant of 10d. school managers, in this particular case, would have obtained books worth 5s. 8d. Their final suggestion was that each child in the top class should be provided with a satchel in which he should be allowed to take three books home every night, to prepare for the next day's lessons.[37] A further concession, in 1850, permitted schools to spend £3 a year in buying books at the reduced price, but without the further assistance of the grant, so that schoolmasters, pupil-teachers and others could make private purchases. Shortly afterwards, school-masters' associations were allowed to buy books at half the pub-lished price for the use of their members.[38]

So strongly was the idea of giving a predominantly secular education distrusted, that school managers took little advantage of the facilities offered them. In 1860, for example, although there were over 800,000 children in school on any one day, the book grant came to only £5,683. Yet, by this time, there were 1,035 books, 210 maps, and 410 diagrams on the list.[39] To administer this scheme there was, the Newcastle Commission reported, a separate office in Great George Street, Westminster, with a staff of clerks. In addition to these expenses, Messrs Longmans, who acted as forwarding agents, charged £1,000 for their services.

Apart from the disproportionate cost of administration, the Commission found other grounds for complaint. 'Those [books] which have come under our observation,' they commented, 'leave much to be desired...Yet schoolmasters have reason to complain that the [Irish reading] books abound with words, needlessly introduced, which are quite incomprehensible to a child; that the poetry is taken from inferior sources, that dry outlines of grammar and geography ... are unsuitably intro-duced, that the history is epitome, destitute of picturesqueness, and incapable of striking the imagination and awakening the sentiments of a child. The fifth book is greatly taken up with science in a form too technical for the purpose.'[40] In short, 'the language of the books was an unknown tongue to the children of the illiterate'.[41]

What, indeed, were children to make of passages like these?

'Stop the thief. Let me help you to a bit of pie. Hie thee home from school. All men must die.'

The First Reading Book, 1865, p. 42.

'Who is it that cometh from the south, thinly clad in a light transparent garment? Her breath is hot and sultry...'

The Third Reading Book, 1865, p. 159.

'The seat of colour is, in fact, a very thin layer of soft substance, which is interposed between the scarf-skin and the cutis, or true skin, and is termed the mucous net-work. In the negro it is of a very dark colour: and the colour is capable of being communicated to water.'

The Fifth Reading Book, 1865, p. 235.

Another fault of the books was that the material they contained was often either out of date or written in poor English. Thus a child in 1860 could still read that railways were just coming into use in England; that the eastern counties of England were a dead flat; or that 'after being washed and dressed in the morning, a slice of cold meat will do a nurse no harm'.[42]

Although the Department was to blame for the unduly heavy expenses incurred in administering the grant, the content of the books was not its responsibility. In an era that distrusted state interference in education, the Education Office had to take the books as it found them. When inspectors wrote books for schools, they did so in their private capacity and not as servants of the state. Their Lordships, moreover, were careful to point out that inclusion of a book on the list did not, in any way, imply that they recommended it.

Nevertheless, the scheme met with opposition from those who feared that undue prominence would be given to secular education. Such an attitude was denounced by the Reverend Richard Dawes who, on the strength of the success with which he had conducted a school at King's Somborne, near Winchester in Hampshire, was presented to the deanery of Hereford by Lord John Russell. 'Why,' he asked, 'is a clergyman thought too secular in his views, as to education, because he introduces books from the suspected list of the Committee of Council or the Irish National Board?' He went on to declare as quite imaginary the idea that 'the system was too probably a nursery for little rebels, and that instead of seeing future good subjects, we ought to see in every little urchin going from a school in connexion with the Committee of the Council, with a satchel on his back, some future Louis Blanc, unfit for the present world, and most assuredly unfit for the next.'[43]

Finally a return of the books bought between 1856 and 1859 throws some light on the day-to-day work of the schools. This return shows that of approximately 1,453,000 books sold, the largest single item consisted of 902,926 reading books and that more than a half of these were ones published by the Irish Commissioners, bought because of their extraordinary cheapness. Unfortunately this was, as we have seen, their main merit. Other subjects that were popular included:

	Copies
Arithmetic	135,323
Grammar and English language	104,974
Political and historical geography	76,696
British history	62,768
Dictionaries and etymological manuals	19,802
School poetry	16,299
Atlases	14,814
Wall maps	14,369

The sales of books on all other subjects (including 9,416 copies of various manuals on the principles of teaching were below 10,000.[44]

The last grant introduced before the Revised Code of 1862—the capitation grant—was, at first, designed to help the rural schools only. In the countryside resources were often so inadequate that managers were unable to meet the requirements in staffing, premises, or equipment to enable their schools to earn a grant at all. That such schools, hitherto outside the grant system, were desperately in need of help, can be seen from the instructions issued to H.M.I.s. Where defects in premises, furniture, apparatus, or books made the schools ineligible for the training of apprentices, but not injurious to the health of scholars, or necessarily fatal to all improvement and progress, 'My Lords will be disposed', the inspectorate was told, 'to look for amelioration from the grant of assistance, and from the influence of your inspection [as a result] rather than as a condition precedent to such aid'.[45] The instructions to H.M.I.s were enforced so leniently that one inspector was able, with some justice, to describe the capitation grants as 'public donations for the improvement of the schools'.[46] In contrast to the earlier grants, the terms of which had had the effect of confining government assistance to those areas most able to help themselves, the capitation grant gave help where it was needed most. Hence the defects of the schools, brought within the orbit of the state for the first time, are evidence not so much of departmental inability to control public expenditure as of the shortcomings of the voluntary system.

The capitation grant had been drafted, in the first instance, to ensure that rural schools received help on terms comparable to those envisaged for urban ones in the Promotion of Education in Cities and Boroughs in England Bill of 1853. Although this measure never went beyond its first reading, country schools were the residuary beneficiaries of this attempt by Lord Aberdeen's administration to aid education out of the rates.

Children were required to attend 192 days a year. This requirement, though, was gradually reduced, firstly by sixteen days' absence, and secondly by allowing children over the age of ten to attend for only eighty-eight days if the inspector approved a scheme of alternate periods of employment and education.[47] However, it came to be widely assumed that children could attend any eighty-eight days they chose. Despite the eventual breakdown of the scheme, the Committee had made an attempt to establish a new principle. It was using its financial powers to induce children to attend school more regularly a generation before it had statutory authority to implement such a policy. 'The mere substitution of public for local money is an evil,' the Committee had explained when the minute was first drafted, 'if it does not stimulate improvement in a greater degree than could otherwise be realized. The attendance required to fulfil the conditions of the grant ought to be fixed at a point beyond the common practice.'

Not only did this grant anticipate the terms of the Revised Code by attempting to impose a minimum school attendance, but it foreshadowed the later measure by imposing an examination. At first three-quarters of the children in the age groups seven to nine, nine to eleven, and eleven or more, had to pass a test. At a later date, inspectors were instructed to test only the two oldest groups. Even this was not always done. 'In a great number of cases that part of the minute [relating to examinations] has never been put into force,' Lowe told the House of Commons in 1862. 'I am not,' he went on, 'blaming the inspectors for that. Their attention was not drawn to it by the Department, and the central office is to blame if there is any blame in the matter.'[48] When Lowe gave this explanation, he was defending his proposals to scrap the existing grants and replace them with the Revised Code. As this required the examination of the individual child, it would have been impolitic for him to have admitted, as had Lingen, that the inspectorate had refused to examine children in groups. 'The inspectors exceedingly objected,' the Secretary had told the Newcastle Commission, 'and declared it to be quite impracticable; they said that the children were not grouped in school according to their age, and that they could not carry out that scheme of examination. The Lord President did not, against that opinion, insist upon that part of the instructions being carried out, and it has remained a dead letter to this day.'[49] Much of the unpopularity of the new code undoubtedly sprang from the fact that those inspectors who earlier had refused to examine children in groups were eventually forced to perform the much more tedious task of giving the individual pupil separate tests in reading, writing, and arithmetic.

At first, teachers had to be certificated or registered,* or if they possessed neither qualification had to obtain one or the other within a year. These requirements were whittled down in 1857, when inspectors were told: 'It should always be a special subject of inquiry whether the numbers and qualifications of the teachers in the school so aided are sufficient.'[50] The Department also abandoned all attempts at allocating the expenditure of the grant. Originally, Lingen had required seven-tenths of all school income, including the capitation grant, to be devoted to the teachers' salaries. This stipulation had been so openly ignored that school managers actually stated in their advertisements, from time to time, that no part of the capitation grant would be allowed to the master.[51]

Lastly, the Department stipulated that the school receiving a grant had to have an income of 14s. per boy or 12s. a girl for each pupil, paying fees of 1d. to 4d. a week, for whom the grant was claimed. Their Lordships admitted that this was not a demanding regulation, but justified it on the grounds that it would become more exacting as the number of pupils eligible for a grant rose.

Because the conditions of the grant were gradually relaxed, many more schools were aided than had been the original intention. Usually schools that had done well under the earlier grants did well under this one, a process that was facilitated by the extension of the grant in 1856 to the wealthier urban areas. For example, of the 479 Lancashire schools that had received a capitation grant by 1860, only fifty-two had not received an annual grant before. Yet despite the imperfections of the schools and teachers, and the unreliability of the registers, only 262,006

* These qualifications are discussed in Chapter 4.

children in England and Wales were eligible for the capitation grant in 1860.[52]

The introduction of the capitation grant marks the peak of the innovating and expansionist phase of the Department. During Lord Derby's administration, with Lord Salisbury as Lord President of the Council, it began to curb the rate at which expenditure was growing by making the first cuts in the grants. In face of mounting criticism the Department, realizing that the system of controls inaugurated by Sir James Kay-Shuttleworth was nearing breaking point, found a simpler and more effective means—the Revised Code.

4   Finding the Teachers

Some doubts were occasionally expressed as to the possible predominance of secular, and consequent neglect of religious, studies.[1]

I have long desired to get rid of the use of monitors, except for such parts of school discipline as approach to what is purely mechanical.

H.M.I. THE REVEREND F. C. COOK[2]

No one who has the least acquaintance with National schools under government inspection would hesitate to prefer the instruction there given to the miserable and pretentious smattering of knowledge promised in the advertisements of private academies for the middle classes.

English Journal of Education[3]

The publication of a series of minutes and regulations in 1846 and 1847, inaugurating the pupil-teacher system, was the occasion of an important extension of public control over elementary education. For the first seven years of its existence, the Education Department had been unable to exercise any supervision over a school once it had been built. Now, under the new regulations, it was able to determine in theory, if not always in practice, the manner in which the day-to-day affairs of a school were to be conducted. Furthermore, the offer of Queen's scholarships to enable students to go to a training college, coupled with the institution of a policy of granting formal recognition to various grades of teachers, gave the state even wider powers. By altering the number and value of scholarships and adjusting the standards of proficiency it expected from the teachers, it was possible to regulate the supply of qualified personnel to meet changes in demand.

Despite these far-reaching consequences, the offer of the new grants was not so much the formulation of a new policy as the delayed implementation of an old one. As early as 1835, £10,000 had been voted for the building of a normal school for the training of teachers. This sum of money, divided equally between the National Society and the British and Foreign School Society in June 1839,[4] remained unused until 1842. In that year, it helped to defray the costs of building projects at the Nonconformist college in the Borough Road and at the new Anglican institution, St Mark's College, Chelsea, now the College of St Mark and St John.*

Moreover Sir James Kay-Shuttleworth, the Secretary of the new Department of State, had already obtained sufficient experience in the training of teachers to be convinced of the value of the scheme he was launching. Shortly after his appointment as an assistant Poor Law Commissioner to the East Anglian district in 1835, he had been able to persuade some of the Poor Law guardians in his area to employ masters for the education of workhouse children. Then, encouraged by the initiative shown by William Rush, a pauper child, who had taken over the running of a school during the teacher's absence, Kay-Shuttleworth had appointed a number of pupil-teachers as assistants.

Fired with a missionary zeal to see the work he was undertaking extended, Kay-Shuttleworth published a paper in which he urged the Poor Law Commissioners to introduce a scheme of apprenticeship. In outline, the plan he advocated was similar to the one eventually adopted in 1846. The pupil-teachers, who 'would receive superior instruction at separate hours from the rest [of the children]', he wrote, 'would constantly acquire a greater degree of skill and knowledge, until they became fitted alike by their attainments and practical address to encounter unassisted the responsibilities and cares of teachers. As the pupil-teachers acquired skill,' he continued, 'they should be permitted to acquire some remuneration...at the termination of their training, a certificate of competency might be given to those who afforded sufficient proofs on examination of skill and general attainments.'[5]

After his transfer to the Metropolitan area in 1838, Kay-Shuttleworth continued with his experiments on a wider scale and with greater publicity than before. As a result, Mr Aubin's

* When the college, founded by Kay-Shuttleworth and others at Battersea (see below), was handed over to the National Society, in 1843, it was dedicated to St John. When the amalgamation of the two institutions took place in 1923, St Mark's College became known as the College of St Mark and St John.

reformatory school at Norwood, for which he secured a grant of £500 a year, became so well known that members of the gentry began to send the prospective teachers for their schools to it for training. Despite the responsibilities that his appointment to the Education Office brought him, he did not give up his private efforts. With the help of his friend and former colleague, E. Carleton Tufnell, and the Bishop of Norwich, he established a college at Battersea for the training of teachers. Here he lived for a while, contributing to its maintenance and supervising the life of the students, until the institution was taken over by the National Society in 1843.[6]

While Kay-Shuttleworth was acquiring first-hand experience in both his official and his private capacity, of the condition of English elementary education, dissatisfaction with the existing state of affairs was expressed more frequently. The contents of the reports of the Department's inspectorate undoubtedly played an important part in this process for they drew attention to the manifest inadequacy of the monitorial system and the deficiencies of the existing schools. Inspectors of schools soon became well aware, as did their colleagues in other departments, of the limitations of their powers and the consequent need for an extension of state supervision. No change, however, could be made until the religious societies were convinced of the need to replace the monitorial system with a better one. Only when this had happened was it possible for meaningful negotiations to take place.

By the 1840s, though, both the National Society and the British and Foreign School Society were beginning to realize that they could not carry on their work without greater help from outside. By the time of the establishment of the Committee of the Privy Council on Education, the National Society, chastened by experience, had lost its early optimism. 'The founders of the Committee had hoped to complete their work in twenty years,' they stated, 'but now the Committee have long been contemplating, with a deep anxiety, the almost boundless sphere of labour and responsibility which has been opening more widely before them.'[7]

The inauguration of the building grants had the paradoxical effect of adding to the problems of the National Society, for they soon found that they were unable to provide sufficient teachers for the new schools. In 1837 alone, they had been unable to supply the managers of thirty to forty schools with trained staff.[8] Two years later, only 212 of the 546 schools built with state assistance since 1833 contained teachers who had 'been regularly trained and instructed for their offices, either in the Central School of the National Society or in District Central Schools for a shorter period'.[9] Yet the new schools presumably were the very ones for which the Society would have made every effort to have found suitable staff.

Furthermore, the training of even those teachers who had been fortunate enough to have been sent to the training school in Baldwin's Gardens, off the Gray's Inn Road, founded in 1812, left much to be desired. The aspirant teacher, first of all, had to learn just as much as he was going to teach. To do this, 'he went to the bottom of the junior class as a boy, and said his lessons with the children until he could get to the top'.[10] A report of the Central Society of Education shows how limited was the secular content of the instruction given even in the principal London schools of the National Society. 'The master at the school in Baldwin's Gardens states that for many years the committee for managing the school resisted the introduction of any map whatsoever; but that at last he prevailed upon them to allow the introduction of a map of the Holy Land, and another of the journeyings of the children of Israel in the desert... In the Westminster model school [to which the training of teachers was transferred from Baldwin's Gardens in 1832], a few maps have lately been introduced, of which, however, very little use is made; but in the great mass of the National schools no map of any kind is ever seen.'[11]

The little that the masters learnt was learnt in an atmosphere of confusion. Monitorial schools were noisy. Noise was part of the 'method'. 'Mr Lancaster had a notion,' Francis Place informed the Select Committee on Education in England and Wales in 1835, '[that] if he could allow boys to make a noise they would never consider it a drudgery to be taught;...there is in the school perpetual noise; strangers think it confusion, but it is perfect order; the boys get the power of abstraction so as to go along with ease, notwithstanding there is noise from the process going on.'[12] In contrast, some attempt was made to give scholars in the Baldwin's Gardens school an opportunity to concentrate. Here 'the School Committee decreed, "that bawling lessons be confined as much as possible to the junior classes, and that important texts of scripture and the doctrines of Christianity be not allowed in any case to form the subject of such repetitions" '.[13] On the other hand the school was frequently left in the charge of a boy of fourteen while the members of the regular teaching staff were spreading the gospel of the 'method' in Ireland and elsewhere.[14] Discipline was further undermined by a succession of visitors; 3,250 signed the visitors' book in 1815, and another 3,922 added their signatures the next year.[15] The evidence of one inspector, J. D. Morell,* suggests that schools were disorderly long after these early days. 'During the early years of my inspection,' he wrote in 1859, 'I was frequently in despair as to the possibility of doing anything or hearing anything in the classroom... The noise of the children, which the teachers had got the singular habit of designating "the hum of work" most effectively prevented any effort which I could make to find out what the work really was, or how far the scholars had advanced in it.'[16] By the late 1850s, conditions such as these were exceptional. Morell only encountered them in new schools with inexperienced teachers.

This improvement was largely the result of the abandonment of the monitorial system. Dissatisfaction with this method of teaching seems to have grown rapidly after the death of Dr Bell in 1832.[17] By the mid 1840s, 'the notion that a few weeks' attendance at an organized school, where what was called the "National system" might be learned, was sufficient to transmute a decayed tradesman, with some knowledge of writing and accounts, into a national schoolmaster' had been largely abandoned. Instead, John Allen wrote in his report in February 1846: 'The conviction is daily gaining ground, that for a supply of well-qualified teachers, we must look to our training establishments, where they may remain long enough to have their characters moulded, and to receive that education which may fit them for their work.'[18]

Both societies soon found that they lacked the resources to meet the challenge of providing more and, at the same time, better trained teachers. Although patrons were ready to subscribe to a school that would benefit the immediate locality, they were less eager to support a training college. Such an institution, often

---

* J. D. Morell, educated at Glasgow and Bonn Universities, was H.M.I. of Nonconformist schools (1848–76).

organized on a diocesan basis, failed to arouse the generous impulses of the more parochially minded.

Although the British and Foreign School Society frequently complained about the quality of the teachers they had to employ,[19] the most thoroughgoing discussion of the problem appeared in the reports of the National Society. In 1844, for example, they regretted that 'the annual income or general fund of the society, which is expended on the various training establishments, compels them to confine their exertions within narrow limits'. The committee could not afford, the report explained, to offer free exhibitions to the many 'best qualified persons [who] are prevented from becoming candidates for admission into training from want of the requisite pecuniary means'. In conclusion they touched on their greatest difficulty, that of 'the deficiency of accommodation available to pupils in training'.[20]

The following year the National Society admitted that by employing monitors they were doing no more than making the best of a bad job. 'Though monitors cannot do all that might be wished, yet at present no equally good substitute is provided.'[21] The remedy required was to use older children. 'It is desirable that the best monitors or pupil-teachers,' the Society thought, 'should be retained in schools till the age of seventeen years, at which age they will often be qualified to enter the training institutions.'[22] This suggestion raised a further problem: if the pupil-teachers stayed at school until they were seventeen, they had to be paid. Unfortunately the National Society could not afford to help a school once it had been opened. Except for a few months after the launching of the special appeal in 1842,* there had never been enough money to spare for such a purpose.[23] Diocesan boards, anxious to improve their schools, turned to the state for help and began to petition for 'special aid in the better training of monitors'.[24]

The way was now open for Sir James Kay-Shuttleworth to implement his long-nurtured plans. In the autumn of 1844, he had had an important meeting with Sir Robert Peel, the Prime Minister, and Lord Wharncliffe, the Lord President of the Council, at which he secured their agreement to the scheme he introduced in 1846. Much of 1845, a year that the failure of the

* See p. 25.

potato crop in Ireland and the controversy over the Maynooth grant made into one of political crisis, seems to have been devoted to negotiation with the National Society. At the end of the year Kay-Shuttleworth was able to inform Sir Robert Peel, 'The proposals as to new measures have been substantially approved by the bishop of London, and have become the subject of an earnest wish among the most influential members of the National Society. I anticipate no opposition in any other direction.'[25] The continuation of the dispute over the repeal of the Corn Laws delayed the publication of the first of the new minutes until 25 August 1846, one month after the fall of Peel's ministry.[26]

As in 1839, so in 1846, the cooperation of the National Society was bought at a heavy price. 'The decisions arrived at in 1846,' Kay-Shuttleworth told the Newcastle Commission in 1860, 'amounted in my conception, to the abandonment of the idea of a common school, and the adoption of the denominational system. It likewise, at least, amounted to a postponement of the consideration of the question of supporting those schools by rates and to an indefinite extension of the Parliamentary grant... The minutes gave a great stimulus to the establishment of denominational schools, hence the difficulty of founding any other class of schools to be supported solely by rates was thereby enormously increased.'[27] By succouring the voluntary schools and giving them a new lease of life, the inauguration of the pupil–teacher system had one unfortunate consequence. Although it did much to stimulate the expansion of elementary education, it did so at the price of delaying the introduction of universal elementary education.

Although the former Secretary to the Education Department did not publicly admit his defeat until 1860, the National Society lost no time in claiming their victory. In their next annual report, they drew attention to the fact that the 'two great principles (1) that it is essential to education that religion pervade the whole teaching of a school; and (2) that the main direction of education should be left in the care of those who would be prompted to approach and handle it from a care for the immortal souls of the children—have been practically recognized....And because due respect has been had to these principles,' they added, 'your Committee will thankfully accept the aid offered in those minutes...[for] they merely offer to develop the existing system of the Society, without invading the province of the clergy and other local managers of the National Schools, and without any attempt at that unnatural and unreal division of knowledge into religious and secular which mars the full efficiency of both.'[28]

The minute of 21 December 1846, which set out the new scheme in detail, is a landmark in the history of English elementary education. Not only did it stipulate the manner in which a school was to be organized; it also introduced the principle of payment by results.[29] A school whose managers wished to take advantage of the new grants had to meet certain preliminary conditions. Above all else, it had to possess a teacher who was capable of teaching the apprentices. The school also had to be well furnished and supplied with books and apparatus. The children in it were required to be divided into classes that received an instruction that was skilful, and graduated according to their age and the time they had been in attendance. Equal care had to be bestowed on each class. Lastly, discipline was expected to be mild and firm, and conducive to good order.

After defining the standards demanded of the school, the minute set out in detail the qualifications expected of the apprentices. These young people had to be in good health, over thirteen years of age, and able to pass a preliminary examination of a carefully prescribed standard. The Department also drew up a syllabus of the course of study, which lasted five years in the case of pupil-teachers, and four years for stipendiary monitors. The shorter indenture was intended for schools in rural areas where the teachers might have found the longer and more demanding syllabus beyond their capabilities.

When Robert Lowe laid down a syllabus in reading, writing, and arithmetic for the Revised Code, he was doing no more than following in his predecessor's footsteps. Kay-Shuttleworth had earlier drawn up a graduated course of study, in considerable detail, for the pupil-teacher to follow year by year. In grammar, for instance, he had to meet the following requirements:

First year   The noun, verb, and adjective; with their relations in a simple sentence.
Second year   The pronoun, adverb, and preposition; with their relations in a simple sentence.

93

Third year	The conjunction, with the analysis of sentences.
Fourth year	More advanced exercises in preceding subjects; with knowledge of prefixes and affixes.
Fifth year	The same subjects.

The full scheme of study was set out on a broadsheet that was displayed in every school in which apprentices were trained. At the end of each year teacher and pupil were paid by results. If the inspector, on his annual visit, was satisfied with his examination in all the subjects that had to be studied, the Department paid an annual stipend to the apprentices and a gratuity to the master who had given them tuition out of school hours. The pupil-teachers were on a scale that rose from £10 a year by annual increments of £2 10s. to £20.* Teachers, in return for an hour and a half's tuition a day, five days a week, received £5 a year for one pupil, £9 for two, and £3 for each child above that number up to a limit of £15 a year.

At first, one pupil-teacher was allowed for every twenty-five scholars 'normally attending'. The new scheme, however, was taken up with such alacrity that the ratio had to be altered less than two years later. On 25 November 1848, Kay-Shuttleworth sent a circular letter to the inspectors telling them that the 2,060 apprentices whom they had already accepted committed the Department to the expenditure of £71,688 11s. 8d. in the fifth year of their training. Furthermore, despite arrears of work, so many pupil-teachers had already been accepted that the parliamentary grant for the current financial year was likely to be exceeded. To prevent this from happening, inspectors were instructed to exercise 'a more critical discrimination in the admission of candidates for apprenticeship'. In addition, schools that already had apprentices were not to be allowed more than one to every fifty children in attendance unless 'the candidates could pass an unequivocally good examination'.[30] Gradually the proportion of one girl pupil-teacher to every forty scholars and one boy to every fifty became the established practice. Then in 1859, for reasons to be explained shortly, teachers were restricted to four acolytes each.[31]

After he had served his articles, the pupil-teacher who won a Queen's scholarship, worth £20 or £25 a year, went to a normal

* Women teachers and girl apprentices were paid at approximately two-thirds these rates.

school or training college. Every teacher who obtained his certificate of merit at the end of his course qualified for an annual augmentation to his salary. This subsidy, paid by the Department, varied between £15 for one year's training and £30 for three years spent at college. This grant was made on the condition that the school managers, for their part, paid the teacher at least twice as much as the government and provided him with a rent-free house. School pence, though, could be used to provide half the locally raised funds. Thus a generation before the school boards were given powers to compel children to attend school, school managers were given an incentive to ensure that they came with regularity.

An important extension was made to the original scheme in March 1847 when those schoolmasters already in the schools were allowed to sit the certificate examination and thus qualify for the government grant.[32] School managers welcomed this concession for it brought them immediate benefit. 'As the only Church Training Institutions at the present open to inspection are St Mark's College, the establishment at Battersea, and those at Chester, York, and Durham, the assistance offered towards the salaries of teachers would have been almost a prospective measure,' the committee of the National Society explained, 'if an important modification of the plan had not been made, by which it is proposed for the present to assist in paying the salaries of any teachers who may prove themselves qualified for the office by examination.'[33]

At first, as the following table shows, more certificates were awarded to 'acting teachers' than to 'students'. Up to the end of 1851, while the first generation of pupil-teachers were still serving their indentures, the training colleges had to accept such students as they could obtain. From 1852 onwards, they were able to recruit holders of Queen's scholarships in increasing numbers. Thus students soon provided the majority of certificated teachers. It has to be remembered, though, that some pupil-teachers never went to college. For this reason the figures for 'acting teachers' for the mid-1850s and later probably include a small number of former apprentices. Since schools did not normally have more than one certificated teacher each, a comparison of the last two columns gives an overall picture of total wastage from the teaching profession. The figures for teachers actually employed and those for teachers in charge of schools, for instance, are identical for the years 1853–8 inclusive.

Table I THE SUPPLY OF CERTIFICATED TEACHERS

Males

Year	As students	As acting teachers	Annual total	Cumulative total	Number in charge of schools
1847	31	102	133	133	120
1848	52	353	405	538	501
1849	98	204	302	840	703
1850	111	146	257	1,097	818
1851	172	150	322	1,419	996
1852	404	224	628	2,047	1,352
1853	249	291	540	2,587	1,541*
1854	538	201	739	3,326	1,859*
1855	439	221	660	3,986	2,242*
1856	438	220	658	4,644	2,726*
1857	490	160	650	5,294	3,206*
1858	810	288	1,098	6,392	3,568*
1859	806	145	951	7,343	4,237

Females

Year	As students	As acting teachers	Annual total	Cumulative total	Number in charge of schools
1847	5	4	9	9	4
1848	19	72	91	100	93
1849	73	100	173	273	227
1850	93	84	177	450	275
1851	107	100	207	657	401
1852	145	109	254	911	627
1853	275	172	447	1,358	756*
1854	370	109	479	1,837	977*
1855	342	164	506	2,343	1,190*
1856	351	155	506	2,849	1,647*
1857	544	157	701	3,550	1,960*
1858	704	102	806	4,356	2,320*
1859	757	148	905	5,261	2,762

* i.e. Numbers actually employed.
Source: *Report of the Royal Commission on Popular Education in England and Wales (The Newcastle Report)*, P.P. 1861. XXI, A, pp. 638 and 676.

The process of amendment and change, which we have already begun to trace, continued until the original minutes were swept away by the inauguration of the Revised Code in the early 1860s. Up to 1859, the main objective of the government was to induce an ever-increasing number of young people to make pupilage, followed by residence in a training college, the gateway to the teaching profession. One of the first problems that had to be tackled arose from the fact that existing teachers had been allowed to sit for the certificate examination. This change in the regulations had virtually deprived pupil-teachers of any incentive to continue their studies at a training college. Since few teachers, at this time, possessed any worthwhile skills, trained apprentices would have had no difficulty in finding posts as teachers. Once they had done so, they would have become eligible to sit the examination for their certificates. Accordingly in December 1851,[34] when the first pupils were about to complete their articles, their Lordships decided to discourage them from thinking of short-circuiting the colleges. They refused to give them their certificates until they had spent either a year at college or three years teaching in a school that was open to inspection. The alternative of a probationary period was offered because not all who wished to do so could go to college.

The number of Queen's scholarships was originally limited to 25 per cent of the number of students who were resident in each college for one year and upwards at the date of the examination.[35] Within a short time it became clear that 'the training colleges were maintained inadequately, with difficulty; were not fully occupied, nor always with the class of students best adapted for training'.[36] When H.M.I. the Reverend H. Moseley made his visits in 1852, he found that only 513 of the 729 places available in Church of England colleges for men were occupied. Yet that same year, a total of 750 young men had completed their apprenticeships in English and Welsh schools. Three hundred and four of the 750 had competed for, and 248 had obtained scholarships. Thus although there were over 200 vacancies in Anglican colleges alone, 502 time-expired pupil-teachers had been left without financial assistance to continue their training. Most of these were lost to the profession. The year before, only 31 of the 570 who did not win scholarships had been able to find some other means of financing their studies.[37]

Steps were taken to deal with the problem of wastage. In December 1846, Kay-Shuttleworth had held out the prospect of employment in the civil service as an alternative career for pupil-teachers. This escape route was sealed off in May 1852.[38] Two months later, employment in a new grade, that of assistant teacher, was offered to those candidates who failed to win scholarships.[39] Although the Department contributed £25 a year towards the salary of the holder of such a post, recruitment proceeded slowly. The Newcastle Commission found that there were only 295 men and women employed in this capacity in 1859.[40]

More effective than either of the changes so far described was the removal of the limitation on the number of Queen's scholarships in 1853.[41] Thus the colleges no longer had to worry about the problem of filling their vacant places because students could not afford to come. At the same time, another cause of considerable wastage, the gap in employment between the expiry of indentures and entry to college, was removed. Apprentices recruited before 1 January 1854 were allowed to draw their fifth-year stipend up to the date of the scholarship examination. Similarly all new indentures had to expire at Christmas, the season at which this eighteen-plus of the nineteenth century was held.

It was one thing to see that the colleges received sufficient students; it was quite another to see that the students received a suitable training. State aid, at first, had done little to encourage the colleges to raise their teaching standards above those of the schools. Assistant teachers had been made eligible for the augmentation grant in August 1851 and, in the following December, a book grant of 10s. a student had been authorized.[42] Thus the offer of a grant in 1853, 'to promote in training schools the study of the subjects proper to elementary education', broke new ground. Not only did it recognize the colleges' need for special treatment; it also attempted to influence the standard and content of the instruction they offered. Each college was allowed to recruit three lecturers, who were to be paid £150 a year by the college and another £100 a year by the Department, for teaching history, English literature, geography, physical science, or mathematics.[43]

The Department also tried to make the course longer. From 1846 onwards, the colleges, in common with the teachers and their apprentices, had been paid partly by results. They received £20, £25 or £30 for each student who passed his first-, second-or third-year examination. Under the terms of the minute of

August 1853, the Department proposed to make no payment until a student had been in residence for eighteen months. This scheme raised such an outcry from the colleges that it had to be withdrawn the following year. A new scale, which sanctioned payments rising from £13 for a first-year student with a third-class pass to £24 for a second- or third-year man with a first-class pass, was introduced in June 1854. This concession was followed by another a year later, which made the prospect of going to college more attractive to the capable student. If he obtained a first-class scholarship, he was given £4 pocket money for his first year, and £6 for his second.[44] Before this, the proceeds of a scholarship had been earmarked exclusively for the cost of a man's tuition. Another way in which the Department attempted to determine the nature and content of the activities of the college was by encouraging them to provide special courses for training mistresses to work in infants' schools.[45] This suggestion met with little response. Only one college, that of the Home and Colonial Society, in the Gray's Inn Road, was offering such a course at the end of the decade.[46]

In June 1856, still further efforts were made to fill the colleges, now capable of taking 1,000 students a year for a two-year course. Those pupil-teachers, apprenticed before 1 January 1854, who had previously been allowed to stay on at school and draw their stipends until they sat their scholarship examination, were given the option of going to college without further delay.[47] To encourage students to stay longer, first-year students, who previously had had to wait three months for their examination results, were permitted to start their second-year course without further ado. Students who failed their first-year examinations were given a second chance. Lastly, the colleges were allowed to give 10 per cent of the Queen's scholarships to private students who had not served their articles. As a result of all these changes, the privately sponsored student had almost disappeared by the end of the decade. In 1859, only 443 of the 2,798 students in residence did not hold Queen's scholarships.[48]

By taking these various steps, the Department had increased the number of students. By manipulating the examination system, it increased the number of successful students. From the following table it can be seen that the pass rate rose from 65 per cent in 1852 to nearly 100 per cent by 1870.

Table II EXAMINATION RESULTS OF MALE STUDENTS IN
CHURCH OF ENGLAND TRAINING COLLEGES

Christmas	Candidates	Passes	Percentage Pass Rate
1852	467	305	65·3
1854	536	411	76·7*
	160	153	95·6
1856	352	317	90·1
	217	184	84·8
1858	503	456	90·7
	236	223	94·5
1860	Not available		
1862	478	471	98·5
	358	355	99·2
1864	367	361	98·4
	419	396	94·5
1866	325	318	97·8
	259	254	98·1
1868	244	240	98·4
	239	238	99·6
1870	228	227	99·6
	365	361	98·9

* From 1854 onwards, the first line of figures gives first-year students and the second line second-year students.

Source: *Reports of the Committee, 1852–70 (passim).*

The first move was taken in 1854 when the Reverend H. Moseley, the inspector of Anglican training colleges for men, produced a syllabus for all the colleges to follow. Prior to this date, the training institutions had developed their syllabuses independently of each other. Because of this the Department had had to set separate examination papers for each college. It now became possible to set the same paper for every student. In drafting his scheme Moseley had been guided by three main principles. His first had been 'not to add to or to take from the existing subjects of the examination'. This left the colleges with the illusion that their independence was not being tampered with. The second objective was 'to give the greatest weight to those subjects which are the subjects of elementary education... If... the course of study . . . be not confined to the subjects of *elementary* instruction,' he explained, '...the grants made to that

[training] school involve a *misappropriation* of public money.'*
The third aim was 'To inculcate the principle of "not attempting
more than can be done well"'.[49]

The last objective soon became the dominant one. In 1857 the
Department told heads of colleges that failure in one of the compulsory subjects—religious knowledge, arithmetic, grammar and
English language, school management, reading, spelling and
penmanship—was 'held to be sufficient to deprive the candidate
of all claim to a place in the class list, however superior his other
papers may be'. The Department, however, left itself an administrative loophole. 'The Committee of Council may...occasion-
ally see fit to retain in the schedule the names of candidates who
have failed in one of the essential subjects, but whose exercises
generally indicate sufficient promise to justify their further
training.'

Lingen explained that the departmental maxim was 'proficiency in a few subjects is valued more highly than mediocrity in
many'. To make quite sure that the future elementary schoolmaster did not become a dilettante he was sternly warned that 'it
is not their Lordships' desire to encourage a large extent of
superficial study, and in no case will two papers marked "moderate" receive as many marks as would have been given to one of
them marked "good"'.[50] So successful was this restrictionist
policy that the Newcastle Commissioners reported that 'a first-
class certificate may be obtained by a candidate, who being perfect in the elementary subjects, takes up none of the higher ones
in the second year'. At the most candidates were only allowed to
choose one of the following: physical science, mechanics,
mathematics, English literature, and Latin. With masterly
meiosis the Commissioners concluded that 'it would be unjust to
say that this part of the syllabus [the higher subjects] is too
ambitious, or that it prescribes subjects unfit for the purpose of
training teachers for elementary schools'.[51] The Revised Code
formalized the situation by dropping the 'higher' subjects
altogether. Instead, candidates were expected to answer questions 'in economy, social, political, and sanitary'.[52]

The state thus enjoyed a remarkable degree of control over the
public educational system at one of its key points. When the

* Moseley's italics.

Newcastle Report was published, the government was providing 76 per cent of the income of Church of England training colleges. A successful college, 'conducted with rigorous economy', was even more dependent on its paymaster. Cheltenham training college drew 94 per cent of its income from public funds and York obtained 89 per cent. 'These contributions,' the Newcastle Commissioners pointed out, 'purchase all the authority over them which the government requires or could beneficially use. By altering it [the syllabus] as occasion may require the Committee of Council can modify the character of instruction given to all the certificated teachers in the kingdom in every point except those which are peculiar to different religious denominations.'[53]

State direction of the education of the masses helped to safeguard the interests of the propertied classes. Hence it was acceptable to public opinion. Middle-class education was another matter. Here state intervention could lead to tyranny. The Taunton Commissioners, accordingly, rejected the idea of training teachers for schools for the middle classes in government institutions. 'The great objection to the establishment of a training school for masters in the endowed schools,' they wrote, 'is that it would almost inevitably give the government an undue control over all the superior education of the country.'[54]

Thus in the search for more teachers, the Department had considerably modified the scheme that had been introduced by its founder secretary in 1846. The greater emphasis that was placed on the acquisition of the basic skills in the training colleges anticipated the needs of the schools under the Revised Code. By 1861, the year in which Robert Lowe laid the first draft of his controversial code on the table of the House of Commons, Queen's scholarships had ceased to be the coveted prizes reserved exclusively for outstanding pupil-teachers at the end of a five-year apprenticeship. A period of five years had ceased to be mandatory. Private students, over the age of sixteen, could be admitted direct to the fourth year of their apprenticeship.[55] The scholarship examination, no longer competitive, had become a qualifying one. For example, at Christmas 1861, 661 candidates competed for 615 vacancies in the Anglican men's colleges, but only 468 were deemed to be worthy of places.[56] When the successful pupil-teachers arrived at college, they found that they had lost their former monopoly of scholarships. Other holders included first- and second-year private students who, together with others on the course for mistresses in infants' schools, had never served their articles.[57] On the other hand, the remaining scholarship holders, assistant teachers of three years' standing,[58] teachers from night schools,[59] and certificated teachers who had not spent more than one year at college,[60] were people of considerably greater maturity and experience than the eighteen-year-olds straight out of the classroom.

When the number of teachers trained annually by the colleges reached 1,500, attention was turned to the problem of framing a manpower budget. Decisions had to be made about both the size of the total labour force required in the schools, and the number of apprentices that had to be recruited each year to make good the annual losses from the profession. The need to do this was made more urgent by the post-war economy drive of the late 1850s. In the search for those areas in which government spending could be reduced, the rapid expansion of expenditure on education that had taken place during the last decade came under close scrutiny.*

As a consequence of this reappraisal of policy, minutes were published in May 1859[61] and January 1860[62] which limited teachers to four pupil-teachers each and withdrew the building grant from all training colleges. After the first cut had been made, the Department justified their action with an argument that also prepared the ground for the next brake that was put on the training programme. They claimed that as the number of apprentices was approaching 15,000, they could expect to have, after allowing for wastage, 2,280 candidates for 1,500 yearly vacancies in the colleges. By a process of special pleading which does not bear close scrutiny, they demonstrated that the output of teachers had already reached its optimum level. After assuming that the largest number of children who would ever have to be taught was 3,000,000 and that one teacher was required for every hundred, they concluded that 30,000 teachers would eventually be needed. Since they already had 6,000 and a further 1,500 were added each year, the gap, without allowing for any losses, would be closed in sixteen years. The number of places in the colleges, they stated, should be determined not by present

* See p. 187.

requirements, but by the ultimate permanent demand for teachers, in other words making good the annual wastage. On this point they took Prussian experience as their guide. Yet at the same time, they admitted that Prussia did not necessarily provide a valid comparison with England and Wales, where 39 per cent of the teachers were women and society had a 'more independent condition'. There were good reasons, however, for ignoring these objections. The Prussian wastage rate was 5 per cent per annum and 5 per cent of 30,000 gave the right answer, i.e. 1,500. Hence they concluded that, 'If 5 per cent is realistic [which they had admitted it was not] the present provision for training teachers ought not to be greatly exceeded'.[63]

The Newcastle Commissoners arrived at the same conclusion but by a different route. After examining statistics relating to 1,851 schools in certain selected areas, they found that there were 58·3 children to each teacher. On the basis of this ratio, they decided that the 2,000,000 children, 'the largest number...for whom trained teachers will be required until a considerable change of feeling has taken place amongst the poor as to the education of their children', needed 33,000 teachers. As the colleges could provide this number in twenty-two years, and twenty-two years, at a conservative estimate, was the probable span of a teacher's working life, 'the supply of teachers,' they averred, 'will soon overtake demand'. 'We think, therefore,' they concluded, 'that the Committee of Council has exercised a proper discretion in resolving for the present to entertain no further proposals for the establishment of training colleges for males.' The only criticism they had to offer was that, although there was no overall shortage of teachers, more mistresses specially trained for infants' schools were needed.[64]

Further support for the Department was provided by the reports of the inspectorate. H.M.I.s, instead of reiterating their perennial complaints about a shortage of teachers, began to suggest that there might soon be too many.[65] In 1863, for instance, Norris welcomed the Revised Code as it would check, he thought, that 'over-supply, and consequent depreciation of the teacher' for which he blamed the old regulations. Under them, his district had been recruiting pupil-teachers at the rate of 180 a year; yet only fifty to sixty new teachers were needed each year. School managers, he believed, were already enjoying a buyers' market. In 1858, the average salary of teachers in his area had been £96 a year. By 1862—one year before the general implementation of the Revised Code—it had fallen to £90.[66] Significantly this trend, which had also been noted by his fellow cleric W. J. Kennedy, was most noticeable in the salaries of new teachers. Over the same period, these had fallen from £65 or £70 to £58.[67] A year or so later the situation was much more serious. 'In several cases which have come under my notice,' Watkins reported in 1864, 'the number of candidates for any vacant situation has been very large, not unfrequently above 100. In one school I was informed that there were 180 applications, for another 163, and for one now lying before me 106.'[68]

The over-supply of teachers that Watkins and others had observed was, in one sense, illusory. Although existing demand may have been satisfied, potential demand, as the events of the 1870s soon showed, was far greater. Considerable though the achievements of the Department had been, much still remained to be done. The 1,825 public day schools in the specimen districts examined in the *Newcastle Report* employed 2,354 teachers. Only 612 (26 per cent) of them possessed certificates.[69] The situation in England and Wales, as a whole, was similar. There were 22,647 public day schools connected with religious bodies but less than 7,000 of them were in the charge of trained teachers.[70] On the other hand, conditions in private schools were far worse. Only seventeen of the 3,594 teachers in the private schools examined in detail by the commissioners possessed certificates of competency issued either by the Committee of Privy Council or the College of Preceptors.[71] The latter qualification, issued by an organization founded in 1848 for the improvement of middle-class schools, was of very little value. No examination was required for membership. Hence membership, as John Robson, the Secretary of the College, was forced to admit to the Schools' Inquiry Commission in 1867, 'carried no guarantee of a member's fitness intellectually, or of his attainments as a schoolmaster'. Yet 473 of the 742 persons connected with the college in 1867 were registered as members. Although a member could attain the higher status of fellow or licentiate by examination, he could do so by taking one subject at a time.[72]

Perhaps the greatest testimony that was paid to the Education Department's efforts to create a corps of trained teachers came from those classes who did not send their children to be taught by them. To them imitation was not only the sincerest form of flattery, but also an act of self-interest. The publication of Charles Dickens's *Nicholas Nickleby*, in 1838, had shown that masters in private schools enjoyed little, if any, esteem. The College of Preceptors, which was founded in 1846 to raise the standards of these schools, received its charter of incorporation three years later. This new organization was established 'for the purpose of promoting sound learning and of advancing the interests of education, more especially among the middle classes...and [to] give certificates of the acquaintances and fitness for their office of persons engaged or desired to be engaged in the Education of Youth, particularly in the private schools of England and Wales'. Its first patron was the Marquis of Northampton, the President of the Royal Society. Amongst its Vice-Patrons was Sir J. W. Lubbock, the distinguished mathematician and astronomer and Vice-President of the Royal Society.[73] The new society, shortly before holding its first examinations for schoolmasters in 1850, warned the readers of its journal of the dangers that lay ahead: 'Unless the teachers of the middle classes, earnestly, and without loss of time, set about reforming themselves, they will cease to be the teachers of the middle classes, and find themselves justly and deservedly supplanted by those whom they are in the habit of regarding as occupying the inferior grades of the profession.'[74] Worse still there was the danger that the whole of the middle classes—and not just their teachers—might be supplanted by their social inferiors. When a meeting was held, in 1861, to consider the promotion of Anglican boarding schools—the Woodard Schools—the editor of the *English Journal of Education* commented, 'There is still ample room for reform in middle class education. The classes above them in the social scale have long been bestirring themselves to justify the claims of birth and wealth by those of intellectual superiority... The classes below them are rapidly gaining upon them, and grudging the traditional respect so unhesitatingly paid by labour to capital before intelligence learnt to assert its independence'.[75] These fears were imaginary. Great care was taken to see that the teachers of the children of the labouring poor were taught to accept the existing social order.

Appendix

TRAINING COLLEGES UNDER GOVERNMENT INSPECTION IN 1858

(a) *For men only*

Name of College	Where situated	Date of Establishment	Date of First Building Grant	Average Number of Students			Number of Tutors and Training Masters	Queen's Scholars as percentage of Total Students
				Queen's Scholars	Other	Total		
Battersea C of E	Battersea	1840	—	106	3	109	9	97·2
Bangor B and F	Bangor	—	1857	18	2	20	4	90
Carmarthen C of E	Carmarthen	1848	1849	14	22	36	6	38·9
Carnarvon C of E	Carnarvon	1846	1858	20	16	36	7	55·6
Saint Mark's C of E	Chelsea (Fulham Road)	1841	1842	93	12	105	14	88·6
Chester C of E	Chester	1839	1843	40	13	53	10	75·5
Chichester C of E	Chichester	1839	1851	10	7	17	4	58·8
Culham C of E	Culham, near Oxford	1853	1853	31	25	56	5	55·4
Durham C of E	Durham	1841	1847	46	1	47	5	97·9
Exeter C of E	Exeter	1839	1854	34	10	44	7	77·3
Saint Mary's R.C.	Hammersmith	1852	1852	25	21	46	—	54·3
Metropolitan C of E	Highbury Park	1849	1850	72	—	72	9	100
Saltley C of E	Saltley, near Birmingham	1852	1852	39	20	59	6	66·1
Winchester C of E	Winchester	1839	—	32	5	37	6	86·5
Peterborough C of E	Peterborough	—	—	14	1	15	3	93·3
			Totals	594	158	752		79

Appendix (Contd.)

TRAINING COLLEGES UNDER GOVERNMENT INSPECTION IN 1858

(b) *For women only*

Name of College	Where situated	Date of Establishment	Date of First Building Grant	Average Number of Students			Queen's Scholars as percentage of Total Students
				Queen's Scholars	Other	Total	
Bishop's Stortford C of E	Hockerill, near Bishop's Stortford	1852	1854	47	10	57	82·5
Brighton C of E	Brighton	1842	1855	28	17	45	62·2
Bristol, Gloucester and Oxford C of E	Fishponds, near Bristol	1853	1854	41	28	69	
Derby C of E	Derby	1851	1851	31	9	40	59·4
Home and Colonial Society C of E	Gray's Inn Lane, London	1836	1856	130	42	172	
Liverpool R.C.	Mount Pleasant, Liverpool	—	—	39	12	51	75·6
St Leonard's-on-Sea R.C.	St Leonard's, near Hastings	—	—	22	9	31	71·0
Salisbury C of E	Salisbury	1840	1852	51	9	60	85
Truro C of E	Truro	1849	1859	6	15	21	28·6
Warrington C of E	Warrington	1844	1854	65	25	90	72·2
Whitelands C of E	Whitelands House, Chelsea	1841	1851	105	1	106	99·1
Durham C of E	Durham	1858	1858	22	15	37	59·5
Norwich C of E	Norwich	1840	1854	35	4	39	89·7
Totals				622	196	818	76·0

Appendix (Contd.)

TRAINING COLLEGES UNDER GOVERNMENT INSPECTION IN 1858

(c) *For men and women*

Name of College	Where situated	Date of Establishment	Date of First Building Grant	Average Number of Students			Number of Tutors	Queen's Scholars as percentage of Total Students
				Queen's Scholars	Other	Total		
British and Foreign School Society	Borough Road, London	—	1842	118	12	130	—	90·8
Cheltenham C of E	Cheltenham	—	1850	155	—	155	—	100
Westminster Wesleyan	Horseferry Road Westminster	—	1852	86	16	102	11	84·3
York and Ripon C of E	York	1846	1846	100	9	109	—	91·7
			Totals	459	37	496		92·5
			Grand Totals	1,675	391	2,066		81·1

Source: *Report of the Royal Commission on Popular Education in England and Wales (The Newcastle Report)*, P.P. 1861, XXI, A, pp. 643–5.

5 Training the Teachers

Although I have met with several instances of the schoolmistress being received at the clergyman's table, I scarcely recollect an instance out of London (except the dean of Bangor) of a clergyman's shaking hands with, or even talking familiarly with, the parochial schoolmaster.

H.M.I. THE REVEREND JOHN ALLEN[1]

Their [the pupil-teachers'] parents are thoroughly respectable persons, of decent habits, and unimpeachable character...; they are the best representatives of the working classes... They... exemplify the virtues which thrive perhaps best in a humble station.

H.M.I. THE REVEREND B. M. COWIE[*][2]

It is no easy task to convert a labourer into a schoolmaster.

H.M.I. THE REVEREND H. MOSELEY[3]

So far the problem of finding and training the first generation of those teachers who served in the rapidly growing number of elementary schools in England and Wales has been discussed mainly in quantitative terms; in contrast this chapter will explore the question of recruitment in a wider context. The functions a schoolmaster was expected to perform, the kind of training he had, and finally his status in society, reflect the political and social climate of the period during which the state first assumed its new responsibilities towards the children of the labouring classes.

The lengthy debate that had preceded this step had turned, as we have seen,† mainly on one issue, the need to protect and preserve the existing social order. At first those who had argued that

* B. M. Cowie, the son of a London merchant, was educated at Passy, near Paris, and St John's College, Cambridge (senior wrangler, 1839; second Smith's prizeman, 1842; Fellow, 1839–43). He was Principal of College for Civil Engineers, Putney (1844–51), Hulsean lecturer (1852–4), Professor at Gresham College (1854–1900), H.M.I. (1858–72), Dean of Manchester (1872–83) and then of Exeter (to 1900), and a member of Owen's College, Manchester.

† See p. 21 et seq.

this objective could best be achieved by keeping the masses illiterate had won the day. In their view, universal education was unnecessary, irrelevant to the needs of the people as a whole, and dangerous to the interests of the propertied classes. To illustrate this point of view, Lord John Russell quoted William Cobbett* as having said: 'What is the use of teaching a ploughboy to read and write? If he wants to mount a carthorse, reading and writing will not give him a leg up. No, he knows better, without reading or writing either: he first leads the horse to a gate, and he gets upon the gate, and then upon the carthorse. That is education, and this is the sort of education which the agricultural labourer wants.'[4] Lord John Russell had done less than justice to Cobbett, the author of *A Grammar of the English Language intended... for the Use of Soldiers, Sailors, Apprentices, and Ploughboys* (1819). Cobbett's quarrel was not with the policy of educating the children of the labourers but with the policy of indoctrinating them with the principles of the Established Church and Ricardian economics. This kind of education, he thought, was failing to achieve one of its declared purposes, that of raising the general standards of morality. Despite its spread since the beginning of the century: 'The number of bastards had increased to a most prodigious extent so that, in this respect, the morality of the people could not be said to have been advanced by education. The people in fact,' he informed the House of Commons in 1835, the year of his death, 'had the intellectual and the bodily enjoyment at the same time.'[5]

The prejudices against one particular form of education that had been so colourfully expressed by Cobbett were shared by many who lacked his fine sense of discrimination. This widespread fear of the consequences of educating the masses had deep roots. From time immemorial, and with few exceptions, those who were literate did not labour, and those who were illiterate performed the menial tasks of a society that maintained the well-being of a privileged few. Hence there was a widespread and deeply entrenched belief that those who became literate would

* William Cobbett (1763–1835), the son of a small farmer and inn-keeper, emigrated to the United States (1793–1800). After his return, he began the *Weekly Register* (1802), and *Parliamentary Debates* (1804). He was the author of *Rural Rides* (1830). An advocate of reform, he entered the House of Commons as member for Oldham in 1832.

thereupon cease to labour. To tamper with the *status quo* by creating a system of public education was accordingly seen as a policy that was fraught with danger. By the late 1830s, however, those who believed that education could be used as a means of preserving the existing social order had won the day. Although this proposition did not command universal support, all could agree on one point. If the lower orders were going to be educated, their social superiors had to ensure that the nature and content of the education offered were carefully controlled. Intellectual instruction, therefore, had to be subordinated 'to the *regulation* of the thoughts and habits of the children by the doctrines and precepts of revealed religion'.*

The writings of Sir James Kay-Shuttleworth leave no doubt about the nature and purpose of this regulation. Because his influence was so great, his views, more than those of anybody else merit careful consideration. They determined not only the function of the schoolmaster but the kind of training he required to equip him to play his allotted role in a society that could no longer rely on the traditional methods of maintaining law and order. Although the unpaid high constables of the counties and the petty constables of the parishes had been able to deal with minor crimes in a rural society, they were not equal to the task of apprehending the urban criminal. Similarly, a policy of relying on the militia and the Army for quelling major disturbances met with growing criticism as the nineteenth century advanced. Despite this, Great Britain was slow to develop a police force. The Metropolitan Police Act had been passed in 1829. Borough police forces were set up under the Municipal Corporations Act of 1835. The Constables Act of 1839, however, was permissive. It was not until 1856 that every county and borough was required to have a police force. In default of an adequate police force, Kay-Shuttleworth and others turned to the Poor Law guardian and the schoolmaster as the saviours of society.

The reports that Kay-Shuttleworth made as an assistant Poor Law Commissioner show that he regarded the hierarchy as the form of organization most proper for society. In his report for 1836, he complained that the earlier lax administration of Poor Law relief had 'so weakened the cohesion of the elements of

---

* Author's italics. See also p. 37.

society, by destroying the connexion between the labourer and his employee, that the social structure must have lapsed into ruin if it had not been upheld by external force'. In contrast, the great virtue of the Poor Law Amendment Act, 1834, he stated, was that it would 'ensure the integrity of the social fabric by restoring that connexion [between master and servant] which is the chief cement of the mass'.[6]

His remedy for the disorders of the day was simple. 'The public peace,' he wrote elsewhere in the same report, 'could only be ensured by the due subordination of the various classes of society.'[7] A rigorous application of the new Poor Law alone was not enough. Education had to be provided as well, for education was 'one of the most important means of eradicating the germ of pauperism from the rising generation, and of securing in the minds and in the morals of the people the best protection for the institutions of society.'[8] Therefore, Kay-Shuttleworth argued, 'The state had the most positive and direct interest in adopting measures to prevent the rearing of a race of felons and prostitutes...[it had] the duty of rearing these children in religion and industry, and of imparting such an amount of secular education as may fit them to discharge the duties of their station'.[9] These he saw as supplying the merchant service with sailors, and the farms and manufactories of the country with workmen, and the households of the upper and middle classes with domestic servants. Lastly, the schoolmaster's staff of office was not so much his proverbial cane as the policeman's truncheon. 'In every English proprietor's domain there ought to be,' Kay-Shuttleworth wrote, 'as in many there are, schoolhouses with well trained masters, competent and zealous to rear the population in obedience to the laws, in submission to their superiors, and to fit them to strengthen the institutions of their country by their domestic virtues, their sobriety, their industry and forethought.'[10]

Since the children of the labouring classes were to be trained in submission to their superiors, it follows that education was not intended to be a means by which they could elevate themselves in society. There was general agreement on this point. When, for instance, J. A. Roebuck, the radical M.P. for Bath, moved a resolution calling for the appointment of a select committee to inquire into the means of establishing a system of national education he explained that 'his desire was, by affording education to the people, not so much to raise them from their proper situation as to make them happy and contented in it'.[11] William Molesworth, another radical who also entered the House of Commons in 1833, agreed. 'It was,' he said, in his opinion, 'the bounden duty of the government to provide for every child born within the realm such an education as was fitting and suitable for the station which Providence had allotted it.'[12] At this time no other view was tenable. Not until the state assumed an overall responsibility for the provision of education, could the elementary and, later, the primary school provide a right of way leading towards the commanding heights of the meritocracy. Despite this, apprenticeship as a pupil-teacher, as we shall shortly see, gave the more perceptive and ambitious child an unofficial route by which he might attempt the social climb.

At the start, elementary schools were intended for those who could not afford to meet the full cost of their children's education: the labouring poor. No serious attempt was made in the educational literature of the 1830s to define the membership of this group. Apparently all who took part in these early discussions knew what the term meant. Such elaborations and explanations as exist are a product of the economically and socially more complex society of the 1850s. One possible explanation of part of the rapid growth of the education vote was that some parents, well able to meet the full cost of their children's education, were taking advantage of the public system. With this consideration evidently in mind, Lord Robert Cecil moved for a return of the trade, calling, or employment of the father of the children in the six schools that had received the largest capitation grants during the year 1857.[13] Although there was little doubt about the social status of the 533 fathers described as labourers, other groups such as the ninety-three clerks, the forty-nine jewellers and silversmiths, and even the three schoolmasters included men whose standing in society was far from clear.

Attempts were therefore made to define the class for whom the parliamentary grant was intended. When the minutes were codified in 1860, Article 4 described elementary education as that education 'suited to the condition of workmen and servants'.[14] Two years later, the Revised Code stipulated that the object of the grant was 'to promote the education of children belonging to the classes who support themselves by manual labour'.[15] Such a statement, however, took no cognizance of the social changes of the last half century. Somewhat belatedly, in 1866, the Department became aware of the complexity of contemporary society. Inspectors were informed that 'children whose parents, though not supporting themselves by manual labour, yet are of *the same means and social level** as those who do so; such as shopkeepers who have only petty stocks, and employ no one but members of their family, are not excluded'. Elaborate instructions were added for the guidance of inspectors. In them, the class for whom the schools were intended was defined partly objectively in terms of status and income and partly subjectively in terms of social esteem. In cases of doubt they were to ask:

(1) Does A.B. work for himself or for a master? If for himself, does he employ apprentices or journeymen? This will apply to masons, carpenters, tailors, blacksmiths, mariners, fishermen, and etc...The class denoted by Article 4 supports itself by its own manual labour only, and not by profit on the labour of others.

(2) Would it be unreasonable to expect him to pay 9d. per week for the schooling of each of his children? [This was]...the estimated cost (Royal Commission's Report, page 345) of elementary instruction in a day school.†

(3) Does he rank and associate with the working men or with the tradesmen of the place? Simple policemen, coast-guards, and dock and railway porters may commonly be regarded as labouring men. But petty officers in those services, excisemen, pilots, and clerks of various kinds, present more difficulty, and must be judged of according to the answers to the preceding inquiries.[16]

The origins of a policy of basing the public educational system on the existing social divisions, and thereby de-limiting them still more firmly, are discernible even before the Committee of the Privy Council on Education was established in 1839.

* Original italics.
† This estimate was used again in 1870. 'The term "elementary school"... does not include any school at which the ordinary payments...from each scholar, exceed ninepence a week.' *The Elementary Education Act, 1870.* Section 3.

In 1835, a select committee had been appointed to 'inquire into the best means of extending a knowledge of the Arts and of the PRINCIPLES OF DESIGN among the People (especially the Manufacturing Population) of the country'.[17] As a result of its recommendations the Normal School of Design was started in 1837 under the control of the Board of Trade. Thus right from the start, technical education intended to provide manufacturers, master craftsmen, and skilled workers, with a training in art, design and industrial techniques, was divorced, socially and administratively, from elementary education which was for the unskilled worker.* In a somewhat similar way the Mechanics' Institutes, intended by their founders to be media of mass education, became select rather than popular institutions. By the 1850s the few that remained faithful to their proletarian origins were to be found mainly in Lancashire and the West Riding of Yorkshire. Generally speaking these institutes attracted the lower middle class and the 'superior order of the working class'. In the country towns and seaside resorts a considerable number had a predominantly middle-class character. Hence they suffered from the fears and prejudices of the privileged and the suspicion of the poor, the latter being the very class that the early enthusiasts had wanted to help.[18]

The assumption that the educational system should be geared to the existing social strata was so firmly accepted that it even influenced the recommendations of the Schools' Inquiry Commission of 1867 on the future structure of secondary schools. The Taunton Commissioners envisaged three grades of schools in which the school-leaving ages were to be fourteen, sixteen and eighteen years, respectively. In each type of school, the curriculum and the subsequent career expectations of the pupils depended on parental ability and willingness to keep the boys at school. These attitudes, in turn, were seen as a function of the father's income and occupation.[19]

---

* The Science and Art Department, formerly the Department of Practical Art, which was responsible for these schools, was transferred from the President of the Board of Trade to the Lord President of the Council in 1856. Yet, except for the years 1873–84, the Education Department, in Downing Street, and the Science and Art Department, at South Kensington, had separate Permanent Secretaries. Effective administrative integration did not take place until 1899 when the Board of Education was formed. (A. L. Lowell, *The Government of England*, (New York, 1908), vol. ii, p. 331.)

In the public sector the schoolmaster was the exception to the rule. He was the one person who, as a matter of policy, had to be given an education that could raise him in society. Once he had acquired those skills of reading, writing, and ciphering that every schoolmaster needed, he could obtain a more congenial and better-paid post outside the classroom. For this reason he had to be given a salary that approximated to what he could earn in the open market. Witnesses to the Select Committee on Education of 1834 were well aware of this problem. They estimated that if competently trained men were to be kept in the schools, teachers had to be paid at least £100 a year in London and the other large towns.[20] The problems created by raising the schoolmaster in society could have been avoided if he had been recruited from outside the ranks of the labouring classes. So little esteem, however, was attached to the occupation at this time that this solution could not be adopted. Those who possessed the educational qualifications that would have made them worthwhile candidates for the training colleges were not prepared to consider teaching as a career. They could do better elsewhere. 'It is found by experience,' Moseley reported in 1850, 'that to men able and willing to pay from £20 to £30 a year for their education, the office of the schoolmaster does not as a general rule offer inducements enough, either in regard to the remuneration, or to the social position attached to it. To such men there are fairer prospects of advancement, unless, by reason of some feebleness of character, or perhaps of intellect, or some bodily defect, they be thought unequal to any more active or enterprising career.'[21] Cook agreed. 'And, if teachers were generally selected from such schools [the commercial schools],' he wrote, 'they would not be from amongst the most promising pupils, those who descend into what they regarded as an inferior position would not be remarkable for "a spirited and cheerful discharge of duty"; unless indeed the descent is made under the influence of strong religious feelings.'[22]

Regardless of what witnesses had said in 1835, H.M.I. the Reverend John Allen found only one schoolmaster, in the 340 schools he visited in the Home Counties in 1845, earning as much as £100 a year.[23] Hence if schoolmasters were to be given an adequate training and then kept in the schools, they had not only to be taught to remain deferential to their social superiors but also to regard their occupation as a divinely ordained vocation. 'The path of the teacher is strewn with disappointment,' Kay-Shuttleworth and E. Carleton Tufnell observed with prophetic irony, 'if he commence with a mercenary spirit. It is full of encouragement if he be inspired with the spirit of Christian charity. No skill can compensate adequately for the absence of a pervading religious influence on the character and conduct of the schoolmaster.'[24]

Guided by the principle that 'the main object of a Normal School is the *formation of the character of the schoolmaster*',[*25] the two friends, Kay-Shuttleworth and Carleton Tufnell, devised a regimen for their college at Battersea to produce the kind of schoolmaster they wanted. 'No part of the training given was more carefully attended to than the moral discipline of the students in humility and self-denial.' With the exception of a matron who acted as the cook, no servants were provided. All the domestic duties were performed by the students. Kay-Shuttleworth was equally concerned about the moral welfare of the teaching staff of the college. 'The teachers assisted personally in such carpenters' and masons' work as was required in the building, and the diet was studiously simple.' The food 'was of the coarsest character, consisting of vegetables, soups, and very brown bread'.[26] 'The conceit of the pedagogue,' Kay-Shuttleworth explained, 'is not likely to arise among either students or masters who cheerfully handle the trowel, the saw, or carry mortar in a hod to the top of the building.'[27] As well as learning the elements of building construction, students practised animal husbandry. 'Animals were bought since the schoolmaster in a rural parish often has a common or forest-right of pasture for his cow or a forest run for his pig or goat,' the college's founder wrote in 1841, 'and might thus with a little skill, be provided with the means of healthful occupation in his hours of leisure, and of providing for the comfort of his family...[Thus] they would be in less danger of despising the labourer's daily toil... and of being led...to form a false estimate of their position in relation to the class to which they belonged, and which they were destined to instruct.'[28]

When Allen visited St Mark's College, Chelsea, in 1842, he

* Original italics.

found the students there leading an equally Spartan existence. Their day lasted from 5.30 a.m. until 10 p.m. The principal, the Reverend Derwent Coleridge, in one respect was clearly a disciple of Kay-Shuttleworth. 'The object being to produce schoolmasters for the poor,' he wrote, 'the endeavour must be, on the one hand to raise the students morally and intellectually to a certain standard, while, on the other, we train them in lowly service, not merely to teach them hardihood and inure them to the duties of a humble and laborious office, but to make them practically acquainted with the condition of the community among whom they will have to labour... The labours of the house, the field, and the garden, are intended to elevate, not depress; the studies of the schoolroom, not to exalt, but to humble.'[29]

Industrial training had other advantages. Not only did it reduce the cost of running a college but, 'It was almost the only mode in which the hours not occupied in study could be profitably and innocently passed by a promiscuous assemblage of youths, almost all of whom had so much both to learn and unlearn'.[30] Authority continued to remain fearful. Twenty years later, the Reverend H. G. Robinson, the principal of the training college at York, admitted that a student's life was unduly gregarious. 'There are reasons,' he darkly hinted to the Newcastle Commissioners, 'why it is inexpedient to give a student free access to his dormitory.'[31] As a result, students had little opportunity either to practise their religious exercises in private or to spend much time in self-recollection and private meditation. In combating the sins of this world, greater reliance was placed on the worldly policy of depriving the students of their privacy than on the efficacy of divine guidance.

Although students were denied the solitary and contemplative life of the recluse, communal worship, based on the chapel, played an important part in the daily round. The Established Church, anxious to prevent any further erosion of its standing in society, knew full well that 'The Religion of a People, in our time of the world, depends upon its schools'[32]—and schoolmasters. Thus Anglican candidates for the teacher's certificates had to be examined in the catechism, liturgy, and history of their Church. At St Mark's College, Chelsea, religious instruction and worship accounted for over a quarter of the fifty-three hours and thirty minutes devoted each week to various forms of academic work.[33]

In the eyes of some members of the Anglican Church, the educational system was a state-subsidized part of the ecclesiastical organization. 'These training schools,' Cowie wrote in the early 1860s, 'are part of the extensive machinery of the Church for the welfare of the poor; they are preparing secular officers of the Church, whom the State certifies for the object of dispelling ignorance, and eliciting the dormant powers of self-help and progress...'[34] Thus classroom and teacher were seen as adjuncts to the pulpit and incumbent with 'the school-house lying, as it ought, under the shadow of the church, as the visible witness and emblem of the relation in which they stand to each other... Among the clergyman's helpers', the same commentator continued, 'there is none so important as the schoolmaster, whose special charge it is, to break up and prepare the soil in young hearts for sowing the heavenly seed'.[35] In the rural areas the new schools provided tangible evidence of the Church's reviving influence. 'It is certainly a remarkable circumstance,' H.M.I. the Reverend F. C. Cook declared with enthusiasm, 'that on entering a country village, the most striking, and frequently the most ornamental building next to the church, should be the schoolhouse for the children of the poor.'[36]

When the pupil-teacher training scheme was introduced, both Church and State had good reason to choose candidates for apprenticeship who were of the right calibre. The school teachers of tomorrow had to be people who would uphold the authority of their Church. In addition, care had to be taken to ensure that those who were about to be raised in society would seek to conserve it and not attempt to overthrow it. Stringent precautions were observed so as to avoid the selection of unsuitable children. A circular letter drew the attention of the inspectorate to the importance of the preliminary inquiries they were to make about the character and conduct of the would-be apprentices. Furthermore, the inspectors were expected to watch over the pupil-teachers' religious and moral conduct throughout the period of their articles. 'Every expedient,' they were told in March 1849, 'should be adopted likely to improve their habits and manners, to promote a sense of order and decorum, a respectful obedience to their parents, teachers, and superiors, to cultivate an intelligent disposition to fulfil the duties of their station in life, and to enable them to see how their interests and happiness are inseparable from the well-being of other classes of society.'[37]

Before the candidates were accepted by the inspectors, the school managers concerned had to certify that the 'moral character of the candidates and of their families justifies an expectation that the instruction and training of the school will be seconded by their own efforts and by the example of their parents'. If the parental home was thought to be unsatisfactory, candidates had to board 'in some approved household'. As well as passing their annual examination, pupil-teachers had to produce evidence to show that their behaviour was beyond reproach. Each year they had to submit three certificates. Two, attesting to their character and attentiveness to their religious duties, came from the school managers. The third, which dealt with their punctuality, diligence, obedience, and attention to their school duties was supplied by their teacher.[38]

Despite all these safeguards, the scheme aroused the apprehension of those who doubted the wisdom of the policy of educating the labouring classes. According to Cook one of the main fears of the critics was that teachers 'selected from the lower orders, as they are called, are not likely to be imbued with the principles and habits…which are requisite in order to raise the moral and intellectual condition in National schools. Their manners [it is asserted] will be less cultivated and their character more liable to be affected by sensual temptations than is the case with those who have been educated with children of a higher station, and amid the associations of more respectable homes…The pupil-teachers', he reassured his readers in a passage the subtlety of which reflects his proficiency as a theologian, 'are raised in, but not out of their station… If they are selected from poor families, they do not belong to a low class, in any sense that implies degradation or unfitness.' The selection of poor boys, he argued, would provide the schools with particularly suitable personnel. Such apprentices 'will be fortified in habits of self-denial and hardihood which will form the best preparation for the discharge of their duties.' Cook concluded his defence of the new grants by pointing out that he had taken even greater care in picking the female apprentices. 'With regard to girls the enquiries have been even stricter and more searching,' he stated. 'Not only should the character of the parents be unobjectionable, but their homes should be decent and respectable. The great scarcity of proper accommodation for large families, which has so much effect in occasioning habits of indelicacy and coarseness, renders this a matter of primary importance.'[39]

There can be little doubt that many children found the teacher training programme a godsend. It opened up new opportunities for social and economic advance both inside and outside the school. On the whole the social origins of the apprentices were humble. 'In the country,' Cook wrote, '[they] are the children of small tradesmen, yeomen, or the upper servants in gentlemen's families. In the towns, and especially in London, they belong to the better and higher divisions of the operative classes...They are the children of respectable artisans, silk-weavers, cabinet

Table I PARENTAL BACKGROUND OF EARLY STUDENTS AT HOCKERILL TRAINING COLLEGE

21 Shopkeepers and artisans		9 Servants etc.
1 Fishmonger	1 Whitesmith	2 Gardeners
2 Shoemakers	1 Printer	1 Groom
1 Grocer	1 Cordwainer	1 Coachman
2 Tailors	1 Van proprietor	1 Servant to the Corporation
1 Shopkeeper	1 Painter	1 Pew opener
1 Smith	1 Millwright	1 Housekeeper
1 Clothmaker	1 Surgical bandage	2 Servants
1 Weaver	maker (Mother)	
2 Carpenters	1 Bookfolder	
	1 Agricultural	
	machine maker	
		8 Unclassified
4 Teachers		1 Miller
8 Labourers		1 Matron (Mother)
		1 Clerk
		1 Retired sergeant (The East India Co.)
		1 'Keeps a school' (Mother) and solicitor's clerk (Father)
		1 Farmer
		1 Esquire
		1 Occupation unknown

Source: *Admission register of students to Hockerill College, 1852–73.*

makers, etc.'[40] Other inspectors mention similar social groups. Moseley considered that the best candidates came from the children of tradesmen, small farmers, and shopkeepers.[41] His colleague, the Reverend M. Mitchell, was also impressed by 'the children of the higher classes, gentlemen's servants, gardeners, sons of widows and mechanics (especially joiners and carpenters) [who] were both by demeanour and intellect, the best fitted for apprenticeships'.[42] An analysis of the parental background of the first fifty students to enter the Hockerill Training College, Bishop's Stortford, Hertfordshire, between November 1852 and January 1855, substantiates the accuracy of the general impressions quoted above.

It is also clear that a minority of the children came from social strata below that of the 'better and higher divisions of the operative classes'. Thus it was with some justice that the Department was able to claim that 'the profession is open to the child of any labourer or common working man upon no harder terms than forgoing higher wages and submitting to a great deal of moral restraint between the twelfth and the twenty-first year'.[43] The Department did its best to see that the necessary degree of moral restraint was shown. Girls who were apprenticed to masters had to be taught in the presence of the mistress 'who was to be the master's wife or near relation by blood'. Despite these precautions the Department remained uneasy. 'It is extremely doubtful,' Lingen added, 'whether such an apprenticeship ought in any case to be recommended where the master is young or unmarried. It ought not to be recommended if he is both young and unmarried. [The school managers] must hold themselves wholly and solely responsible...for the moral consequences.'[44]

The girl who successfully survived these hazards eventually became a schoolmistress earning around £60 a year, and lived in a rent-free house. Although she usually only earned two-thirds the salary of a certificated master, she had an income that could equal, if not exceed, that of her father. Moreover, entry into a college, such as Hockerill, opened up new horizons to a working-class girl. She was able to obtain financial independence at a time when even few middle-class women enjoyed such an advantage. She also avoided a life of ill-paid domestic drudgery or manual work in industry or agriculture. For example, the maids at Gorhambury, the Hertfordshire home of the Earl of Verulam, received between £10 and 14 guineas a year, plus their board, in 1847.[45] Hertfordshire women working in the near-by fields were paid 3s. 6d. a week in 1860 and 4s. 6d. ten years later. In the 1870s the top rate for women in the cotton industry in Manchester seems to have been 20s. to 24s. a week. This was earned by women on piece rates minding four looms at a time. A more normal wage was that of the card minder who earned 12s. a week or that of the warehouse hand who obtained 14s. 6d. for a fifty-nine hour week. Lastly in Sheffield, female scissor dressers and burnishers received between 7s. and 13s. for a fifty hour week.[46]

As the following table shows girls and women were quick to take advantage of the new opportunities presented them. The number of first-year girl apprentices exceeded that of men in England for the first time in 1860. Boys from the economically less advanced parts of Great Britain redressed the sexual balance.

Table II RECRUITMENT OF FIRST YEAR APPRENTICES IN 1860

	Boys	Girls	Total
England	1,072	1,123	2,195
Wales	82	26	108
Isle of Man and Channel Islands	11	7	18
Scotland	299	126	425
Grand Totals	1,464	1,282	2,746

Source: *Report of the Committee*, P.P. 1862, XLII, p. liii.

The next year's intake had an overall female majority (1571 girls, 1521 boys). By January 1864 the sexual revolution had reached the training colleges. Six hundred and ninety-four women and 594 men were admitted that month.[47] Eight years later, the classroom, the last stronghold of male numerical superiority fell to the advancing forces. There were 7,778 certificated mistresses and 7,632 qualified masters in the elementary schools of England and Wales.[48]

Another result of the limitation on the occupational opportunities available to women in the nineteenth century was that some of the schoolmistresses were very well qualified. 'Many female teachers,' Cook reported, 'are persons whose education in early life fitted them for the situation of governesses in families of distinction, and in schools for the highest classes of society. They preferred the independence, the comfort, and the security attached to the position of a well trained National school-mistress; and...in most cases they are themselves convinced that they have chosen well and wisely, and would not, were the alternative again open to them, make a different choice.'[49] No inspector ever suggested that any certificated master had a social background that made him a suitable person to employ as a tutor in a gentleman's family.

Thus it was with some justification, but pardonable exaggeration, that the journal, the *Pupil-Teacher*, claimed that 'The system has established a distinct class in society. They [the pupil-teachers] are the apprentices of the nation; they are destined for the public service in a department honourable and most important... Many a country boy, whose highest ambition, ten years since, would have been to be the village innkeeper or the village blacksmith...will now aspire to a profession... He has [now] at least a fair chance of raising himself in the social scale. ...Many a country girl will now, by becoming a pupil-teacher, be first in her family, for many generations, to be accounted of a higher grade than that of peasants and domestic servants... In short the pupil-teacher system is probably working a social change of far greater magnitude than perhaps even the most imaginative or far sighted amongst us supposes.'[50]

After satisfying themselves that the candidates presented by the school managers were suitable for training, the inspectors had to make sure that their teachers were capable of giving the necessary instruction. Here the main problem was that the tuition had in many cases to be conducted by the schoolmasters whose shortcomings had previously been so roundly condemned. The Committee accordingly decided that 'where the teacher did possess a certificate of merit my Lords would be satisfied if the inspectors could report that his character and attainments were such as to enable him to qualify himself for success in an examination at the close of each year of the apprenticeship, in those subjects in which the pupil-teachers would be instructed in the ensuing year'.[51] Once a schoolmaster had been allowed to have apprentices, it was very difficult for the inspector to refuse to allow him to carry on. Pupil-teachers, through no fault of their own, would have been left high and dry in the middle of their training. Moreover, the unhappy plight of the apprentices would have given school managers, ever ready to bite the hand that fed them, a splendid excuse for complaining to the Education Office of inspectorial officiousness.

A reading of the reports suggests that Watkins' action in cancelling the indentures of seventeen of his 513 pupil-teachers in 1852, because of the incapacity of their teachers, was the exception rather than the rule.[52] On the other hand, the same inspector's contention that 'sixty per cent of the schools receiving grants were in some striking points deficient'[53] seems to be valid. Similarly, although Moseley rejected about 10 per cent of all the applications made by school managers to have pupil-teachers, he did not think that the majority of teachers in his district reached the standard required of them. In other words, they did not keep a year ahead of their apprentices.[54] In 1850, when Moseley made this statement, there were only 1,173 certificated teachers in all the schools of England, Scotland and Wales,[55] and only 1,127 schools in England and Wales employed pupil-teachers.[56]

The problem facing the Department was that it had undertaken the proverbially impossible task of making bricks without straw. It was attempting to build up an adequate supply of teachers without the initial resources of skilled manpower that were required for such a task. Moreover, the Department could not afford to alienate the school managers on whose cooperation and goodwill it was dependent. Consequently inspectors had no option but to countenance low standards. The most they could do was to weed out those teachers who were manifestly incapable of undertaking the training of their apprentices. As for the rest, the inspectors had to hope that they would use their annual visits as occasions for exhortation and encouragement. Given these considerations, it is not surprising that only a few pupil-teachers ever 'failed' their examinations. Brookfield, for instance, in 1850, disqualified two for bad papers and a further two for copying, out of a total of 380 he examined that year.[57] In that same year, Kennedy refused to pass six of his 400 apprentices.[58] A couple of years later, Tinling removed three for bad papers and a further five of his 300 pupil-teachers for misconduct.[59]

Despite the difficulties that faced the Department, an attempt was made to bring pressure to bear on school managers to remedy the worst of the abuses in their schools. Between 1847 and 1849, for example, the Department refused to sanction pupil-teachers in one school held in a rented cottage less than seven foot three inches high, in a second where the space for each pupil was less than four square feet, and in a third where the schoolroom had been described by the inspector as 'a miserable, low ill-ventilated room, under which there is a stable, the smell from which is extremely disagreeable'.[60] Similarly some of the least efficient teachers were expected to mend their ways before apprentices were assigned to them. 'Your master should be warned,' the Department told the managers of the Kentish Town National School, London, 'that the inspector does not consider the discipline of the school, or the elementary instruction of the children to be in a satisfactory state…[and that this] arises…from some degree of [the teacher's] ignorance of the best methods of imparting knowledge to his scholars. Before commencing a lesson… he ought to have made up his mind not only of what he is going to teach but also how he is going to teach it…If at any future date your master's efforts should have succeeded in raising the standard of instruction and discipline in the school the Committee of Council will be glad to receive a renewal of your application for the apprenticeship of pupil-teachers.'[61]

During the course of the 1850s the Department began to demand a higher standard of competence from the schools. One of the main improvements made was that of removing the less competent teachers from the working of the scheme. In June 1851, R. R. W. Lingen, Kay-Shuttleworth's successor, decided that those teachers who failed to keep ahead of their pupil-teachers were to be refused any further apprentices.[62] Three years later, when the category of registered teacher was introduced, the unqualified teacher was eliminated altogether. Members of this new group had to be over the age of thirty-five and to possess 'sound, if humble, attainment'.[63] Those who passed an examination of a standard approximating to that required of a pupil-teacher at the end of his fifth year were recognized for the purposes of the capitation grant.*[64] If they presented an additional paper in geometry or algebra, they were allowed to have

* See p. 82.

apprentices. After the end of 1854, only those teachers who were certificated or, in the case of those over the age of thirty-five, qualified by registration, were permitted to have apprentices.[65]

Lingen also brought pressure to bear on the more wayward school managers. Those who persisted in ignoring the Department's recommendations about the provision of furniture, books or maps were refused any more apprentices after the summer of 1851.[66] The following February, the acceptance rate for new pupil-teachers was limited to 100 a month.[67] In addition, mistresses under the age of twenty-one were to be refused payment, after the end of 1852, for any apprentices they taught.[68] Then finally, in an attempt to close all loopholes, he minuted: 'In admitting candidates to apprenticeship insist rigorously and literally on the standard prescribed by the minutes both as regards the individual and the school... There should not be the slightest relaxation of this rule.'[69] This decree may have had the desired effect, as he did not return to the subject again until 1858. In that year, he reminded his staff that there could be no exceptions to the minimum age at which apprentices could be accepted.[70] Six months later, they were told that if they received reports of unchastity amongst the pupil-teachers, no further indentures were to be granted without the strictest inquiries.[71]

Apart from all his other responsibilities, the inspector had the important duty of conducting a series of examinations for pupil-teachers and for those practising teachers who wished to become certificated or, at a later date, recognized as assistant or registered teachers. It is difficult for us today, living in an examination-ridden society, to realize how novel was the idea of a public examination in the 1840s. When Allen examined the students at the Battersea and Chelsea training schools in 1842, he set what were probably the first public examination papers connected with elementary education in the nineteenth century.[72] The Department's example was soon copied. The College of Preceptors held its first examination at Nottingham in 1850. It began to arrange exams on a nation-wide basis in 1854, the year in which the Society of Arts set its first papers.* Although this last venture was inspired by Harry Chester, the Assistant Secretary, it was a disaster. Only one candidate turned up.[73] Three years

* The Society of Arts received its Royal Charter in 1908.

later, two of Chester's colleagues, H.M.I.s the Reverend F. Temple* and J. Bowstead,† met with greater success. The Department lent their services to a committee in Exeter that ran examinations for children in the middle-class schools of the West Country in 1857. On the basis of this experiment Temple put forward a plan that was adopted by the University of Oxford for running their first local school examinations in the following year.[74] The Department's innovation is noteworthy for another reason. Perhaps as an act of divine retribution, the profession that was to inflict the examination system on the rest of society was the first to be its victim. The first tests for a teacher's certificate, for instance, were held almost a decade before either the Civil Service Commissioners or the General Medical Council began their work.

Some of the early candidates were almost overwhelmed by their experience. A number of the schoolmistresses whom Watkins examined told him 'that in this, their first public examination, they were so nervous as to be quite unable to do themselves justice. Two of them', he added, 'were so unwell that they were absent during the greater part of the hours allotted to one or two subjects'.[75] The mistresses whom the Reverend M. Mitchell supervised were made of sterner stuff. 'Their dress and general appearance,' he reported, 'conveyed a most favourable impression of their characters, and they set to work at the papers in so steady and businesslike a fashion as both pleased and surprised me. There was no affectation of any kind. Each seemed fully aware of their position, and determined to exert their powers to the full.'[76]

One inspector, H. Longueville Jones,‡ found that he was so

* Frederick Temple, son of the Lieut-Governor of Sierra Leone, was educated at Balliol College, Oxford (First class Lit. Hum. and Maths 1842, Fellow 1842–8). He joined the Education Office (1849), was Headmaster of Kneller Hall (1850–55), H.M.I. (1856–7), Headmaster of Rugby School (1858–69), and successively Bishop of Exeter (1869–85), Bishop of London (1885–96), and Archbishop of Canterbury (1896–1902).

† Joseph Bowstead was educated at Pembroke College, Cambridge (second wrangler 1833, then Fellow). He was called to the Bar (1839) and was H.M.I. (1852–76).

‡ H. L. Jones was educated at Magdalene College, Cambridge (thirty-first wrangler 1828, later Fellow and Dean). He was the author of *Illustrated History of Caernarvonshire* (1829) founded the Cambrian Archaeological Association (1847) and edited its journal *Archaeologica Cambrensis*. He was H.M.I. (1848–64).

much the object of popular curiosity that he wrote to ask how to deal with 'the inconvenience which occurs from overcrowding the schoolroom at the time of the examination'. The Department recommended him 'to marshal all the spectators together, at once out of his way and that of the children, by courteously explaining the reasons which would make it an unkindness to the children if they talked, moved about, or interfered, until the examination was over... As the system goes on', the letter continued, 'the absence of novelty will keep away mere idlers, and those who attend will better understand the conditions on which they are invited to be present'.[77]

As well as having to control an audience, the supervising inspector had to deter candidates from cheating. The evident prevalence of this habit was more probably the result of the novelty of the situation than of the moral shortcomings of the candidates. The introduction of the public examination system, one of the major growth industries of the nineteenth century, required the establishment of a new code of morality. To foster such a development, the Department adopted the practice of suspending culprits for three years from all examinations.[78] In 1854, the year by which this penalty had become the general rule, the inspector conducting the Christmas examination at Battersea was given special instructions. He was told to send the Department a list of the names of the candidates in their order of sitting, 'as such a list was often wanted in deciding upon cases of copying'. To deter the less scrupulous, he had also to explain to those assembled that 'as all the papers on the same subject are read over together, there is little or no chance that delinquency of this kind will escape detention.'[79] Two years later, inspectors were told to take the preventive measure of issuing clean blotting-paper. 'In cases where the presumption of fraud has been strong (e.g. where the fifth proposition of Euclid has been found written on the blotting-paper in pencil) the candidate has argued that he has written out the proposition in this manner in the course of practising himself before the examination, and that he had never thought of bringing the blotting-paper with him. However improbable this and similar tales may be, it is next to impossible for a department that is administrative only, and which has no pretence to be judicial, to act penally upon any evidence short of such as enforces a confession of the fact.'[80] In dealing with one candidate, the Department did not find its hands tied by this nice regard for constitutional propriety. He complained that although he had helped another and successful candidate to spell 'necessity' and 'Manasseh', he had failed the examination. This was unfortunate. He did not have another chance for three years.[81]

Some examinees were more fortunate and escaped this close supervision. In 1859, the journal *School and the Teacher* complained about the way in which the examination of the pupil-teachers was often conducted. 'Cases have come under notice,' it was stated, 'in which even the papers set by the master were left with him, and his own estimate of the result [of the apprentices' work] was accepted by the inspector.'[82] On another occasion, the Reverend A. B. Nicholls, the husband of Charlotte Brontë, of Haworth, Yorkshire, complained about the lax way in which the examination of a schoolmaster had been conducted. The candidate in question had been able to consult a neighbouring colleague before dispatching his scripts to his 'supervisor'.[83]

It is difficult to assess the standard required for either a Queen's scholarship or for a teacher's certificate. Although examples of the question papers survive, it is not easy to decide from them the kind of answer that was required. The problem is further complicated by the fact that standards undoubtedly changed over the course of the years. There was also a wide range of ability within the profession. The contributions made by some teachers to their journals show that many could write fluently and intelligibly. On the other hand, the first question in each section of the paper for the teacher's certificate was 'of such a character as that ignorance of it would be inexcusable in any person professing even a moderate acquaintance with the subject of the paper'.[84] Yet the candidate was required to answer only one question in each section.[85] The papers were marked, or more probably just generally assessed, by the inspectors who wrote on the front of each script 'excellent', 'good', 'fair', 'moderate', 'imperfect', or 'failure'. Some idea of the meaning of these grades is given in a letter sent to a schoolmaster in 1848. 'With regard to the entry which describes your spelling as moderate, I am to inform you that it is by no means intended to convey the impression that you are ignorant (in which case "imperfect" would have been used) but, that in that respect your papers appear to be careless.'[86]

By the end of their term of apprenticeship, pupil-teachers 'were expected to be able to read with proper articulation and expression, to be acquainted with English grammar, to be prepared to compose an essay on some subject connected with the art of teaching, to work sums in arithmetic, and to be acquainted with the first two books of Euclid, and algebra to the end of simple equations, if boys; or to be acquainted with arithmetic up to decimals and simple interest if girls, and with the geography of the habitable world.'[87] These standards, though, were not always reached. For example, in the mid 1850s, Lingen complained that the second-year students at training colleges were unable to work out the average weekly attendance on a school register. They were frequently unable, he stated, to distinguish between a weekly total attendance and an average attendance.[88] Lingen also found out that the pupil-teachers read badly. At one training college, not one of the nine Queen's scholars was capable of reading the lessons in chapel. He accordingly instructed the inspectorate to make a special point of hearing the apprentices read during the annual inspection. This basic skill was apparently neglected in the schools for he added: '*It is, however desirable that every school time-table should contain an entry of one daily lesson for each class in the art of reading as such.*'*[89]

Finally, one inspector thought that the schools did their job so badly that the students went to college without having had a sound elementary education. Consequently, he alleged, the course in some subjects for a Queen's scholar was precisely the same as that given to the apprentices in the college's practising school.[90]

To some extent this state of affairs was the fault not of the apprentices, but of the schoolmasters and managers who not only neglected their duties, but also imposed an undue burden on the young people. The children's commitments to the Privy Council were heavy enough without the addition of other tasks by the school managers. They had to do a full day's teaching, prepare their lessons for the next day, and receive an hour and a half's tuition from their teacher. In addition to all this, the

* Original italics.

school managers usually expected them to keep the schoolroom clean and on Sundays to help with the Sunday school and the church services. Unfortunately the school managers did not always keep their part of the bargain. They did not ensure that the schoolmaster earned his gratuity properly by giving the obligatory tuition every day.[91] Frequently the apprentices, if they were taught at all, received their instruction while the schoolroom was being swept and cleaned, or while the children were eating or playing in it. So frequently did the schoolmaster neglect his duty that inspectors were told to make a special point of finding out what sort of instruction was given and how it was given.[92]

The commonest criticism of those hostile to the pupil-teacher training scheme was not that the Committee was content with too low a standard, but that it demanded too much of those 'who are intended to educate those who for the most part are to be domestic servants, or who will occupy some subordinate situation in life'.[93] That such complaints were made is not surprising when the standards of education outside the schools are considered. The report of the Clarendon Commission on certain public schools, for example, suggests that these schools, in their particular field, were little if any more efficient than the socially inferior elementary ones. The Dean of Christ Church, Oxford, told the Commission that the answers to questions in arithmetic, set in the matriculation examination, were of such a low standard that the College did not feel encouraged to examine the candidates in Euclid and algebra. As for their performance in the classics, the staple fare of the public schools at this time, he said it would have been useless to have set an unseen passage of Latin or Greek. Yet despite the limited scope of the university examination, a third of the candidates usually failed. At the next university examination, responsions, the candidates faced a syllabus comparable to that laid down for a fifth-year apprentice. They were examined in 'arithmetic to vulgar fractions and decimals, the first two books of Euclid, and algebra to simple equations'. Yet shortly before the Commission took evidence, this hurdle proved too much for sixty-seven of the 168 examinees.[94]

Similar educational deficiencies were found amongst those of humbler social origins. Between May 1855 and December 1856, the newly appointed Civil Service Commissioners examined

2,566 candidates for various clerkships. Of these 1,686 were successful. One hundred and forty-seven of the failures were in arithmetic, a subject in which the questions 'for the higher class of junior situations did not reach beyond vulgar and decimal fractions'. In the English papers, the Commissioners found 'but few instances in which a candidate has shown great facility in composing a letter'. They found a similarly low level of attainment in history and geography. Candidates, for instance, were unable to list either the principal manufacturing districts of England, or state which countries produced cotton, tobacco, tea, mahogany, sherry, or currants, etc.[95]

The performance of candidates for the office of letter carrier* or mail guard is of particular interest. The examination for these applicants was in the basic skills of writing from dictation, reading manuscript, and elementary arithmetic. The level was roughly that of standard three or four of the Revised Code. The Commissioners, however, could pass only 321 of the 509 applicants. Those who failed 'were [so] grossly ignorant of arithmetic and writing', they reported, '[that] both the Post Office and the public would have sustained great inconvenience'.[96] Yet it was largely from this same social group that the Committee of the Privy Council on Education was recruiting its pupil-teachers. The difficulties of the Civil Service Commissioners and of the Committee of Council were part of a problem that confronted mid-Victorian England as a whole. 'It was one thing to pass legislation which involved the performance of special duties; it was another to find the men capable of carrying out the duties.' This conclusion, reached after reviewing the difficulties of setting up a county constabulary in the 1850s, a task that involved the 'turning of half literate farm labourers into reasonable and reliable policemen', might equally well have been written of the problem of turning children from a comparable social background into schoolmasters or minor civil servants.[97]

The Education Department, school managers and chief constables alike, were faced with the problem not only of finding suitable recruits but of retaining them after training. Both occupations were relatively poorly paid. Hence those moral and

---

* The term 'postman' was not generally used until the parcel post service was introduced in 1883. (P. S. Bagwell, *The Railway Clearing House in the British Economy, 1842–1942*, (1968), p. 113.)

intellectual qualities demanded of efficient pupil-teachers, schoolmasters, and constables alike, could command higher incomes elsewhere. Largely for this reason, a quarter of all apprentices abandoned the profession before they reached the training college. The Newcastle Commissioners found that 87·32 per cent of the young people completed their articles but only 76·02 per cent went on to try for a Queen's scholarship.[98] They did not feel that the money spent on the missing 23·98 per cent had been wasted. Not only had the children rendered their services year by year, but the salary was not excessive. More could be earned elsewhere.

It is probable that the apprentices whose stipends, computed on a weekly basis, rose from 3s. 10d. at the age of fourteen to 7s. 8d. at eighteen, were poorly paid from the day the scheme started. Cook, for example, as early as 1844, had thought that 'about 9s. a week will be required in London'.[99] At first, despite an occasional complaint, the inspectors seem to have been satisfied with the quality of the recruits. The increasing diversification of the economy, together with its recovery from the depression of the late 1840s, soon created difficulties. A crop of complaints appeared in the reports published in 1854. Watkins, who inspected Yorkshire, wrote that because of the low stipend, 'we must take what we can get, and where we can get it. I do not say it lightly', he added, 'the maimed and the lame, and the nearly blind, have been offered at my examinations during the year, and rejected to the visible and sometimes very audible dissatisfaction of those who proposed them'.[100] The Reverend D. J. Stewart, who covered the counties of Northumberland, Durham, Cumberland and Westmorland, thought that the position was even worse. 'Your Lordships' stipends are so far below the market value of a boy's services,' he charged, 'that, in many schools which I could mention, no candidates for office can be found.'[101] The Reverend J. J. Blandford, the inspector for Lincolnshire, Nottinghamshire, Leicestershire, Northamptonshire, Derbyshire and the County of Rutland, pointed out, as had Watkins, that managers were advertising for apprentices. Such a practice Blandford condemned as being contrary to the spirit of the 1846 minute under which apprentices were supposed to be selected from the schools in which they were going to serve.[102] To complete the score for that year, the Reverend W. J. Kennedy, whose area was Lancashire and the Isle of Man, also joined in the chorus of complaints.[103]

Apprentices and would-be apprentices soon saw, as did their parents, that they could do equally well in other occupations. To many, the pupil-teacher system became 'a means of getting, at the public expense, that general education which any good elementary school ought to supply'.[104] Watkins, perhaps because he inspected a rapidly expanding industrial area, was more concerned with this problem than were any of his colleagues. The average weekly wage earned by boys leaving school, just before the age of ten, he reported, was between 3s. 9d. and 4s. 9d. This was as much as a pupil-teacher received at fourteen.[105] He also made an extensive survey of wage rates in Leeds, Sheffield, Huddersfield, and Rotherham. From this he demonstrated the extent to which apprentices were at a financial disadvantage. Messrs Walker of Bradford, for instance, paid 4s. 9d. a week to boys of thirteen and 10s. a week at the age of eighteen. In Leeds, boys could earn between 3s. and 4s. a week, as errand boys at the age of twelve, and 16s. either as warehouse boys at eighteen or as butchers' apprentices at twenty-one. These figures could be doubled by working overtime. However, the boy who abandoned the security of the classroom for the excitement and high wages of the outside world found one drawback. 'In industry his life might be shorter, as in the printing trade where there was the danger of lead poisoning, or in pottery or glassware where he was subjected to considerable ranges of temperature.' One compensation remained. Industrial and other workers had a freedom that the carefully supervised pupil-teacher lacked. Many an apprentice sitting in church, Sunday after Sunday, must have envied the young man whose way of life was denounced by Watkins. 'One youth, only eighteen years of age, who had earned in four weeks the sum of £4 16s. 4½d...is living with a married woman, whose husband has left her in consequence. This wretched pair pass their evenings and Sabbaths in drinking from public-house to public-house.'[106]

The growth of the economy created a demand for employees who were sufficiently literate and numerate to fill a wide range of clerical and minor supervisory posts in industry and commerce. In particular a job with a railway company became the goal of many a working-class youth. With its promise of regular and secure employment it had all the attractions that the civil service had for his social superiors. So highly valued were these openings that families developed a tradition that lasted up to three generations of putting their sons and later their daughters 'on the railway'. Thus the railway companies were able to take the *élite* of the labouring classes. Stewart found that 'railway offices, in some parts of England, are managed mainly by boys...' 'There are railway stations in this district,' he reported, 'where the whole work is done by boys whom I have known as scholars in a neighbouring school.'[107] At a slightly higher level, the Department competed with the railway companies and a wide range of commercial offices for the services of lads who were of potential schoolmaster calibre. Watkins thought that the railway companies, in particular, were 'formidable competitors with us for the services of these youths'. He went on to describe how 'One chairman had asked him to recommend twelve to eighteen lads who could write with a good hand and had "such a knowledge of geography as would enable them to spell the names of places correctly". He wanted them', Watkins explained, 'for telegraph offices at 10s. to 11s. a week, with the prospect of gradual but certain increase. Other offices, merchants', lawyers', canal and etc.,' he added, 'are almost as enticing to young lads.'[108]

When Stewart took over the predominantly agricultural counties of Cambridgeshire, Huntingdonshire, Bedfordshire, Hertfordshire and Buckinghamshire in 1856, he found as great a shortage of pupil-teachers there as in the industrial north. 'In many districts,' he wrote, 'no candidates can be found except the managers are prepared to pay £5 per annum to eke out the stipend offered by the government... The managers of schools have no power to select this or that child for training; they must take what they can get, or go without.'[109] In addition to the low rate of pay offered, the government scheme, as Stewart pointed out, had another drawback. Since the payments were made annually, often after a delay of three months, apprentices had to live for long periods on credit. This procedure had the added disadvantage of making inspectors reluctant to fail the apprentices. If they did so, the apprentice lost a year's pay. The solution usually adopted was to terminate the indentures at the time of the inspection so that the pupil-teacher was paid for the year's work. A further difficulty was that the apprentice was tempted to break his articles without warning and go off with £10 to £20 in his pocket.

To some extent one's sympathies are with the young person who incurred his inspector's wrath by abandoning his chosen career. Although some of the rigours of the 1840s had been alleviated, life at a training college remained austere. Students at York, whose routine seems to have been typical,* spent sixty hours a week at their studies in the 1860s. Their day's programme began at 5.30 a.m. in the summer and 6.00 a.m. in winter, and continued until 9.30 p.m.[110] On the other hand, they had two days off a week, a concession that the earlier generation of students at Battersea had never known. Less time was spent on industrial training. This change was not so much the result of the deliberate adoption of a new policy as the outcome of a need to devote more time to literary and professional studies. The Newcastle Commissioners, for instance, barely concealed their regret at the passing of the old order when they wrote: 'The precautions against personal ambition which he [Kay-Shuttleworth] tried to establish, in the shape of extreme plainness of diet and hard manual work, have been largely given up.' The end, however, remained the same. 'Now that the training colleges have abandoned the routine of self-denial inaugurated by Kay-Shuttleworth,' the Commissioners commented, 'they should [still] impress on the students a sober estimate of their future prospects.'[111]

Sobriety was certainly the order of the day at the Wesleyan College, Westminster. The founders had put the college in Westminster, close to a slum area, because 'they did not wish their students to be spoilt in training, and by a lengthened residence away from the dwellings of the poor...disinclined and rendered unfit to take the arduous and self-denying duties of school teachers. They hoped that, surrounded as the students are at Westminster, by the families of the poor, their want of education, with its attendant degradation and misery, would excite their best feelings'.[112] Students had little else to excite them. Their daily routine, the Reverend H. G. Robinson, the principal of the training college at York stated, left 'little room

* A thoroughgoing and critical account of the growth and work of the training colleges, together with an analysis of the academic and professional background of their lecturing staff, is badly needed.

for indulgence in frivolity or dissipation'.[113] Unlike their contemporaries in offices or workshops, the students had scarcely any opportunity 'to indulge in irregularities or to consort with improper companions'. No set of young men, as far as he knew, were kept under such close restraint. Within the college, 'money was not wasted on superfluities'. The diet remained very plain, the furniture very simple. The staff were not overpaid, Robinson assured the Commissioners, nor were the students greatly indulged.[114] As a result of this frugality, Robinson claimed 'a well trained schoolmaster can be manufactured for about £90'. This, the cost of maintaining a student for two years at college, compared favourably with the expense incurred in training an infantryman. 'Every soldier in Her Majesty's regiments of foot has cost £100 by the time he becomes efficient.'[115]

Under the guise of fiction, *Schools and Scholars*, published in 1887, gives a somewhat colourful account of life at a training college. The college described possessed the minimum of furniture. 'There was not a picture or an ornament in any room; the asceticism of a workhouse was blended with the solidity and ugliness of a gaol... No man could have a moment of privacy until he was in bed. The barren, foetid rooms, with their greasy forms and notched desks, were the only place where a letter could be written... At dinner...silence was enforced...and the food passed down in rough platefuls...Manners were forgotten, and the greediest men grabbed at the vegetables with vulture-like eagerness.'[116] After dinner the students went up carpetless staircases to their dormitories. 'Long lines of cells stretched like rows of horse-boxes from right to left... The men were separated from each other only by a low partition, so that privacy was practically unknown. No candles were allowed so that those furthest away from the gas had to grope their way to bed.'[117]

The drabness which permeated the students' surroundings embraced their professional training as well. Annesley, the chief character in *Schools and Scholars*, 'was shocked to find that he was expected to learn his country's history from a tiny fivepenny book, which contained strings of dates and names arranged in horrifying sequence, which he was expected to learn by heart'.[118]

'Vast demands are made on the memory,' the Commissioners stated, 'little is done for the improvement of the judgment or reasoning powers.'[119] In criticism of the examination papers set for the students they wrote: 'There is too much of minuteness; too much which appeals to mere verbal recollection, and too little attention to the real importance of the subject matters inquired into. We think that in questions...it should always be borne in mind that they are addressed to persons who are to be appointed to no higher office than that of teachers of children of the poorer classes.'[120]

Robinson saw the effects of the training given in the colleges stretching down into the classroom. 'The present course tends *to impart information* rather than to *develop the faculties and to discipline the mind*. The principle in short ... is to pour into the students' minds a large supply of knowledge which they in turn may discharge into the minds of their scholars... The great feature of the course...is cram. The master has been *crammed* himself, and so he *crams* his pupils.'*[121] Thus the introduction of the Revised Code did not suddenly make English elementary education uninspiring, it merely intensified the use of bad teaching methods already in existence.†

Even when the student left the training college, his difficulties were by no means over. As a schoolmaster he found himself in the unhappy position of neither belonging to the social group he had left nor being accepted by those to whom he now felt himself equal. The dilemma confronting the teacher was described by Robinson in unsympathetic terms to the Newcastle Commission. 'They naturally think,' he wrote in evidence, 'more of what education has made them than of what it first found them. They easily lose sight of the fact that they have risen from a very humble social position, and they crave for that status which education seems generally to secure. I think that in some cases they are apt to forget that they owe the culture they have to the public provision made for them.'[122] The lot of the schoolmistress was even harder. Cook described her social position as a very peculiar one: 'It separated her very much from the class to which she had originally belonged, while it did not bring her socially into contact with a different class, and therefore she was very much isolated. She could not marry a labourer, nor an artisan who was not an educated man, and she was not very

* Original italics.
† This point is discussed more fully in Chapter 7.

likely, generally speaking, to marry a person very much above herself.'[123].

Much of the schoolmaster's unhappiness arose from the fact that too much was expected from him. During his seven years of training, he had to forgo the opportunity of earning the wages his contemporaries were receiving. In making this long-term decision he was conforming to the norms of the *bourgeoisie*. The young professional man, however, who accepted comparative penury early in life so as to reap later a dividend of a higher income and social esteem had the support of his family and class ethos. Whereas in deciding to become a teacher, a young person often had to show exceptional foresight, initiative, and ambition, in breaking with the traditional patterns of working-class behaviour and accepting those of an alien culture.

The Newcastle Commissioners failed to realize this. 'We may observe...,' they said, 'that the occupation of an elementary schoolmaster is not well suited for a young man of an adventurous, stirring, or ambitious character, and that it is rather a misfortune than otherwise, when persons of that temper of mind are led into it by the prospect...of rising in the world socially as well as intellectually.'[124] In expecting the unadventurous or unambitious to undertake seven years of training, the Commissioners were asking for the moon. Needless to say the more ambitious sought an outlet for their energies outside the classroom.

If the Commissioners had been able to enlist the services of a sociologist, he would have diagnosed one of the teacher's complaints as that of role conflict. On the one hand the teacher was expected to defer to the existing social order, on the other he was required to exercise a leadership role in relation to his social inferiors. As was the case with his house,* he had to be given an income that set him above those whose children he taught but did not allow him to vie with the traditional holders of authority. In rural society he was expected to occupy a position next to, but below, that of the clergyman. 'I really think,' Robert Lowe told the House of Commons in 1861, 'that the schoolmaster should be taught some political economy in these days of strikes; so that the person who is looked up to as an authority next to the

* See p. 70–1.

clergyman in his village should be able to give some sensible opinion on those melancholy contests about wages.' Since the Disraelian quip of *sanitas sanitatum* had yet to be enunciated,[125] Lowe also saw the schoolmaster as a substitute for a rural sanitary authority. He should be able, Lowe said, 'to demonstrate the advantage of good drains and sewers in preventing disease and death; and the advantage of vaccination'.[126]

A further cause of social tension lay in the substantial progress that the schoolmaster had made. In 1862, the journal *Pupil-Teacher* stated: 'His social position is respectable in the estimation of every right-minded person. His income is, perhaps, rather less than it would be were he a policeman; but it is, perhaps, something more than it would be were he a curate.'[127] A few months later the same journal thought it worthwhile to review Henry Gaze's book *Switzerland: How to see it for ten guineas*. 'If any of our readers intend,' the anonymous reviewer began, 'now that the summer sun shines in all its glory, to visit that land of mountains...he cannot do better [than to buy this book].'[128] Moreover, while he was defending the Revised Code, Lowe quoted from a statement made by an association of schoolmasters in which it was asserted that 'A goodly proportion of the 9,000 certificated teachers are in possession of the franchise'.[129] In other words they lived in a house that had an annual value of at least £10. Lastly, some crossed the great social divide by putting their earlier training and experience to another use. 'The bishops have begun to admit them to holy orders,' one assistant commissioner stated in 1861, 'the dissenting bodies are talking of their admissibility to the work of the ministry amongst them.'[130]

Here was a generation gap with a vengeance. A schoolmaster could be the son of a nearly illiterate labourer who had never travelled more than ten or fifteen miles from the parish in which he had been born. In contrast, his son was able to taste those delights of foreign travel that, a generation earlier, had been experienced only by a privileged few. Tourist promoters were quick to exploit the expansion of the railway system that was occurring both in Great Britain and on the Continent. Such institutions as temperance societies and mechanics' institutes gave them a ready-made market of customers zealous to combine pleasure with self-improvement. Many a schoolmaster, for instance, must have been able to afford 36s. to go on Thomas

Cook's four-day trip to Paris to visit the exhibition held there in 1867.[131] Similarly the first Polytechnic tour, twenty-seven days in Switzerland for £5 19s., was organized in 1889 for the benefit of its students attending classes in Regent Street, London.[132]

The fact that some schoolmasters were able to live in moderate comfort shows how hard it is to generalize about their lot. Furthermore, Watkins demonstrated the wide range of salaries that was concealed by the average figure for Great Britain which in 1854 was £85 15s. $6\frac{1}{2}$d.[133] He quoted the following examples:

Middlesex and the Metropolitan area		£132
Lancashire	Nearly	£122
British schools in the South East	„	£121
British schools in the North and North West	„	£99
Hants. and the South East (C of E)	Above	£94
Yorkshire (C of E)	„	£66
Somerset and the South West (C of E)		£65
Roman Catholic schools		£60

Thus despite the recent development of the railway system, the market for the services of schoolmasters remained a surprisingly local one at a time when posts were already being advertised nationally through such journals as the National Society's *Monthly Paper*. One possible explanation is that regional differences in dialect were greater than today. Hence a man from a small mining village in Yorkshire and cockney children, for example, would have found each other incomprehensible. On the other hand the contents of the professional journals suggest that the services of certificated masters were eagerly sought in the colonies and India where pay and prospects were better.

Apart from suggesting to the schoolmaster who stayed in England that hard work brought its own compensations, his social superiors could offer him little help in resolving his social dilemma. One assistant commissioner thought that: 'The character of their work, if engaged in with an earnest hearty purpose, ought...to elevate them above morbid fears as to their position in society, as well as fortify them against any sense of disproportion between them and the quality of their education and personal ability.'[134] Over another grievance they were even less helpful. Since the schoolmaster reached his maximum earning capacity at an early age, he had little chance of promotion. 'He reaches in early life a table land,' the Newcastle report stated, 'and may tread it till he dies.' The remedy they proposed possessed one merit, that of simplicity. 'If the emoluments of the young schoolmaster were smaller, those of the older schoolmaster would appear greater, and there would be no complaint of the absence of promotion.'[135]

The Taunton Commissioners offered a consolation prize to the certificated teacher whom they saw as 'apt to be mechanical, apt to explain too much, prone to recognize only one form of excellence, that of conforming to a closely defined type, and to judge progress, not by the hesitating results of silent growth, but by the readiness of superficial display'.[136] He could teach the children of 'the smaller tenant farmers, the small tradesmen, the superior artisans'. In the third-grade school, which these pupils would leave at the age of fourteen, the certificated man could provide 'a clerk's education—a thorough knowledge of arithmetic, and an ability to write a good letter.'[137]

In the 1860s, the occupation was in a state of transition. Earlier it had enjoyed little esteem. 'Men were generally made schoolmasters because they were unfit for anything else,' one M.P. told the House of Commons during the 1847 debate on the pupil-teacher system. 'If a man lost an arm or a leg; the first thing he did was to look for a turnpike; or failing an empty turnpike, he next applied for the situation of village schoolmaster.'[138] In the same debate Lord Macaulay (then T. B. Macaulay, Member for Edinburgh) had described schoolmasters as 'the refuse of all other callings...to whom no gentleman would entrust the key of his cellar'.[139] Thanks to Kay-Shuttleworth the trade of schoolmaster, that last refuge of the unemployable, gradually became a profession. Because of the basic characteristics of the English elementary school system, the profession remained a low status one for a considerable period. Schools had originated as charitable institutions that ministered to the welfare of the labouring classes. Under the voluntary system the schoolmaster depended for part of his income on the goodwill of the propertied classes. This was a humiliating situation for a man who had stayed at school until the age of eighteen and had then spent two years at college. What was virtually a caste system still differentiated the elementary school from all others.

Since it was believed that too much education would endanger the existing social order, the education proper to the children of workmen and servants was a strictly limited one. The school-master's task was to prepare 'the children of the poor for their future life by appropriate religious and moral discipline, by teaching them to write, to read their own language with interest, and with an intelligent perception of its meaning, and to per-form common arithmetical operations'.[140] During the short time that children could attend school, the teacher could do no more than give them 'a mere groundwork of plain reading, a still less practice in writing, and less of practice in the elementary rules of arithmetic...the grinding of which into the pupils is the most repulsive part of the task of the educator'.[141] Inevitably, the public image of the man who performed these duties was an indifferent one.

For as long as the elementary schoolmaster was unable to shake off the legacy of the past, his social, economic, and pro-fessional status remained incongruous. The passing of the Education Act, 1870, gave him a new confidence. He no longer needed to depend for part of his income on the generosity of his social superiors, nor did he have to endure a master-servant relationship with the incumbent. He could go and work for that institutionalized employer, the school board. For these reasons it is no coincidence that the National Union of Elementary Teachers, the first effective national non-denominational teachers' organization, was founded in 1870.

With the development of higher grade schools, which was accompanied by the growth of opportunities for promotion to well-paid posts in large schools that were controlled by the rate-assisted school boards, the schoolmaster's status rose and with it his self-confidence. In 1889, the N.U.E.T. emancipated itself from its working-class stigma and became the N.U.T.[142] The wider world outside the classroom accepted the schoolmaster's new self-evaluation. In 1861 the Newcastle Commissioners had hoisted the certificated master with his own petard. 'It is abso-lutely certain,' they wrote, 'that the inspectors should be fitted, by previous training and social position, to communicate and associate upon terms of equality with the managers of schools and the clergy of the different denominations. It is one of the alleged grievances of the schoolmasters that these persons do not recognize them as equals; and that state of things is in itself conclusive against the suggestion that they should be made inspectors.'[143] In 1888 their successors, the Cross Commissioners, reported: 'We are, however, of opinion that it is neither fair nor wise to debar elementary teachers from rising to the ranks of inspectors . . .'[144]

6   A Mid-Victorian Bureaucracy

How pleasant it is to have money.

ARTHUR HUGH CLOUGH[1]

What influenced him [F. C. Hodgson] in the choice of a profession was the wish to support his nearest and dearest relatives in real comfort.

J. R. MOZLEY[2]

When he [an examiner] found any difficulty in making his recommendation [to an assistant secretary about a reply to a letter], it was customary for him to 'pigeon-hole' the papers or to put them into a drawer, either for consideration in the distant future or in the hope that future developments might providentially render any consideration unnecessary.

SIR GEORGE W. KEKEWICH.[3]

Structure and organization

The nineteenth century saw a revolution in government. In a predominantly rural society, it had been sufficient to provide such services as education, the maintenance of law and order, the relief of the poor, and the upkeep of the king's highway on a local and voluntary basis. Industrialization and urbanization made these methods obsolete. They had to be replaced by institutions and bureaucracies that were under the control of the central government. In the course of this process new departments of state, of which the Education Department was one amongst many, had to be set up and extra duties had to be given to existing government offices. This chapter will show how, in one particular instance, the so-called unreformed civil service* responded to the demands imposed on it by the challenge of a changing and dynamic society.

The early history of the Education Department is unlikely to be typical of that of other government offices at this time. Although the new office began as an offshoot of the Privy Council Office it was, in effect, a new department administering a new

---

* To call the pre-Northcote-Trevelyan civil service unreformed is to ignore the substantial improvements made from the 1780s onwards.

service. For this reason it never had to slough off an inheritance of inefficiency bequeathed it by the eighteenth century. Moreover, it had the additional advantage of controlling the recruitment of its own staff. Patronage was vested in its political chief, the Lord President of the Council. Since the Department was in the political limelight, it had to be staffed by men who were reasonably competent. For these reasons Sir James Kay-Shuttleworth never experienced the misfortunes suffered by Major Graham at the General Register Office. When his office was set up in 1836 the Treasury appointed 'a great many persons who were certainly very incompetent'.[4] One of the Treasury nominees had earlier in life been imprisoned as a fraudulent debtor. Two more had to be kept in rooms by themselves, one because of his health, and the second because the clerks found him so offensive that they refused to work with him.[5]

Ultimate political control of the Education Department was exercised by the Committee of the Privy Council on Education. Its membership – the Lord President, the Lord Privy Seal, the Chancellor of the Exchequer and one of Her Majesty's principal Secretaries of State – closely followed the recommendations made by Lord Brougham four years earlier. This champion of popular education had proposed the setting up of a Board of Commissioners consisting of the Lord President of the Council, the Lord Privy Seal, the Home Secretary, and 'if it were deemed necessary', the Speaker of the House of Commons.[6]

Only one minute book of the committee that was formed in 1839 has survived. Fortunately it is the very interesting one covering the formative period, April 1839 to March 1841.[7] The early meetings of the Committee were remarkably well attended. The only absentee during the first eight was the Lord Privy Seal who failed to come on two occasions. By present-day standards much of the business transacted was of a trivial nature. The agenda even included consideration of the applications made by individual school managers for building grants. The inclusion of such items, even if they were passed 'on the nod', evokes a picture of an unhurried and undemanding public life. Such a view is a mistaken one for, although the Committee's annual budget was only £30,000, great issues were at stake. The fate of Lord Melbourne's administration, confronted by the resurgence of the Tory party, was in the balance. The survival of the government and of its education policy, to some extent, depended on the success with which the Committee arbitrated between the conflicting interests of the religious societies. Consequently, an event such as the appointment of the first school inspectors was a matter of considerable political significance. Hence, when John Allen and Hugh Tremenheere were summoned for interview, they faced a Committee that had recently been enlarged by the inclusion of a further three leading members of the Whig party.*

By the mid 1850s the practice of appointing a large Committee had become general. When the Earl of Derby, for instance, took office in February 1852 he included eight of the thirteen members of his Cabinet.[8] Lord Palmerston's Committee was even larger and more unwieldy. He omitted only four from his Cabinet of fourteen.[9]

The growth in the size of the Committee which was accompanied by a steady rise in the education vote began to alarm Members of Parliament. Earlier the appointment of an *ad hoc* Committee had helped to win over those who would have opposed such a definite and permanent move as the setting up of a Ministry of Education. Now friend and foe of education, alike, began to demand that one man should be responsible for all educational matters. Some saw this as a means whereby the size of the vote could be reduced. On the other hand Sir John Pakington,† one of the staunchest parliamentary allies the children of the poor possessed, argued that the concentration of responsibility into the hands of one man would lead to an improved educational service. A precedent for such a move, he pointed out, already existed. In 1847, the Poor Law Commissioners had been replaced by the Poor Law Board which was headed by its president who sat in the House of Commons.[10] In response to this pressure a Vice-President was appointed in 1856, 'to be responsible for all matters relating to education'.[11]

Unfortunately, this step raised more problems than it solved. Given a Lord President, a Vice-President sitting in the House of

---

* See p. 40.
† J. S. Pakington, created First Lord Hampton (1874) was M.P. for Droitwich (1837–74), Secretary of State for War and the Colonies (1852), First Lord of the Admiralty (1858–9 and 1866–7), Secretary of State for War (1867–8), and first civil service commissioner (1875).

Commons, and a Committee whose powers and functions were obscure – where did ministerial responsibility lie? Furthermore, were the powers of the Committee advisory or executive? Last, what was the relationship of the Vice-President, theoretically the responsible minister, to the Lord President and the Secretary of the Department? Such a situation was not in accord with current constitutional practice. The growth of public business, and with it public expenditure, required the concentration of responsibility into the hands of one minister who was accountable to the House of Commons for the affairs of his department. Yet the Education Department, one of the major civil spending departments, was a constitutional hydra. As Pakington pointed out when he returned to the attack nearly ten years later: 'Under our Parliamentary system, it is the object and the desire of the country that at the head of each Department there should be a man whose time, attention, and mind are concentrated on it, and who has full control over it, subject only to the general check of the Cabinet and of the responsibility which he owes to Parliament... That is the system under which the great Departments of State are administered; but what is the state of affairs in the Education Office? In the Education Department there are eight or ten ministers instead of one, and as to responsibility, there is none.'[12] His persistence was rewarded the following year. He became the chairman of a select committee to inquire into the constitution of the Committee of the Privy Council on Education.

The members of the newly appointed Committee heard evidence for two sessions before submitting their report. They found the system of having a Committee of four departmental heads to administer education peculiar and without precedent.[13] 'The Board of Trade,' they observed, 'is similar only in name, as the Board never meets. The Poor Law business,' the report continued, 'is practically conducted by the President of the Poor Law Board. The Admiralty is managed by a Board, but the members of it are connected exclusively with that office, and their whole time is given to its duties; and the same could be said of the India Council.'[14]

Earl Granville though, in his evidence, had compared the Committee with the former Board of Control for India.* Both

* The Board of Control was set up under Pitt's India Act, 1784, and abolished when the government of India was reorganized after the Indian Mutiny.

bodies, he argued, had at their head a President and a Vice-President who were also members of the Privy Council. The examples of this board and that of the Board of Trade had been copied by the Melbourne administration, Earl Granville stated, when the Committee on Education was formed.[15] Granville also compared the Committee of Council on Education with a Cabinet committee. 'My notion of the Committee of Council,' he said, 'has been...that of a committee of the cabinet... It is a common thing,' he continued, 'to call committees of the cabinet. I have been on committees of the cabinet at different public offices, and every year there are such committees at the Office, the Admiralty, at the Treasury and at other offices,' he ambiguously added, 'almost as often as the Committee of Council is assembled.'[16] The committees to which Earl Granville referred, however, were of an ephemeral nature and never outlived their political progenitors.

Although much about the structure and functions of the Committee of the Privy Council on Education was obscure, one point at least was clear. Its members, unlike those of the Admiralty Board, did not have to give the whole of their time and attention to its duties. Many of them seldom, if ever, attended a meeting. Lingen, who by this time had been secretary for seventeen years, was closely questioned on this point. According to him the most active members had been the Home Secretary and the Chancellor of the Exchequer. During his early years at the Education Office the Committee had met three or four times a session. Just recently the controversial nature of the Revised Code had brought a renewal of interest and activity. There had been between six and ten meetings on that item alone. One of them had been particularly noteworthy. It seems that all the members had attended. Usually, though, these more recent meetings had been attended by the Lord President, the Home Secretary, the Chancellor of the Exchequer, and as a somewhat unexpected fourth, the First Lord of the Admiralty. The Lord President's colleagues could probably have spent their time with greater profit in their own departments. On occasion the Lord President and the Vice-President ignored the necessity for a quorum of three and transacted business on their own.[17]

Lord Salisbury's evidence shows that some members realized that their presence was not essential. While he was Lord

President of the Council* he had called, he thought, three or four meetings of the Committee of Council. None of the members had attended and he had accordingly acted on his own responsibility. Later in his evidence he modified this statement by admitting that one meeting had actually taken place.[18] C. B. Adderley,† who had been Lord Salisbury's Vice-President, described the occasion when the members, despite their complaints at being summoned, had actually come. 'I recollect quite distinctly,' he said, '[that] what we had to do in consultation was to explain to the Committee upon what subject we wanted their advice, and the advice they gave was very much to sanction the conclusion to which we had come already.' In the light of this experience Adderley thought the Committee 'absolutely useless and worse than useless'. Individual members, he found, were neither well informed nor interested in educational problems.[19] This was unfortunate for, as Lingen had stated, 'the satisfactory solution of the questions submitted to the Committee required a great deal of accurate knowledge of the educational systems of the country'. It is therefore strange that the obvious precaution of circulating draft copies of the minutes before a meeting was not always taken.[20]

As well as knowing little about the problems they were supposed to be discussing, members were further handicapped by being uncertain about the constitutional status of their Committee. On this issue there was wide disagreement. Lingen, a senior civil servant of considerable service, understandably saw the Committee as the Lord President's creature. It was, he said, 'a merely consultative body'.[21] It met at the discretion of his political master and discussed those items that were put before it. If the Lord President wished to do so, he could ignore the Committee altogether and take his business straight to the Cabinet.[22]

Robert Lowe disagreed violently. The Lord President was the Committee's servant. In his opinion the Committee was the depository of all those executive and administrative functions that were, in practice, delegated to the Lord President. In addi-

* From February 1858 to June 1859 as a member of the Earl of Derby's second administration.
† C. B. Adderley, created 1st Lord Norton (1878) was Vice-President (1858-9), Under-Secretary of State for the Colonies (1866-8), and President of the Board of Trade (1878).

tion the Committee possessed a legislative power. Hence the Lord President had the duty of submitting any new minute or important change in the Revised Code to it for approval. Moreover, such a meeting was no mere formality. If members wished to do so, they could overrule the Lord President.[23]

Earl Russell was in broad agreement with Lowe. Once a member had concurred with a minute, the Earl stated, that member became responsible to 'a certain degree' for its general contents.[24] Earl Granville, however, disagreed with his former political junior colleague. He did not attach much importance to the Committee. Individual members had no more responsibility for education than they had, as members of the Cabinet, for affairs that did not concern their departments. Furthermore, if he had been overruled by the Committee, he would not necessarily have taken such a decision as final. If he had wanted to, he would have appealed to the full Cabinet.[25]

These differences did more than 'afford additional proof of the anomalous position and uncertain functions' of the Committee.[26] They made it impossible to determine where ministerial responsibility lay. If Lowe's interpretation was the correct one, the responsible body was the Committee of the Privy Council on Education. The appointment of a Vice-President on education, therefore, had been a meaningless gesture. On the other hand if Earl Granville was right, responsibility rested on someone within the Department.

If we are to carry this discussion further, we must now look at the powers and functions of the main office holders. Before 1856, the position had been reasonably clear. If there was a Minister of Education, that person was the Lord President. It was to him that Lingen had taken all important matters before 1856. Furthermore, the Lord President had signed all the money orders for the payment of building grants until the appointment of a Vice-President had relieved him of the chore. Lingen, as Secretary, was saddled with the tedious task of signing all the orders for the payment of the annual grants. For this purpose post office orders, made out to the individual teacher or pupil-teacher, were used. As the largest denomination issued was £5, the amount of clerical work involved was considerable.[27] In addition he drafted and signed all letters except for the few that were referred to the Lord President.

The coming of a Vice-President had deprived Lingen of much of his earlier freedom. He found that he now had to refer much more to his immediate senior, the Vice-President, than he had earlier to the Lord President. Residual power, albeit largely dormant, still lay with his former master. 'I consider the Lord President to be the senior officer,' he told the Select Committee, 'when he chooses to give an order, but the greater part of the current business is transacted by the Vice-President.'[28]

No witness successfully solved the constitutional problem. Even Lowe, the most forthright witness, was unhappy. In 1864 he had apparently accepted the doctrine of ministerial responsibility by resigning after the House of Commons had passed a vote of censure. Later, however, he maintained that he had resigned as a matter of honour because the House of Commons had refused to accept his explanation concerning the alleged mutilation of the inspectors' reports.[29] In 1865 he somewhat inconsistently told the Select Committee that he was constitutionally irresponsible. 'I think I should have been arrogating too much to myself,' he said in evidence, 'if I had stated myself to be responsible for anything connected with the Department except for administering it with honesty and to the best of my ability, and for obedience to my official superiors the Lord President and the Committee of Council. I consider myself neither more nor less than an Under-Secretary,' he added, 'with the single exception of having a seat in the Committee of Council.' Yet as such he was a member of a body that he said could over-rule his chief.[30] Moreover, although Lowe had resigned ostensibly because the House had refused to accept his word, he had not felt it appropriate to apply for the Stewardship of the Chiltern Hundreds.

H. A. Bruce,* Lowe's successor, probably made the most realistic appraisal of all. He thought the office of Vice-President was unique. 'Finding the practice of the office to be what it is,' he said, 'and finding the position of the Vice-President—as a member of the Council—to be what it is, I conceive there is a substantial amount of responsibility vested in the Vice-President;

* H. A. Bruce, created 1st Baron Aberdare (1873) was Liberal M.P. for Merthyr Tydfil (1852–68) and Renfrewshire (1869–73), was Vice-President (1864), Home Secretary (1869–73), Lord President of the Council (1873–4), and Chancellor of the University of Wales (1894).

although there may be something anomalous in it. In my opinion the office of Vice-President has no actual counterpart in that of any other office of the government.'[31] Bruce had found that Lingen, whom he saw as occupying the position of a Permanent Under-Secretary, referred matters to him for decision. Usually Bruce's decision was final and the Lord President was not consulted. In addition, Bruce considered that he was answerable both to the Lord President and the House of Commons.[32] Thus his relationship with Lingen made him something more than an Under-Secretary; his subordination to the Lord President made him something less than a full Secretary of State.

If we look at the day-to-day working of the office we find that the Lord President was far less concerned with its running than was the Vice-President. Yet all witnesses had agreed that the former had some degree of responsibility for the Department, while some thought that the latter had none. There was no doubt, for instance, that the Lord President was responsible for the exercise of patronage.[33] Similarly it was generally accepted that the Lord President had to be consulted on any proposed change of policy. Earl Granville, for example, expected to be consulted before any alterations were made in the rules or their application.[34]

Such a directive suggests that the initiation of policy came from the Department rather than from the Lord President. A study of the way in which the Revised Code was promulgated substantiates this thesis. The initiative for the change seems to have come from the officials of the Department who were seeking a way of simplifying their work. As early as December 1859, Harry Chester, the Assistant Secretary, told the Newcastle Commissioners, 'I do not see how it is possible to relieve the Committee of Council on Education from the multiplicity of details which are involved in the present system, unless you give up the plan of inspecting the schools...and substitute...a system of simply testing by examination, and paying for results.'[35] Granville's opinion at this stage is not known. What is known, though, is that Lingen was instructed by Lowe, not by Granville, to draw up the new code. Lingen's draft proposals were then discussed several times by the Committee of Council. On only one occasion, it seems, were they revised by Granville.[36]

Similarly when Lingen drew up the equally important

instructions to inspectors on the administration of the Revised Code, Granville's role was only a minor one. Lingen discussed his directive to the inspectorate paragraph by paragraph with Lowe; Granville made no amendments and merely remarked that the instructions were very voluminous.[37]

Lingen was closely questioned about the part played by the Lord President and the Committee in these episodes.

Question and answer 538.	Did any of the Committee of Council suggest any alterations [to the Revised Code]? There were many discussions about it, and many opinions pronounced.
Question and answer 510.	Had he [the Lord President] made any note in the margin to indicate that he had read them [the instructions to inspectors]? I am sure he had read them.

On each of these occasions Lingen's evasion of the question is as revealing as a direct answer.

The evidence of the Secretary's minute book broadly confirms the impression derived from a study of the particular instance of the introduction of the Revised Code. Although the Secretary occasionally referred matters relating to the interpretation of the new code to the Vice-President,* he seems never to have had to go to the Lord President for a ruling.

Further confirmation of the Lord President's aloofness from the affairs of his Department is provided by Lingen. The appointment of a Vice-President had made his nominal political chief such a shadowy figure that often Lingen did not even know if he was in the building. Moreover, even if he was there, Lingen did not know what branch of the Privy Council business was engaging his attention.†[38] Despite his varied duties his office 'was not a hard worked one'.[39] Lord Salisbury thought that the work of the Science and Art Department had taken more of his time than had popular education.[40] Yet Granville found that these particular duties could usually be discharged in the course

* See p. 217 for an example.

† The work of the Privy Council, apart from its formal functions, included duties relating to health transferred from the short-lived Board of Health, oversight of the Science and Art Department, the work of the Judicial Committee of the Privy Council, and the representation of the government in the House of Lords. A cattle plague department was added in 1868-9.

of a three-hour meeting, held once a week at South Kensington.[41] The remaining miscellany of duties apparently took up very little time.[42]

It is thus possible to suggest that the extent to which the politicians participated in policy-making varied over the course of time. During the period covered by the first minute book the Committee met frequently. At this stage Kay-Shuttleworth's role may only have been a minor one.[43] Some time later, Kay-Shuttleworth and, after his retirement, Lingen, had greater freedom. They were statesmen in disguise.[44] A further change came when a Vice-President was appointed in 1856. Lingen suffered the fate of those great reforming civil servants, Edwin Chadwick and John Simon. He lost much of his former discretion.[45] Despite the anomalies of his office, the Vice-President, Lingen's immediate departmental superior, was his effective political master. After 1856 the Lord President, at the apex of the power pyramid, knew little of what happened in his Department. The extent to which responsibility had been devolved in this particular department may not have been typical of the civil service as a whole. Both the Select Committee's concern over this point and the *naïveté* of some of the school managers* suggest that the structure of the Department was exceptional. If this was so, the Education Department pointed the way to the future. It was the prototype of the modern government office in which political heads do not know of, and cannot supervise, every action of the subordinates.

In contrast the origins of the Department had been humble enough. As was so often the case, a new government service was provided by attaching new duties to an already existing institution.[46] Three clerks, who for pay purposes remained on the establishment of their old department, the Privy Council Office, formed the nucleus of the Education Office. The loss of some of its staff in 1839, the year in which it assumed the additional responsibility of running the Judicial Committee of the Privy Council, did not inconvenience the parent office. 'Previous to the existence of the Education Office,' the Select Committee on Miscellaneous Expenditure reported in 1848, 'it is obvious that the establishment of the Council Office was redundant, as the

* See pp. 47–8.

duties of this new and onerous department have been performed, with a small addition of labour, by gentlemen already upon the staff of the office.'[47] Those who were transferred certainly had to work harder. According to C. C. F. Greville,* 'the staff of the Education Office come at about ten o'clock, and the others [those on Privy Council Office duties only] come about eleven, and stay till between four and five, and sometimes particularly in the Education Department, very much later; [but] it varies very much, just as the amount of business varies, so the attendance varies'.[48] Harder work brought its reward. Those who were shaken out of an eighteenth-century lethargy by the administrative needs of the nineteenth, drew a supplementary salary from the education vote. From the start Harry Chester received an extra £100 a year for acting as Kay-Shuttleworth's assistant.[49] By the late 1840s the situation was as follows:

Table I SALARIES PAID TO MEMBERS OF THE EDUCATION OFFICE

	1847			1848		
	Salary from			Salary from		
	Privy Council Office	Education Office	Total	Privy Council Office	Education Office	Total
H. Chester Third clerk	£450	100	550	450	250	700
E. Harrison Fourth clerk	350	50	400	350	150	500
C. G. V. Bayley Sixth clerk to the Privy Council	220	50	270	220	130	350

Source: *Appendix to the Report from the Select Committee on Miscellaneous Expenditure*, P.P. 1847–8, XVIII, B, pp. 100–1 (106–7).

The remaining six established members of the staff drew salaries that ranged between £120 and £300.[50]

* C. C. F. Greville (1794–1865) was educated at Eton and Christ Church, Oxford, was private secretary to Lord Bathurst (1810), and also secretary for Jamaica, an island he never visited. He was clerk to the Privy Council Office (1821–59), an eminent political diarist, and a founder member of the Jockey Club.

It soon became clear that the Department demanded greater expertise from its staff than that offered by three clerks who had been recruited by the methods of the late eighteenth century to serve a largely pre-industrial society. Therefore Kay-Shuttleworth was instructed on 6 August 1840 to prepare 'an act for facilitating the conveyance of sites for schoolhouses', to obtain the help of a barrister to examine the deeds and to start a registry of trust deeds and 'to procure such assistance for the examination of plans and specifications as the Board of Works may advise'.[51] By 9 November an architect, S. Kempthorne, and a barrister, W. G. Lumley, had been appointed. Both men came from the Secretary's old department where they had had to face problems similar to those now confronting the Education Department. Each department had to verify titles to land and supervise the erection of buildings on a countrywide basis. Thus the qualifications and experience of these two made them well, if not uniquely, qualified for their new duties.

The Secretary had been equally well chosen. Kay-Shuttleworth's experiences amongst the poor of Manchester and East Anglia, together with his long-held interest in education, marked him out as the obvious man to head the new Department. In addition Harry Chester, the Assistant Secretary, shared his chief's interests and convictions. Largely as a result of Chester's efforts, the Highgate Literary and Scientific Institution had been opened in January 1839. In his inaugural speech as President he had made it clear that, like Kay-Shuttleworth, he believed that the diffusion of education would act as an antidote to social disorder.[52]

By the end of 1840 the initial staffing problems of the Department had been solved. Daily work had become more organized through the inauguration of a series of office books and forms. These included letter books, a counsel's ledger and record books for the applications, trusts, and grants departments, as well as one for a statistical abstract.[53] In addition, some control had been established over the inspectorate who were required to forward a weekly diary of their journeys and visits.[54] Lastly an important victory had been gained over the National Society. Their Lordships discovered 'that the National Society had in many cases granted aid for the erection of schoolhouses on condition that if the applicants afterwards applied to the Committee of Council for aid, and obtained it, these conditional grants should be subject to review and reduction or reclamation by the Society, and that these promoters of schools had in many cases been subsequently urged to apply to the Committee of Council for aid'. The matter was taken up with the National Society and the errant school managers were informed that My Lords 'will not proceed to a decision on any case, until they are informed whether it is the intention of the applicants to apply to any other source for aid, and until the decision of such Society or other body is communicated to them...'[55]

The inauguration of the pupil-teacher system in 1846 brought the Department extra work and the need for more staff. The next few years were, for both the inspectorate and the office staff, ones of strain. The British educational system had already begun to develop one of its outstanding characteristics: allowing commitments to outstrip resources. Only a decade later, Kay-Shuttleworth was asked by the Newcastle Commissioners if the office was once again in danger of breaking down under the sheer volume of work. In reply, he referred to the difficulties that had led up to his collapse in the late 1840s with great bitterness: 'If I were in charge of the department and encountered the usual difficulty of obtaining an efficient staff and adequate accommodation then such an apprehension would not seem to me quite chimerical.'[56] Kay-Shuttleworth had not been alone in his suffering. 'Mr Armitage', he wrote, 'is the victim of chronic congestion of the brain and practical paralysis on one side. Mr Harrison had a very sudden attack of congestion of the brain threatening paralysis, which was only averted by active treatment. Mr Lingen has left the office in a state of nervous exhaustion.'[57]

The victims of Treasury parsimony, though, had one consolation. The three predecessors of Charles Trevelyan, the Assistant Secretary to the Treasury, had all suffered similar misfortunes.[58] To suggest, as the civil servants naturally did, that their illnesses were solely the result of overwork is to ignore other factors. With a crude system of sanitation the general standard of health, even of middle-class civil servants, must have been poor by present-day standards. Imprecise medical diagnosis, sheer ignorance, and the prescription of ineffective remedies must have caused many minor complaints to escalate until they reached crippling proportions.

When Kay-Shuttleworth finally retired in 1849 Harry Chester, the senior man in the Department, was passed over. The choice of the new secretary apparently lay between two relative newcomers, Lingen and the Reverend F. Temple. Both were men of outstanding and demonstrable ability. In contrast Chester, the son of a sinecurist, had left Cambridge without taking a degree.* Temple, however, was never seriously in the running. Since he was in Holy orders, his appointment as secretary would have offended Nonconformist opinion.[59] Lingen had the further advantage of having shown his capacity for hard sustained work on joining the Department. The report he had made on the state of education in the counties of Carmarthen, Glamorgan and Pembroke ran to nearly 500 pages of foolscap print. Yet he had begun his inquiry on 18 October 1846, completed it on 3 April 1847, and had written his report by 1 July of the same year.[60]

It is unlikely that the majority of the staff ever had to work as hard as Lingen did during those months he spent in Wales. Yet the pace of official life began to quicken when he started to enforce a stricter discipline in the mid-1860s. The instructions he then issued show how undemanding many must have found the daily routine before he began requiring a higher standard of conduct from his assistants. In February 1865 he minuted: 'The Lord President cannot allow the present practice of introducing beer during all hours of the day and from all quarters to continue. The passages of the office are, at times, more like those of a public house. The Treasury kitchen is established to furnish such refreshment as is necessary; and the office keeper and messengers have orders to let no persons, except from that kitchen, enter the office after today with beer or baskets. The heads of rooms are held responsible for preventing drinking in their rooms, except at the time of lunch or dinner...Officers are not to absent themselves during office hours on the plea of refreshment... These rules apply to the messengers. Trays, plates, pots, and the like are not to lie about in the passages.'[61]

The following July the staff were in trouble again. 'I must remind the examiners that the time to be at their posts is 11 a.m.—At 11.25 this morning,' Lingen wrote, 'I found two visitors but no examiner. It is exceeding probable,' the Secretary

---

* His father, Sir Robert Chester, had held the post of the Master of the Ceremonies under George III, George IV, William IV, and Queen Victoria (Burke's *Landed Gentry*, 1855).

warned, 'that sooner or later, complaint may be made to the Lord or Vice-President upon the subject, and I am quite certain that, were such to be the case, they would feel the necessity of laying down some rule about attendance, that in itself would imply a censure.'[62] Two years later, leave of absence was granted on stringent terms to members of the Volunteer forces to take part in a review held one Saturday afternoon before the Sultan of Turkey. Those not taking part were allowed to leave at 4 p.m. Those who were to be on parade were allowed to leave at 2 p.m. All arrears of work, however, had to be cleared by the following Monday afternoon without any extra assistance. The Lord President insisted, Lingen emphasized, 'that it is part of the arrangement that all who take advantage of it fulfil their obligations'.[63]

At an official level leave was granted sparingly; at an unofficial level French leave was taken more freely. The absentees did not always escape notice. Sir George Kekewich* found that 'Some officious member of the Government or Parliament might happen to see one or more of us whom he happened to know taking his ease at some place of amusement or social function...during office hours and be base enough to write to the Secretary or minister'.[64] The work that had been missed during the day was made up in an hour or so at night. When he first entered the office in 1868, the daily allocation was one of assessing the grants for eight schools. This was hardly a day's work. Once when he was in arrears, Kekewich dealt with seventy schools in a day.

The absence of 'open plan' offices added considerably to the problem of maintaining effective control over the staff. 'The public offices are, in general, very ill arranged as regards construction,' Lingen wrote in a paper on the reorganization of the civil service in 1855. 'The rooms are far too numerous for the purpose of ready reference and supervision. The principle of construction...should be to make large halls for the main body of the clerks, with side-rooms opening out of them for a few superior officers... In my own department there are sixty per-

* G. W. Kekewich, the fourth son of S. T. Kekewich, M.P. for South Devon, was educated at Eton and Balliol College, Oxford (second class Lit. Hum., 1863) was examiner (1868), secretary (1890-1900) and of the Board of Education to 1903. Then was M.P. for Exeter (1906-10) and was created K.C.B. (1895).

sons (including messengers and copying clerks) scattered on four different floors, throughout twenty-five separate rooms.'[65]

As well as ensuring the regular attendance of his staff, Lingen had to teach them the elements of office routine. Even such a basic office task as filing was badly done. In March 1858, for example, he had to point out that letters were to be tagged on the files consecutively with the minute to him at the top. Two years later he minuted: 'In filing papers always put enclosures in front of and not behind the letters to which they belong.' In 1863 he returned to the attack. 'The several directions of a minute,' he instructed, 'should follow one another in a distinct order...and not [be] screwed into odd corners, and...where there is more than one direction they are to be numbered consecutively...It is frequently very difficult, in consequence of the slovenly manner in which letters are sometimes minuted, and noted, to tell whether they are really ready to be put away.' Lingen's stream of admonitions had little effect. In 1868 a file was put away by mistake and, as a result, no action was taken on a particular letter for three months. 'I hold it out of the question,' Lingen wrote when he found out, 'to expect the clerks to find minutes scattered up and down the portfolios and to decide which is the last of them...I find it, myself, most extremely difficult and open to error, in dealing at much greater leisure with references. The only remedy is to observe strictly the directives at folios 240 and 253. [Here Lingen referred to instructions he had issued earlier the same year.]...The neat and orderly writing of the agenda is one of the essential parts of the office work.'[66] Despite all his efforts the standard of clerical work remained low. Instructions and comments continued to be screwed into odd corners of the working papers in the files. For this reason it is very difficult at times to follow the sequence of events even when examining the much later parish and school files of the 1880s and 1890s. In comparison with present-day standards in the civil service, many of the surviving departmental files were very badly kept.

Despite the difficulties that Lingen had with his staff, it is likely that recruits to the Education Department were of a particularly high calibre. The Education Department was fortunate for its period of most rapid expansion came at a time of great concern over the reform of the civil service. As we have seen, in 1839 there were three clerks who had been transferred from the Privy

Council Office. By 1848 the established clerical strength was nine. In addition a number of provisional appointments had been made.[67] Five years later, there were eleven clerks and seventeen supplementary ones on the establishment of the Privy Council Office. To deal with the new work caused by the introduction of the annual grants, there were four examiners and two supplementary clerks whose salaries were carried on the education vote.[68] This gives a total of thirty-four. To arrive at Lingen's figure of sixty, there must be added Lingen himself, Chester, the part-time architect and counsel, a statistical clerk, a varying number of temporary copying clerks, and the messengers. A further increase took place by 1860. In that year the establishment stood at 127. This figure included the political head of the Department, sixty-nine 'sub-heads' (the Vice-President, the Secretary, two assistant secretaries, nine examiners, and the inspectorate), fifty-five clerks, and the architect and counsel whose services were still shared with the Poor Law Board. In addition there were the messengers and the temporary clerks. With only one established clerk less than the Foreign Office, the Education Department had become one of the largest civil offices of the state.[69] The introduction of the simplified procedure of the Revised Code for the payment of the annual grants brought this period of rapid expansion to an end. By 1875, despite all the extra work that followed the passing of the 1870 Act, the permanent clerical staff had grown by only another five to sixty. On the other hand the number of examiners had increased by fourteen to twenty-three.[70]

The practice of keeping many of the staff of the Department on the strength of the Privy Council Office had one considerable tactical advantage. It concealed both the total size of the departmental staff and the real cost of education from critical and hostile M.P.s. For this reason the figures that are traditionally given for the cost of public education before 1853 are incorrect. The procedural reforms of the late 1840s and early 1850s gradually brought the true state of affairs to light. Following the report from the Select Committee on Miscellaneous Expenditure, full civil estimates were laid before the House of Commons, for the first time, in 1849.[71] Those for the financial year 1849–50 reveal that the Privy Council Office vote bore £5,355 of the expenses of the Education Department.[72] By the year 1853–4, this figure had risen to £7,670.[73] During the course of 1853 the Committee of Inquiry into the Privy Council Office published its report. In accordance with its recommendations a Treasury minute was published which separated the two offices.[74] From then onwards the Department carried the full cost of its staff.

The recruitment of the staff

There were two important ways of recruiting additional clerical staff. One method was by offering permanent posts to some of the Department's temporary employees. Additional clerks were obtained for short periods of time from firms of law stationers. By 1870, the main supplier was the firm of Vacher who performed the function of a modern secretarial bureau. They hired out the clerks, whom they themselves employed, to the Education Office at a shilling an hour.[75] This system allowed the Department to adjust the size of its staff to meet the seasonal fluctuations in the volume of work. As the establishment gradually increased, the best of the hired clerks were offered permanent posts. 'The consequence was,' Harry Chester told the Select Committee on Civil Service Appointments in 1860, 'that before the competitive system was introduced, we had got in the Education Office a body of assistant clerks of a very superior character. Very few indeed of them,' he added, 'had been selected in the way of patronage by the Lord President.'[76]

The second method was by competitive examination. In 1855 the Civil Service Commission was formed and given the task of supervising limited competitive examinations for vacancies in the lower grades of the public service. For the first few years, the process of selection was little more than a slightly modified or disguised form of nomination.[77] Of the 10,860 nominations made during the first five years, 8,039 were of one candidate only for a particular vacancy. Hence only 2,821 nominees had to sit a competitive examination. This figure, though, includes 391 persons who competed for nine clerkships at the India Office in the first entirely open examination ever held. As only 732 vacancies were competed for, the number of candidates in any examination would seldom have exceeded four. Many of those who failed, it was thought, would have been rejected under the former system of absolute nomination.[78]

This was not true of the clerical recruits to the Education

Office. Whereas in the Civil Service, as a whole, one vacancy in eleven had been filled by competitive examination, in this department two thirds of all clerical vacancies were so filled between 1855 and 1859.[79] Moreover, the high quality of many of the candidates made competition much keener than the figures, given in the following table, would suggest.

Table II RECRUITMENT OF CLERKS, 1855–9

	Vacancies	Candidates examined
November 1855	10	31
June 1856	1	5
January 1857	7	21
August 1857	6	15

Source: *Report from the Select Committee on Civil Service Appointments*, P.P. 1860, IX (H. Chester's evidence) Q. & A. 4003.

The appointment of Lord Salisbury as Lord President of the Council in 1858 brought a temporary end to competitive recruitment.[80] As well as the twenty-four vacancies that were filled by competition, a further twelve were filled by straightforward nomination.

Competition was severe because the right to nominate candidates was frequently given to the Society of Arts. Although Chester, who was a keen and active member of the Society, must have played a large part in this decision, he had an ally. Lord Granville, the Lord President, was also a member. Between 1856 and 1864, nineteen of the Society's nominees entered the Education Department and other government offices. These men had usually been outstandingly successful in the Society's own examinations before they were nominated. In a later age they would have done well in their G.C.E. 'O' level or civil service clerical class examination.[81]

When they entered the Education Department they found that their salary scales, which had been fixed in 1857, were as follows:

		Numbers
Class III	£100 × £5 to £150	As business required
Class II	£150 × £10 to £250	12 promoted by merit
Class I	£250 × £10 to £300	6 promoted by merit[82]

The young man who came to London on a salary of £100 a year

had to watch his money carefully. When these new rates were being fixed Lingen had protested against the old rate of £80. 'The salary at entrance into the service [£80] payable...at the end of each quarter,' he informed the Treasury, 'has been ascertained, by careful calculation, and by inquiry into the experience of steady, prudent officers, to afford a very narrow provision for a youth who has no home in London, nor independent means, but whose dress, habits, and mode of life, ought all to be respectable, and who ought to be exposed, as little as possible, to the temptation of running into debt.' The young clerk who possessed sufficient patience to make the long haul up to a salary of £250 a year was eventually rewarded with a moderately comfortable standard of living. In 1855 the Statistical Department of the Registrar-General's Office produced this budget for a clerk earning £200 a year, his wife, two children, and a family servant.[83]

BUDGET OF A LONDON CLERK (Summarized)

Expenditure			£	s.	d.
Rent of a six-roomed house in London plus house tax, rates, etc.			31	10	9
Food, cleaning materials, fuel, etc.			100	5	8
Servant			8	0	0
Clothing	Clerk	£15			
	Wife	£9			
	Children	£8	32	0	0
Miscellaneous			11	11	0
		Total	£183	7	5

This expenditure, 'regulated with the strictest regard to economy', did not make any allowance for such items as the cost of educating the clerk's children, pew rent, excursions into the country during his holidays, or life insurance. Another £25 to £50 a year, however, brought spiritual as well as spirituous consolation within his reach.

In 1867, Lingen requested a further revision of the salary scales. He pointed out that the clerks in the Treasury and the General Registry Office were earning more than his own staff. The Treasury accepted the force of his argument and sanctioned the following:

$$\text{Class III} \quad £100 \times £10 \text{ to } £150$$
$$\text{Class II} \quad £150 \times £10 \text{ to } £250$$
$$\text{Class I} \quad £250 \times £15 \text{ to } £360[84]$$

Thus although the Treasury had not yet established a common salary structure for the whole civil service, departmental rivalry helped to bring some degree of uniformity to the conditions of employment in the various government offices.

A year later a new grade, that of boy clerk, was introduced to replace the hired copying clerks. The clerks, who entered the Department between the ages of fourteen and sixteen, started at 12s. a week. This rose by a shilling a week until they reached the age of nineteen. They were then discharged. By January 1870 the Office had recruited twenty-seven boys who had passed a simple examination that involved 'copying manuscript with due regard to accuracy, handwriting and neatness and arithmetic in the first four rules, simple and money, with trials in addition in long columns'. The number of clerks from Vacher's, whose employees were 'inferior in every way to those whom the permanent service attracted', had fallen from an average of twenty-five or twenty-eight to five.[85]

Both Lingen and Chester were pleased with their new recruits. 'The new entrants,' Lingen told the 1860 Select Committee on Civil Service Appointments, '[were] free from those examples of gross inefficiency which occasionally occurred under the old plan; but many of the clerks appointed before 1853 are unsurpassed for practical usefulness and trustworthiness, by any who have been appointed since; and I have no fault whatever,' he went on, 'to find with the nine who, since 1855, have been directly nominated; nor do I consider them to be below the average of the others, in respect of their power to do what is wanted from them.'[86] Chester's only concern was 'whether they will be sufficiently robust; whether they may not spend too much time in their evenings in improving their education to do justice to their health.' His remedy was simple. 'To avert this risk I have promoted the establishment of a cricket club...'[87]

Chester did not have to worry about the men in the next grade—the examiners. Indeed he might well have agreed with the witness to the 1860 Select Committee who had complained that many of the highly educated civil servants 'appear to think that education is all that is required, and look on their duties as beneath their abilities... They are generally fond of discussion, argumentative displays, and private reading and writing during office hours'.[88] The examiners, Kekewich wrote, formed 'exactly the same society that is to be found in any college common-room'.[89] Yet one of the main duties of these highly gifted men was that of examining the inspector's report on a particular school and calculating the amount of a school's annual grant. Even under the Revised Code this was a simpler task than many that are performed by clerical officers today. In the local offices of H.M.I.s of Taxes, for instance, tax officers (clerical officers) compute the income tax assessments of most wage and salary earners. Higher tax officers (executive officers) calculate the amounts payable under the capital gains tax.

When Kekewich entered the Department in 1867, there were ten examiners. Five handled the annual grants, two the corre-spondence relating to the payment of the building grants, a further two dealt with the rest of the correspondence, and the tenth, usually the most senior, acted as private secretary to the Vice-President.[90] In only the last post would an honours graduate be employed today, and then only while he was an assistant principal undergoing training.

To add to their frustration the examiners had little oppor-tunity to assume any responsibility for the work of the Depart-ment. Although they drafted letters, they never signed them. Only the Secretary and the assistant secretaries signed letters. This rule even applied to the *pro forma* letters informing school managers of the amount of their annual grant. Yet this figure had been calculated by the examiners and checked by the clerks under them.

It seems that there was little except their social and official status to distinguish the examiners from the more experienced clerks. When the clerks complained to the Civil Service Inquiry Commission of 1875 that they were debarred from promotion to the examiner grade they stated: 'It is a plain matter of fact that while perhaps no other staff in the service comprises so many brilliant instances of academic success, their [the examiners'] duties afford no field for the display of other qualities than are to be found in civil servants who do not possess these distinctions. On occasions, clerks have done the work of examiners... Clerks are continually doing work which the examiners' initial

169

without checking, or work which the examiners have already done, and have sent back to the clerks to check. In short,' the clerks argued, 'the so called higher work is, after all, no higher than a clerk with the requisite experience might do.'[91] The clerks gave the Commission a specific instance. The Christmas examination of the pupil-teachers, formerly the responsibility of an examiner, was now supervised by a first-class clerk.[92]

As far as one can tell, the examiners had only two duties that they did not share with the clerks. Normally the letters were drafted by the examiners. This arrangement Patrick Cumin* regarded as essential. He told the Commissioners that, as a result of the Elementary Education Act, 1870, they had to deal with 'town councils, managers of voluntary schools, squires, clergymen, peers, bishops, in fact, every class in the country. Now if an examiner were not careful', he warned, 'and if the correspondence were not conducted in a judicious way, there would probably be a flame all over the country in a very short while.' He pointed out that he had to sign seventy-two letters a day, 'and if they were not minuted and recorded by men of the capacity which I have described,' he continued, 'I simply would not do it, and could not do it.'[93]

The other duty which the examiners did not share with the clerks was that of examining the reports made by the inspectors of returns. These men had conducted a census of school accommodation throughout the country after the passing of the 1870 Act. From these reports the examiners calculated the number of school places that a particular locality needed. When this had been done, it was possible to decide if a particular area needed a school board. This was a routine task that could have been carried out by experienced clerks. Cumin, however, justified the Department's employment of examiners on this work on the grounds that none of their decisions had been challenged in Parliament.[94] Although this was meant as a tribute to the political *finesse* of the examiners, it also suggests that excessive deference was being paid to the susceptibilities of the voluntary societies. Certainly the Education Office was always aware that it was

---

* Patrick Cumin, the first son of a Glasgow doctor, was educated at Balliol College, Oxford (Third class Maths, 1845), was Assistant Commissioner to the Newcastle Commission, private secretary to W. E. Forster (1868–71), Assistant Secretary (1871–84), and Secretary (1884–90).

handling political dynamite. 'Have not clerks at the Foreign Office,' Cumin was asked, 'to deal with ambassadors and consuls, and have not the clerks at the Admiralty to deal with admirals and captains?' 'Yes, but not with vestrymen, which is a very different thing,' he replied.[95]

In 1839 the Church of England had been reluctant to accept inspection of its schools. Hence the Education Department had had to recruit its inspectorate from those who were socially acceptable as gentlemen. In turn the examiners, who had to cooperate with both the inspectors and the school managers, had to have an equally acceptable social and academic background. The Committee of Inquiry of 1854 drew attention to the unusually high qualifications that the examiners possessed.

'The qualifications required of those who are employed in supervising the administration of the annual grant are peculiar; inasmuch as it is necessary that they should not only have received a high university education, but should also have kept up their acquaintance both with classics and mathematics, so as to give them weight and authority in communicating with the inspectors and managers of schools on matters connected with the examinations and with the course of study in general.'[96] The Committee added an argument of their own. The examiners controlled the expenditure of some two-thirds of the education grant. They accordingly recommended a salary scale of £300 × £20 to £600 which they thought 'would suffice to attract young men of the highest attainments and reputation from the universities'.[97] A salary of £300 was also fixed as the upper limit for those clerks who had been recruited to the establishment of the Privy Council Office 'with exclusive reference to the Education business'. Future clerical appointments were to be made in the 'supplementary clerk' grade at a salary of £80 × £5 to £150 and then, on merit, by £10 to £250.[98] There was thus achieved, at a salary level of £300, a division between the 'intellectual' and 'mechanical' work of the Department.

Such an arrangement may have been suggested by Lingen, 'A main point in my opinion,' he wrote a year later, 'is gradually to abolish all the situations under £300 a year which are now held by persons in superior establishments of offices; to delegate the whole of the work now done by these gentlemen to a class who, beginning at £80 or £100, shall rise to £300 or £400 as a maximum, being analogous to the clerks of merchants, bankers, or actuaries; to reduce the highest class of officers very greatly in number, and to make the lowest appointment to it begin at not less than £300 per annum.'[99]

The Committee's expectation that the salary they recommended would attract young men of high attainments was largely fulfilled. The names of thirty-one men who served, as examiners or senior officials, between 1848 and 1871 have been extracted from the Secretary's minute book. Twenty-eight of those whose careers have been examined were graduates of either Oxford or Cambridge. The three non-graduates were Chester (1839),* who left Cambridge without taking his degree, C. W. Merrifield (1851)† and W. Severn (1848)‡. Although the last two entered the Department before the grade of examiner was formally created, their extra-mural activities show that they were men of some ability. Nineteen of the graduates obtained first-class honours, five were awarded seconds, two thirds, and two are classified as passmen.§

Normally the Department required a first-class honours degree from its entrants. Those who did not possess this qualification were either early recruits, as were the non-graduates Chester, Merrifield and Severn, or they owed their posts to some special circumstances. The two residually classified as passmen are H. S. Bryant (before 1860),¶ and H. L. Whateley

---

* In the following discussion the date in brackets indicates the year of entry into the Department.

† C. W. Merrifield, the son of a barrister, was called to the Bar in 1851, entered the Education Department in 1847, was examiner (1851–67 and 1873–83), principal of a school of naval architecture and marine engineering (1868–73), Vice-President of the mechanical section, British Association (1875–6), and Hon. Sec. and contributor of 100 papers to the Royal Institute of Naval Architecture.

‡ W. Severn (1830–1904), the son of the British Consul in Rome, was educated at Westminster School. He was a water-colourist of some repute. He entered the Education Office in 1848, and in later years devoted himself to designing furniture, textiles and wallpapers at the possible expense of his official duties.

§ The number of pass degrees may be slightly overstated as the register of Cambridge graduates, *Alumni Cantabrigienses*, does not always give full details of a man's degree. Where the university and college registers, together with the *Annual Register*, do not show an honours degree, the graduate has been classified as a passman.

¶ H. S. Bryant, the son of Major Sir J. Bryant, was educated at Eton and Trinity College, Cambridge (B.A., 1850).

(1868).* The two holders of thirds were P. Cumin (1868) and G. W. Randolph (1860).† Cumin had already earned a reputation by writing two reports for the Newcastle Commission. He had come into the Department as W. E. Forster's private secretary in 1868. Randolph served the Lord President, Earl Granville, in a similar capacity in 1860.

The five men who obtained seconds were A. H. Clough (1853),‡ C. M. Cowie (1870),§ S. Joyce (circa 1862),¶ G. W. Kekewich (1868), and J. White (1865).‖ Clough, the first of the five to obtain an examinership, only did so after considerable difficulty. Sidney Joyce was an amateur essayist of sufficient local repute to earn the sobriquet 'the Charles Lamb of the Office'.[100] Kekewich was lucky. When he was appointed the Lord President thought that he had obtained a first.[101] White, despite his second, had been fellow, tutor, and classical lecturer in his university before joining the Department. Lastly, Cowie did not necessarily owe his job to his father. He had narrowly missed a first. He had been bracketed with five others at the top of the *senior optime* class of his year.

Up to at least the late 1840s it was still possible for men without high academic qualifications to join the Department. By this time, however, a policy of recruiting men with firsts was being adopted. Twenty years later, the man who did not

* H. L. Whateley was educated at Balliol College, Oxford (B.A., 1859), and was an examiner (1868–96).

† G. W. Randolph, the fifth son of a clergyman, was educated at Christ Church, Oxford (third class Lit. Hum., 1849), was Fellow of All Souls' College (1851–63), private secretary to Earl Granville (1860) and examiner from 1860 to 1863, when he died.

‡ Arthur Hugh Clough (1819–61), the second son of a Liverpool merchant, was educated at Rugby School, and Balliol College, Oxford (Second class Lit. Hum. 1841). He was a Fellow of Oriel College (1841–8), Head of University College Hall, London (1849–52), and examiner (1853–61).

§ C. M. Cowie, son of the Reverend B. M. Cowie, H.M.I., was educated at St Paul's School, London, and Jesus College, Cambridge (B.A., 1869). He entered the Education Office in 1870.

¶ S. Joyce, the sixth son of a clergyman, was educated at Christ Church, Oxford (second class Lit. Hum., 1856) and was admitted to Lincoln's Inn in 1860.

‖ J. White, the son of an Antrim landowner, was educated at Balliol College, Oxford (second class Lit. Hum., 1862; Sacred Poem prize, 1869), became a barrister in 1866, was a Fellow of Queen's College, temporary H.M.I. (1865, 1869–70) and also worked as an examiner. He later became assistant principal secretary.

possess a first was only admitted under exceptional circumstances. When the examiner grade was expanded around 1870 to deal with the new Act, the number of holders of firsts admitted to the Department almost doubled. Up to 1869 ten first-class-honours men had joined the administrative staff. Within two years another nine had been recruited.

An analysis of the academic background and achievements of those who became inspectors reveals a similar tendency. By 1860 there were thirty-six Anglican inspectors on the strength of the Department.[102] These men had begun their careers at various dates from the early 1840s onwards. Twenty-two were graduates of Cambridge and thirteen of Oxford. The thirty-sixth, B. J. Binns,* came from Trinity College, Dublin. The thirty-five English graduates obtained thirteen firsts, six seconds, two thirds, and fourteen pass degrees.

Although the religious exclusiveness of the older universities was not breached until the reforms of 1854 and 1856 were enacted, a substantial proportion of the Nonconformist and Roman Catholic inspectors of the pre-1860 period were Oxford or Cambridge men. Four British inspectors took their degrees at Oxford; one British and two Roman Catholic inspectors came from Cambridge. T. W. M. Marshall, one of the Catholic inspectors, however, had not abandoned his Anglican faith until five years after leaving Cambridge. The academic careers of two suggest that they were not prepared to compromise by subscribing to the Thirty-Nine Articles. J. Laurie, the son of an Anglican clergyman, went to that third university, the Inns of Court. The Nonconformist, J. D. Morell, who later in life wrote extensively on German philology and philosophy, went to Glasgow and Bonn. One inspector, J. Bowstead, was the second wrangler of his year, three obtained thirds, the two Roman Catholic inspectors were content with thirds.

Between 1860 and 1871 at least another twenty-two Anglican, four British, and one Roman Catholic inspector joined the Department.[103] One Anglican inspector went to King's College, London where he obtained a first, a second went to Trinity College, Dublin, and the remaining twenty were divided equally

---

* B. J. Binns, educated at Trinity College, Dublin, was principal of the Caernarvon Training Institution (1849–55), incumbent of St Ann, Llandegai, Caernarvon (1855–7) and H.M.I. (1857–81).

between Oxford and Cambridge. Excluding the Dublin graduate and the inspector of Roman Catholic schools, eight men obtained first-class honours degrees in public examinations, nine obtained seconds, six thirds, and two were passmen. All four British inspectors were awarded firsts. Three were at Cambridge and one at Oxford.*

It has to be remembered that the early recruits to the Department had been undergraduates when honours degrees at Oxford, if not also at Cambridge, were taken by very few. 'The average number of candidates for honours in classics,' the Royal Commission on Oxford University stated in 1852, 'is not less than ninety out of nearly five hundred for a degree. Of these ninety, about ten obtain a first. The honour, then, is no mean distinction.'[104] An ordinary degree carried little weight. 'The minimum of knowledge required is so scanty,' the same report stated, 'as to leave all but the dullest and most ignorant unoccupied for the greater part of their academical course and therefore exposed to all the temptations of idleness.'[105] Following the publication of this report, the university introduced more rigorous requirements for the ordinary degree. Despite this improvement, the pass degree did not lose its unfortunate reputation. 'So low is the standard,' Robert Lowe told the House of Commons in 1877, 'that a young man going to Oxford might live there all his time in idleness, and yet be able to satisfy the standard required for a degree.'[106]

Since so few undergraduates read for honours in the 1840s and 1850s it would be unrealistic to criticize the Department for taking on men with pass degrees. Such men may well have been the 'under-achievers' of an era in which there was little incentive to read for honours. There is no doubt that the Department preferred to employ men of high ability. The comparative absence of men with poor honours degrees is particularly striking. Moreover, many of the examiners and inspectors had had distinguished academic careers before joining the Department.

At least ten of the examiners had at some time been Fellows of Oxford or Cambridge colleges. Three had held fellowships at Oriel or Balliol, the only Oxford colleges where all the fellowships were open before the mid–1850s.[107] Five were held at Cambridge. 'The perfect integrity and impartiality' with which

* I have not been able to trace the academic background of W. S. Coward, an inspector of Roman Catholic schools.

Cambridge fellowships were usually awarded had been commended by the Royal Commission on that university. 'A student however friendless and unknown,' the report stated, 'was as sure of obtaining his fellowship as another of better family or wealthier connexions.'[108] The only fellowship held by an examiner that was not indisputably an award for academic distinction was held by Randolph who had obtained a third. Four of the examiners were prizemen. Two examiners, W. J. Courthope* and F. T. Palgrave became professors of poetry, a distinction shared by H.M.I. Mathew Arnold.

The inspectors were proportionately slightly less successful in obtaining academic distinctions. Of the thirty-six Anglican inspectors serving in 1860, nine had been Fellows at Cambridge and a further three at Oxford. Two of the Oxford fellowships, those given to the Reverend W. P. Warburton and the Reverend F. Meyrick,† had clearly been awarded for academic distinction. Two British inspectors, J. Bowstead, the second wrangler of his year, and C. H. Alderson‡ became Fellows. Five Anglican and one inspector of British schools were prizemen. Despite their high proportion of firsts and seconds the recruits of the year 1860–71 produced only one prizeman. This was W. Baily, a British inspector, of St John's College, Cambridge.

From the above discussion, it can be seen that the Department was quick to take advantage of the expansion of the honours schools at the older universities. Long before 1870, it was recruiting men as inspectors and examiners who were virtually indistinguishable from those who later entered other departments through the medium of an open competitive examination. This conclusion is true not only of its senior staff but, as has already been shown, of its clerks as well.

* W. J. Courthope, the son of a clergyman, was educated at New College, Oxford (English verse prize, 1864; first class Lit. Hum., 1865; English essay prize, 1868) was examiner (1869–87) civil service commissioner and first civil service commissioner (1887–1907) and Professor of Poetry (1895–1905).
† F. Meyrick, the son of a clergyman, was educated at Eton and Trinity College, Oxford (second class Lit. Hum., 1847; Fellow, 1847; Dean, 1853). He was H.M.I. (1859–69).
‡ C. H. Alderson, the second son of Sir E. H. Alderson, Baron of the Exchequer, was educated at Eton and Trinity College, Oxford (second class Lit. Hum., 1853), was Fellow of All Souls' College (1857), H.M.I. (1859–85), second Charity Commissioner (1885–1900) and chief Charity Commissioner (1900–1903).

Inspectors and examiners alike came from substantial middle-class homes. Although the fathers of six were titled, none was the direct descendant of the hereditary landed aristocracy.* With the exception of H.M.I. W. Jack,† all the senior officials of this new and rapidly expanding government department were the sons of the gentry, the clergy, civil and military officials, and professional men.

Only fathers with substantial means could have sent their sons at this time to Oxford or Cambridge. Cambridge, the first of the two to adapt itself to the needs of a changing society, was slightly cheaper. A degree there cost between £300 and £400, plus the cost of private tuition.[109] At Oxford the father who did not have to spend more than £600 while his son was up, and pay off his debts afterwards, was a lucky man.[110] Yet Thomas Arnold, the headmaster of Rugby School, managed to send all three of his sons to Oxford. Birley, Kennedy, Moncrieff and Warburton were fourth sons, T. W. Sharpe‡ a fifth son, and Joyce a sixth son. Perhaps some of them emulated Temple who 'lived at Balliol with stern and brave frugality, maintained himself by scholarships, denied himself a fire in the winter, kept close and careful accounts'. During his first year he spent £88 17s. 8¼d. and in his second year £88 11s. 3½d.[111]

Even when a father had paid off his son's debts his worries were by no means over. The son had to be found employment offering a salary that was high enough to justify the expense of his education. An expanding civil service, that was beginning to recruit men more for their proven intellectual ability than because of their aristocratic connexions, seemed an obvious choice. The demand for posts in the public service was high.

* Alderson was the son of a Baron of the Exchequer, Moncrieff the son of a Lord of Session and Justiciary of Scotland, Bowyer the heir to a baronetcy which he held for three months before his death in 1883, Chester, Palgrave, and Sir F. Sandford were the sons of knights.

† W. Jack, the son of a carpenter of Irvine, was educated at Glasgow University (1848–53) and Peterhouse, Cambridge (fourth wrangler; Smith's prizeman, 1859; Fellow, 1860). He was H.M.I. (1860–66), Professor of Natural Philosophy, Manchester (1866–70), editor of the *Glasgow Herald* (1870–6) and Professor of Mathematics, Glasgow (1879–1909).

‡ T. W. Sharpe, the fifth son of a Vicar of Doncaster, was educated at Rossall and Trinity College, Cambridge (twelfth wrangler, 1852). He was Fellow of Christ's College (1852–8), H.M.I. (1859–97), and principal of Queen's College, London (1898–1903).

When Sir Robert Peel became Prime Minister, in 1841, he is said to have spent much of his time replying to applicants. So great were the demands made on him that he protested: 'Such is the number of applications addressed to me for employment that I should only be deluding applicants for office by holding out expectations which it will never be in my power to realize.'[112] The experience of the Education Department was similar. 'The offices [of H.M.I.] are extremely sought after,' Earl Granville stated in 1864, '...I have myself appointed twenty-eight... with the exception of one clergyman whose treatment of education matters I have had an opportunity of observing, I do not think I knew of one of the persons I appointed, even by sight, at the time of their receiving their appointment from me. Even now I have no idea what the political opinions of these gentlemen may be.'[113]

The high academic standing of many of the recruits shows that the Department was, indeed, able to recruit its senior staff in a highly competitive labour market. It was thus able to choose with discretion and exclude the grosser forms of political pressure. This does not necessarily mean that educational facilities for the sons of the middle classes were expanding more rapidly than were the opportunities for their subsequent employment.[114] Nobody would seriously argue, for instance, that because 2,500 graduates applied for sixty-four vacancies with the firm of Unilever, in 1968, we are faced with the problem of graduate unemployment.[115] It merely shows that many young men find the prospect of working for an international concern an attractive one. Similarly, the Education Department had much to offer. An examinership or an inspectorship based on London gave Matthew Arnold, A. J. Butler,* Courthope, Clough, Palgrave, and Severn time to pursue their literary, scholarly and artistic interests.

Moreover, it has to be remembered that, before 1877, Fellows of Oxford and Cambridge colleges were required to remain celi-

* A. J. Butler, the son of a Dean of Lincoln, was educated at Bradfield, Eton, Trinity College, Cambridge (eighth classic, 1867; Fellow, 1869), was examiner (1870–87) and then joined the publishing firm of Rivington & Cassell. He was Professor of Italian, University College, London (1898–1910). While at the E.O. he edited and translated Dante's *Purgatory* (1880), *Paradise* (1885); then *Hell* (1892); he was editor of *Calendars of Foreign State Papers* (1899–1910), and contributed to the *Cambridge Modern History*.

bate. In the past the eager bachelor had had to await a vacancy in a living to which his university held the right of presentation. In the more secular atmosphere of the mid-nineteenth century, an inspectorship or an examinership provided another means by which he might make an honest woman of his *inamorata*.

Similarly a number of curates found that an inspectorship offered a substantial increase in salary. W. Birley's curacy had been worth £120 plus a house; N. Gream* had earned £122 a year as a curate in South Devon; G. R. Moncrieff had come from a living worth £277. Other ex-curates include J. J. Blandford and R. L. Koe.† Similarly many returned to the Church for solace in their old age. B. M. Cowie eventually obtained a deanery at Exeter worth £2,000 a year. R. Temple‡ augmented his pension for thirty-five years' service with the living of Ewhurst, near Guildford, worth £600 a year. E. D. Tinling, who had inspected schools for forty years, secured the canonry of Gloucester and an additional £600 a year. W. P. Warburton supplemented his pension with the yearly £910 he drew as Canon of Winchester.[116]

Young men just down from Oxford or Cambridge, impecunious curates and Fellows wanting to marry provided the Department with a wide choice of suitable candidates. Their exact number cannot be determined. All that one can say is that by the mid-1880s there was a list of 200 to 300 names that was handed down from one Lord President to another.[117]

Although personal contacts undoubtedly helped certain candidates, contacts alone were seldom enough. The Education Department did not provide jobs for the boys but merely for the right sort of boys. Unfortunately the matter cannot be discussed exhaustively. Only one personal file, that of Matthew Arnold, has survived. Sufficient examples, however, can be cited to give us an adequate picture of how the patronage system worked before 1870.

* N. Gream, the son of a clergyman, was educated at Magdalene College, Cambridge (B.A., 1843), held various curacies and was H.M.I. (1859–78).
† R. L. Koe, the son of a Q.C., was educated at Rugby School and Christ's College, Cambridge (B.A., 1843), was a curate at Yeading, near Uxbridge, Middlesex and H.M.I. (1853–93).
‡ R. Temple, the son of a barrister, was educated at Trinity College, Cambridge (B.A., 1850), held clerical posts (1853–7), was H.M.I. (1857–92), and was rector of Ewhurst, Guildford (1892–7).

Walter Severn, who seems to have developed his artistic interests at the expense of his official duties, owed his appointment to the friendship that existed between Lord Lansdowne and his parents. So close was this connexion that Joseph Severn, the father, had been able to borrow £200 from the Lord President to tide him over hard times. Furthermore the young Severn and Lord Lansdowne were old boys of the same school, Westminster. Because of this bond, the Lord President indulgently overlooked the two black eyes that the applicant had acquired in a fight just before his interview.[118]

Similarly the Marquis of Salisbury knew two of his nominees personally. The Reverend C. J. Robinson, whom Salisbury made an H.M.I. in 1859, was a curate in the Lord President's home parish of Hatfield. The Reverend F. Meyrick, who also became an H.M.I. in 1859, was a friend of the Lord President's son.[119] There is, however, no reason to doubt the ability of either man as an inspector. Two better documented cases of influence can be quoted. Sir George Kekewich became an H.M.I. after his father, the M.P. for South Devon, had asked Sir Stafford Northcote, then Chancellor of the Exchequer, for a post for his son.[120] Lastly, E. M. Sneyd-Kynnersley owed his appointment to a bit of horse-trading. His father knew two of the ministry of the day. One of them was in the Cabinet – Gladstone's first administration, 1868–74. 'In a few days,' Sneyd-Kynnersley later wrote, 'a letter from the Lord President to the friendly cabinet minister was forwarded to my father; it ran thus:

'Dear...
I have had great pleasure in putting your friend Mr Kynnersley's name on my list.
                        Yours sincerely,
                                    "Carabas".'

And on a folded corner was a note: "Thanks for appointing X.Y." It was evident,' Sneyd-Kynnersley commented, 'that X.Y. and I had been bartered.'[121]

In a number of cases it is difficult to state with any confidence exactly how a particular appointment was made. Members of the executive, legislature, and administration came, as Kekewich's comment on the perils of taking French leave reminds us, from a small circle. Consequently candidates often had a large number of strings they could pull. E. Carleton Tufnell, who had taken a first at Balliol, had the additional advantage in his father who had made three useful marriages. His fathers-in-law were a former Governor of Ceylon and two earls.[122] Such a combination of parental social discrimination and filial academic success must have made the son's appointment as an assistant Poor Law Commissioner a relatively simple matter.

Similarly many officials shared a common educational background. Nine inspectors of schools* and one examiner passed through Thomas Arnold's hands while he was the headmaster of Rugby. Moreover, twenty-one men who had been members of Balliol, 'the smallest and most distinguished' college at Oxford, had joined the Department by 1870.[123] The most important of these was Lingen who was a fellow of Balliol from 1841 to 1846 or 1847. His contemporaries included some of those who were well known for their enthusiasm to reform the university. Here the influence of Thomas Arnold who, for the last year of his life, managed to combine the tenure of the Regius Chair in Modern History with his headmastership of Rugby, was an important factor. He was the 'father figure' to a large group of Oxford liberals who were full of a sense of mission to 'leaven the whole lump' at Oxford. The Arnold faction was a part of a larger whole that included Jowett, another fellow of Balliol and a friend of the liberally minded Lingen and Temple, and H. B. Barry.†[124]

Because the officials of the Department came from a small, closely knit society it would be unwise to attribute the appointment of any of the Oxford men solely to Lingen's influence. Naturally any Lord President, anxious to run his department efficiently, would have given considerable weight to what Lingen knew about his friends at Oxford. Frederick Temple, for example, certainly owed his appointment to Lingen's influence.[125] On the other hand Arthur Hugh Clough, another Oxford man, had a long and anxious wait before he became an examiner. During a two-and-a-half-year struggle to find employment he enlisted the help of his former pupil, Matthew Arnold. By this

* This includes Thomas Arnold, the second son, who inspected Tasmanian schools.
† H. B. Barry, the son of a clergyman, was educated at Queen's College, Oxford (second Lit. Hum., 1842; English prize, 1843; Ellerton prize, 1845) and was H.M.I. (1855-84) and Chief H.M.I. (1884-96).

time he was clearly a desperate man. As a tutor he had accurately but unflatteringly prophesied that Arnold would obtain a second. 'This is above his deserts certainly but I do not think he can drop below it and one would not be surprised if he rose above it in spite of all his ignorance.'[126] As well as giving Clough a testimonial Arnold advised his old tutor to try the Education Office: 'An inspectorship would be better suited to you than an examinership, besides the pay being better. Hard work, low salary, stationariness and London to be stationary in under such circumstances, do not please me.' In the end it was the intercession of Lady Ashburton, a successful society hostess, that proved decisive. In 1853, after unsuccessfully trying his luck in the U.S.A., Clough at last found employment in the Education Office.[127]

Francis Palgrave, another Balliol man, had a number of influential contacts and did not necessarily owe his appointment primarily to Lingen's influence. While he was still an undergraduate he became a private secretary to Gladstone, who was a friend of his father. He then entered the Education Department as an examiner and for a while was the vice-president of Kneller Hall, a training school for workhouse schoolmasters. He had a wide circle of friends. 'On March 31, 1849,' an entry in his diary runs, 'in the evening to Mr Brookfield's. Found there Lingen, A. Tennyson; afterwards Thackeray and H. Hallam [Brookfield's brother-in-law] came.' Other friends included Frederick Temple, who was then the principal of Kneller Hall, Carlyle, Arthur Stanley, Jowett, Courthope, W. E. H. Lecky, and Lord Frederick Cavendish with whom Palgrave later served as private secretary to Lord Granville.[128] The Reverend W. H. Brookfield, whose wife was a hostess of some renown, was a fashionable preacher. He had held curacies at St James's, Piccadilly and St Luke's, Berwick Street before entering the Education Office. During his inspectorship he was the morning preacher at the Berkeley Chapel, Mayfair.[129]

Another point at which these social groups overlapped was the Athenaeum Club. Amongst its members were H.M.I.s Alderson, Matthew Arnold, T. B. Browne,* Fearon, Norris, Temple and

* T. B. Browne, son of Pryce Jones, changed his name to Browne. He was educated at Harrow, and Brasenose College, Oxford and was H.M.I. (1847–74) for Poor Law and industrial schools.

Warburton. Here they had a chance of meeting two of the examiners, G. Miller* and Palgrave, and assistant secretaries Chester and Cumin. A number of political figures that were connected with the Department were members as well. These included W. E. Forster, Earl Granville, the Marquis of Salisbury, Viscount Sandon and Earl Spencer.†[130]

Some of the inspectors had the added qualification of possessing useful professional experience. Cook, for example, had spent two years as secretary and inspector to the London Diocesan Board of Education.[131] Later on, his successor at the London Diocesan Board, J. D. Glennie,‡ also became an inspector for the Department.[132] Another inspector, the Reverend W. J. Kennedy, had been secretary to the National Society before joining the Department. Over some of these appointments the Church probably obtained a better bargain than did the state. Kennedy, for instance, was allowed to leave at such short notice that the National Society must have been inconvenienced. On 9 November 1848, 'Mr Kennedy expressed a wish [to the Society's committee] to be relieved of his present duties at as early a period as possible on account of the nature of the office to which he expected to be appointed... Mr Kennedy stated that he should probably be desirous to give up all his duties in the National Society's office in the course of a fortnight.' The Society obligingly found a substitute.[133] Another key figure who became an inspector was Joshua Fitch,¶ the principal of the Borough Road training college. He was offered a post after Earl Granville had visited the college in 1863 where he had been

* G. Miller, the fourth son of Sir T. Miller, Bart., was educated at Harrow and Exeter College, Oxford (First class Lit. Hum., 1855) was examiner (1865–84), Assistant Secretary (1884–97) C.B., 1897.
† W. E. Forster, Matthew Arnold's brother-in-law, was Vice-President, (1868–74), Viscount Sandon, Vice-President (1874–8) and Earl Spencer, Lord President (1880–2 and 1886).
‡ J. D. Glennie, the son of a secretary of the S.P.C.K., was educated at King's School, Canterbury and Christ's College, Cambridge (Tancred scholar, 1846; B.A., 1848). He held various curacies, was diocesan inspector, London (1853–7) H.M.I. (1857–60) and Vicar of Croxton (1869–1903).
¶ Joshua Fitch (B.A., London, 1850) was lecturer and then principal of Borough Road training college H.M.I. (1863–5), Assistant Commissioner to the Taunton Commission (1865–7) Assistant Commissioner of elementary schools in northern towns (1869), Assistant Commissioner of endowed schools (1870–77), Chief H.M.I. (1883–5) and Inspector of Female Training Colleges (1885–94). He was knighted in 1896.

'much impressed by the teaching power of the principal and the inspiring influence which he exercised over his students'.[134]

It is common to criticize the inspectorate of the pre-1870 era on the grounds that the officials had had little or no experience of teaching. To some extent such criticism is irrelevant for it implies that the duties of an H.M.I. in the 1840s are comparable to those of his successors a century later. Yet the main function of the Church schools was seen as that of rearing the young in the principles of the Anglican faith. Since much of their work was concerned with inspecting religious education, 'The inspectors became, in fact, itinerant curates, paid by the state, and were used to consolidate and strengthen the already powerful diocesan and parochial organization of the church'.[135] As all Anglican inspectors were in Holy orders, they were all admirably suited to their duties in what many saw as the secular arm of the Anglican Church. Some even had the added advantage of having spent a short period as a curate during which they had undoubtedly supervised the Sunday school. Finally, it has to be remembered that in 1855 the Macaulay Report had 'extolled the merits of young men from Oxford and Cambridge who had read nothing but subjects unrelated to their future careers'.[136] Hence the appointment of a man who had read Greats at Oxford as an inspector of elementary schools, however incongruous such an action may appear a century later, was in accordance with the most enlightened administrative practice of the day.

In contrast, previous teaching experience was regarded as an essential qualification for the would-be inspector's assistant.* He had to possess a teacher's certificate and also pass an examination conducted by the Civil Service Commissioners. 'The examination,' the minute of 19 May 1863 stated, 'will be based on Standard VI and to that extent will be extremely rigorous. No candidate will pass who cannot read well, as regards pronunciation, stops, and tone; who cannot write and tabulate neatly, legibly and quickly; who cannot work sums, with neat and legible figures, quickly, accurately, and by good methods. The examination will be conducted by the Civil Service Commissioners; there will be no appeal from it.'[137]

We have seen, as far as possible, how one government depart-

* The duties of members of this grade are described on p. 44.

ment recruited its staff in the days of the 'unreformed civil service'. There is little reason for believing that patronage was exercised in a way that harmed the interests of the Department. Departmental procedure seems to have been slow rather than inefficient. Contemporaries complained of delays in answering letters and paying grants. There is an absence of complaints of straightforward clerical errors. Eventually the right person was sent the right sum of money. Similarly the administration of the examinations for the Queen's scholarships seems to have been conducted without any major errors.

Individual civil servants have left evidence of their industry and ability. At least twenty reports for some of the major commissions of inquiry held in the middle of the nineteenth century were written by members of the Department. A number had distinguished careers either on transfer to other departments of state or in new pastures such as the academic and publishing fields. Collectively they have provided one testimony to their efficiency: the successful implementation of the Education Act, 1870. This was one of the great administrative triumphs of a civil service that had been recruited before the introduction of open competitive examinations.

7   The Revised Code Revised

SIR JOHN PAKINGTON: Can not you trust your inspectors?
ROBERT LOWE: Certainly not.[1]   HANSARD

I must admit that my reports upon many schools were rather approximations
to accuracy than accuracy itself.

H.M.I. THE REVEREND H. W. BELLAIRS.[2]

The [simultaneous] method errs when the lesson is returned by or
supposed to be returned by the whole class in one collective voice. This
peccant part of the simultaneous method quite disappears under the
necessary preparations for the individual examination.

H.M.I. J. GORDON*[3]

By 1860 the Education Department had become one of the
largest civil establishments of the state. A staff of 127, which
included the largest inspectorate yet in existence, controlled an
annual expenditure of nearly a million pounds. The vote for
Education, Science and Art, in the financial year 1860–61, came
to £1,305,912. This was nearly a fifth of the total amount of
£7,492,329 needed for all the civil estimates. The Department's
main sub-head, 'public education in Great Britain', £798,167,
was the largest civil one. A second item, £94,951, the vote for
the Science and Art Department, put a total of £893,118 at the
Lord President's disposal. This was nearly twice as much as the
£484,012 that was spent on maintaining the country's colonial,
consular and other services. Expenditure on schools had also far
outstripped the earlier much-quoted cost of repairing the Royal
stables at Windsor. Public works and buildings took £621,990 in
1860–61. On the other hand the state spent £2,565,301 dispens-
ing law and justice to those whom the schoolmaster had been
unable to rear 'in obedience to the laws'. The subsequent so-
journ of his wayward pupils in 'prisons and convict establish-

---

* J. Gordon was H.M.I. of schools connected with the Established Church
in Scotland. He had earlier been secretary to the Committee of the General
Assembly of the Church of Scotland.

ments' required £408,029, the second largest sub-head in the civil estimates.[4] This was less than half the cost of the preventive measures being taken with the next generation in England and Wales. What many saw as another closely related service, the relief of the poor, required £5,454,964 for England and Wales in the year ending Lady Day 1860.[5] Since the central government contributed only £222,969, the bulk of this expenditure was met out of local rates.[6] At the parochial and union level any tendency to extravagance was inhibited by a system of election that was heavily weighted in favour of the propertied classes.

In contrast, critics of the Education Department, who had seen the total education vote rise at an annual rate of £100,000 for a decade, wondered if there were any checks at all upon its extravagance. Up to the mid-1850s the Department had been able to prosper largely through salutary neglect. Since there were few Members of the House of Commons who had any real interest in education the Department, lacking adequate ministerial representation, had thrived in its constitutional obscurity. The appointment of a Vice-President in 1856, coupled with a search for a means of reducing public expenditure after the Crimean War which had ended the same year, brought the Department's activities into the limelight.

Because of their growing concern over the size of the estimates, M.P.s began to scrutinize one of the largest items, Class IV (Education, Science, and Art), much more closely. Amendments to reduce the education vote were regularly moved from 1854 onwards. The discussion that took place in 1859 was particularly revealing. At the end of the debate many members must have wondered if they could put any reliance at all on the methods by which they thought they controlled expenditure on education. During the course of the proceedings, Sir Stafford Northcote, the Member for Stamford, pointed out that formerly the Treasury had been represented in the Committee of the Privy Council on Education by the Chancellor of the Exchequer. With the appointment of the Vice-President the Treasury, he alleged, had ceased to exercise any real control over the departmental minutes. The minutes which sanctioned the expenditure of public money were now passed, he maintained, solely by the President and Vice-President.[7]

As Northcote had been Financial Secretary to the Treasury in

1859, his charges could not be lightly ignored. In reply the Chancellor of the Exchequer, W. E. Gladstone, made a speech that, by present-day standards, was remarkable both for its candour and its failure to foster ministerial duty. Such a situation, he said, was one 'that well deserved the attention of the government, because it was not regular; it was not conformable either to precedent or to our principles of administration that important documents, forming, as one might say, standing contracts with parties all over the country, should take effect and raise expectations which could not be disappointed, when they had never in any way been submitted to the consideration or the approval of the minister of finance'.[8] Robert Lowe then argued that since the minutes were standing contracts they had to be fulfilled. The only effect of a reduction in the estimates, he told the House, would be a deficit that would have to be met the following year.[9] Although the House then voted supply, the debate had disturbed many members. It had revealed what the Hon. J. W. Henley, the Member for Oxfordshire, had described as 'an awkward state of affairs, for whereas the Chancellor of the Exchequer had just told them that he had no control over expenditure, the Vice-President now said the House of Commons had no control'.[10]

In the July of the following year, a select committee was appointed to 'inquire into the Expenditure for the Miscellaneous Services, and to report to The House whether any Reduction can, in their opinion, be effected in that branch of the Public Expenditure'.[11]

The evidence the committee heard seemed not only to confirm the findings of the 1859 debate, but also to suggest that the education vote provided ample opportunity for economy. Between 1849 and 1859, the civil estimates had risen by £2,500,000. The education vote for the United Kingdom accounted for over a third, £931,000, of this increase.[12] Most of this sum, £711,000, was being devoted to the education of the children of Great Britain. S. Laing, the Financial Secretary to the Treasury, who had provided these figures, compared the cost of English and Irish public education. In England the *per capita* cost was £1, in Ireland it was only 10s. Similarly English schoolmasters cost more to train than did their Irish counterparts. For every pound spent on aiding the education of children, two were spent on the training of the schoolmaster. For Ireland, the corresponding figure was only two to three shillings. In addition, while grants to English pupil-teachers were running at £294,000 a year, Irish pupil-teachers cost only £8,500 a year.[13] Laing then went on to endorse the views put forward by Gladstone and Lowe during the previous year's supply debate. The Treasury, he contended, had no control over the education vote nor of calculating what would be the expenditure in a given year. 'Certain minutes...are conditions of the grant; and they constitute a pledge to the public that while those minutes exist, all who like to avail themselves of them may get the money.' He believed, he stated in reply to a further question, that the Department of Education could pass a minute without reference to the Treasury. Not surprisingly he recommended that all minutes should in future be referred to his department.[14] Apparently his advice was not followed. Thirteen years later, a witness told the Select Committee on Civil Services Expenditure that he could not recollect a single occasion on which the Treasury had been consulted on the rate at which the school grant should be paid.[15]

The fears that members of the House of Commons and Treasury officials had expressed can be largely discounted. The Department was always aware of its delicate relationship with Parliament. Hence it is unlikely that the Department ever seriously considered expanding its activities during a period of post-war financial retrenchment. After the extension of the capitation grant to the urban areas in 1856,[16] only minor changes were made to the terms of the grants. In 1858 the building grant was extended to include the provision of rooms for the teaching of science and art. The last mentioned change was in accord with the greater emphasis that was given to the teaching of these subjects after the Great Exhibition of 1851. In 1853, the old Department of Practical Art, which it will be remembered was set up to supervise the Normal Schools of Design, marked the occasion of its acceptance of new functions by changing its name to the Department of Science and Art. By the time of its transfer from the President of the Board of Trade to the Lord President of the Council, its tasks included the encouragement of the teaching of science and art in elementary schools.[17] Another concession made in 1858 allowed small parishes to employ certificated mistresses in mixed schools. Finally, children under the age of sixteen were permitted to start as pupil-teachers in the fourth year of their training.[18]

A year later the first cuts were made.* The era of financial stringency had begun. To simplify and improve the administrative process, the existing minutes, dating from 1839 onwards, were published as a code in 1860. This innovation was accompanied by an instruction from Lingen telling his staff to enforce the terms of the code strictly. 'Now that there is a code,' he wrote on 12 June 1860, 'every examiner minuting should hold himself bound absolutely by the letter of the code, whenever the subject falls under any express provision. Under no circumstances whatever (this is absolutely without exception),' he continued, 'should the letter of the code be dispensed with, except after reference to one of the Assistant Secretaries, who will speak to the Secretary, and the other assistant secretary together, if he sees sufficient reason for not enforcing the strict and literal rule. This direction should override all existing precedents whatever which vary the letter of the code.'[19] A month earlier, he had reminded the staff that the capitation grant ought not to be paid, and still less continued, when the inspector reported that there was not a sufficient staff of teachers.[20] As a result of these measures, the rise in the education vote began to be contained. Thus when Lowe introduced the estimates in 1861 he was able to claim: 'Within the three years during which I have moved these estimates the number of children has increased by 141,000 while the estimate has only increased by £42,000.' This slow growth, he argued, compared favourably with an annual rise of £100,000 for the three years previous to his holding office.[21]

Other forebodings were equally groundless. Although the Treasury witnesses had stated that their department was never consulted about the draft minutes, the Chancellor of the Exchequer still attended occasional meetings of the Committee of the Privy Council on Education.† Similarly the minutes setting out the terms of employment of the schoolmasters and pupil-teachers were not binding contracts. Lowe had used this term to persuade a somewhat reluctant House of Commons to vote supply. In his first draft of the Revised Code, published two

* See p. 103.
† See p. 151.

years later, he proposed to abolish them outright. Legally, though not morally, he was perfectly entitled to do this, for at this time no contract could have been enforced against the Crown.* The concessions he later made to safeguard the position of the existing pupil-teachers and their instructors were not made out of a regard for constitutional propriety. They were granted to mollify an irate House of Commons and to secure the acceptance of the Revised Code.

The criticisms that were made in committee and on the floor of the House of Commons failed to reach the heart of the problem. The real difficulty was that the Department was the prisoner of the voluntary system. It depended mainly on the goodwill of two social groups whose prejudices made them distrustful of any form of state control. They were the landowners of the shires, who by temperament and tradition opposed the encroachment of the Benthamite state, and the clergy. The latter were protected by that highly successful pressure group, the Established Church. Although the landowners were usually ready to contribute to the cost of building a school, their interest soon waned. The bulk of the day-to-day work fell on the local incumbent. In addition, the clergy frequently had to make good any deficit in the school funds out of their own pockets. An analysis made by the Rev. J. Fraser, an assistant commissioner to the Newcastle Commissioners, suggests that, in proportion to their income, they contributed far more generously than did any other group in society. He found that in 168 parishes in South West England 169 clergy gave £1,782 to their schools, an average of £10 10s. 0d. each. This was nearly twice the average contribution (£5 6s. 0d.) of 399 landowners, eleven times that of 217 farmers (18s. 6d. each) and six times that of 102 householders (£1 15s. 6d.). Furthermore, the total contribution of the landowning class—at least 200 of whom had given nothing—was less than the product of a one-third per cent levy on their landed income.[22]

In these circumstances it is hardly likely that any clerical inspector would have refused a school the annual grant. Apart from other consequences, such an action would have put a still greater financial burden on one of his fellow clergy. Moreover, under the terms of the Concordat of 1840, the state shared

* This remained the situation until the passing of the Crown Proceedings Act, 1947.

control over its inspectorate with the Established Church. Yet the expenditure of public money was sanctioned in accordance with the recommendations in the reports made by these officials. The result was that the minutes committed the Department to an expenditure whose rate of growth it was almost powerless to control. The initiative in making demands on the Exchequer came from the school managers. Once a school had started to obtain an annual grant, it seldom lost it.

Only a year after becoming Vice-President, Robert Lowe told the House of Commons that he could not trust the inspectorate to perform their duties efficiently. During a debate on 14 August 1860, he rejected a proposal put forward by Sir John Pakington to allow ragged schools an increased subsidy, on the report of an inspector, on the grounds that 'There would be a run upon the government for these grants'. In answer to Pakington's interruption, 'Can not you trust your inspectors?' Lowe replied, 'Certainly not.' 'Without wishing to cast any reflection upon the inspectors, who were men of great intelligence and ability,' he continued, 'the experience of the Department was that they could not afford to spend the enormous sums of money voted by Parliament merely on the reports of these gentlemen... They were satisfied,' he added, 'that, partly from good nature on the part of the inspectors, and partly from other causes, such a system would not be trustworthy and that no one having a proper regard to economy could safely administer the grant on such a principle.'[23] A year later, C. B. Adderley, Lowe's predecessor as Vice-President, told the House of Commons that he shared the same opinion. He had never known an instance, he stated, in which an inspector had reported that the general character of a school was so bad that it ought not to have received any assistance from the state. Under the denominational system, he added, no other result could have been anticipated. This, he explained, was because it would have been unreasonable to have expected an inspector to have given a general account of schools of his own denomination which would have contrasted unfavourably with the state of schools managed probably no better by some other denomination.[24]

The existence of sectarian rivalry, however, provides only part of the explanation. The conditions under which the annual grants were offered had been deliberately designed to preserve the autonomy of the school managers. At times this freedom was abused. Less scrupulous managers mistook liberty for licence and indulged in sharp practices. Between one annual visit and another, the inspector had to rely on the good faith of the local manager. When he made his visit he could only use as evidence what he actually saw. Lingen told his staff to 'be careful whenever the inspector reports on *moral* qualities [of the pupil-teachers] to confine the letter to what *he observed at his visit** and to refer these observations to the managers for future notice. The managers', he continued, 'are the recognized judges of character, and, even if they were not so, H.M.I. has not time to do more than record phenoma [*sic*], which may, or may not, be in accordance with the general character of the person under examination.'[25]

Unfortunately the recognized judges, in their eagerness to obtain the grants, were not always reliable ones. In one such case Lingen was directed 'to express the pain and surprise with which their Lordships had learnt of the contradictory testimonials' given about a schoolmaster who had left the correspondent's school. Although the manager had testified that he was satisfied with the teacher so that his school could obtain the annual grant, he had then proceeded to give his employee a bad reference for another post. On this occasion, the errant cleric was warned that 'since the moral side of public education rested upon the strictness and fidelity with which testimonials were given by the school managers their Lordships, whose confidence was much shaken, would find it impossible to continue the grants to a school in respect of which the same weak indulgence were repeated.'[26]

Similarly, the Department could do little once a manager had certified that he was satisfied with the moral qualities and family background of a particular pupil-teacher. Cook, for instance, knew that he could not openly question another clergyman's trustworthiness. 'The religious principles and character of the candidates,' he reported, 'are of course the main considerations which guide the managers in making the selection. [If the inspector disagrees]...it does not affect the candidate's success if the [secular] examination is successful and the school

* Lingen's underlining.

managers press the appointment... It is not to be supposed,' he added with gentle irony, 'that any clergyman would sign the certificate if he had not very clear and safe grounds for his opinion.'[27] The Reverend F. Watkins was much more blunt. He stated that school managers, on more than one instance, had signed the necessary certificates without making adequate inquiries.[28] Another clerical inspector, the Reverend W. J. Kennedy, was equally disillusioned when he wrote: 'The chief matter of regret is, that in several cases the apprentices were not such as seemed likely to become valuable schoolmasters and mistresses... For the future, however, I trust that only those boys and girls will be proposed to the Inspectors, and, to the Committee of Council, as candidates for apprenticeship, whose dispositions are thoroughly known and approved by the local school committee.'[29]

School managers showed an equal disregard for the Department's regulation that 'A constitutional infirmity such as scrofula, fits, asthma, deafness, great imperfections of the sight or voice...are to be regarded as positive disqualifications'.[30] The main difficulty arose from the fact that teaching was believed to be an easy option. Hence 'the child too delicate for manual work', Watkins warned, 'or too slow for the bustling intercourse of the trading world, will be offered as a pupil-teacher'.[31] Although he had rejected 'the maimed and the lame, and the nearly blind' in 1853, one is left wondering where he and the other inspectors were able to draw the line. On one such occasion, in 1848, the inspector had described a candidate for apprenticeship as 'very small, sickly-looking, and deficient in health'. The school manager, however, maintained that his health was good. The Department resolved this particular dilemma by asking for a medical certificate.[32] At this stage in the emergence of the practice of medicine as a profession, it is unlikely that the manager had any great difficulty in meeting the Department's request. From 1860 onwards, a tougher line was taken with the managers and a certificate was demanded of new pupil-teachers as a matter of course.[33]

The system was open to other abuses. Both school managers and masters wanted as many pupil-teachers as possible. School managers obtained assistants towards whose salaries they did not have to contribute a penny. The more apprentices the master had to teach, but in practice frequently failed to teach,* the greater his gratuity. Since the number of apprentices a school could have depended on the average number of children in attendance, school registers were falsified on a widespread scale. So flagrant was this practice that the figures of average attendance in Great Britain, before the introduction of the capitation grant, exceed the number of children actually present at the yearly inspection. Yet one would have expected the opposite to have been the case. School managers, anxious to 'put on a good show', must have gone all out to secure a bumper attendance on the day the inspector made his long-heralded appearance. The capitation grant brought the compiler of the register a further problem. He could not make his average attendance exceed the number for whom he claimed the new grant. Schools were open for 220 days a year, but the capitation grant was claimed for those pupils who had attended for 176 days—in certain circumstances children over the age of ten qualified after eighty-eight days—and who were present when the inspector came. Although the inspectors now began to see more children than were usually in attendance the margin between the two figures, as the following table shows, remained suspiciously narrow.

Table I STATISTICS OF SCHOOL ATTENDANCE IN GREAT BRITAIN

Year ending	Average attendance	Present at inspection
31 October 1850	225,389	214,873
31 October 1852	373,159	354,442
31 July 1854	461,445	473,214
31 July 1856	571,239	645,905
31 July 1858	672,728	725,738
31 July 1860	837,212	900,587

Source: *Minutes and Reports of the Committee, 1850–60, passim.*

It is possible to give some idea of the extent to which the managers of annual grant schools inflated their attendance figures. The Newcastle Commissioners concluded that 63·7 per cent of the children on the registers of schools in England and Wales attended for 100 days or more a year.[34] Since sixty-four of every

---

* See p. 133.

100 children made the necessary 200 half-day attendances to be eligible for examination in the first year of the operation of the Revised Code, this estimate seems to have been remarkably accurate.[35] In England and Wales, 'the annual grants in 1860 promoted the education of about 920,000 children'.[36] This suggests that 584,040 attended a minimum of 100 days a year. Yet if the school managers are to be believed, there were 712,199 regularly attending school in England and Wales in 1860.*

Doubt may be cast on the figures supplied by the school managers in another way. To have achieved the average attendance they claimed, the children the inspector saw would have had to attend for approximately 200 days a year in the late 1850s. Yet the Newcastle Commissioners found that 1,549,312 children in public elementary schools belonging to the religious denominations made the following attendances:

269,581	less than 50 days a year
292,819	50 to 99 days a year
323,806	100 to 149 days a year
378,033	150 to 200 days a year
285,073	201 days or more a year.[37]

By 1860, the administrative disadvantages of the system of annual grants, inaugurated by Kay-Shuttleworth in 1846, had become manifest. The effective employer, the possessor of the power to hire or fire, was the school manager. The sole paymaster of the pupil-teachers and part paymaster of the certificated teacher was the Department. However, except in the case of a gross breach of the regulations, the Department could do little but acquiesce in the manager's choice of staff for the schools. The Department's authority was doubly circumscribed. Firstly, it was limited by the vested interests of the voluntary societies. A second restriction it shared with the school managers. Both were the victims of economic circumstance. The increasing occupational diversification of the economy offered the ambitious adolescent many openings that provided a greater and more immediate return than did apprenticeship as a teacher. As a result, neither party was able to exercise any real discrimination in recruitment.

Moreover, critics of the Department had been deeply suspicious

* This figure includes attendances at Roman Catholic schools in Scotland.

196

of the pupil-teacher training scheme from the day it was launched. 'Parliament has been set aside,' one pamphleteer claimed in 1847, 'the constitution has been violated; the powers of the Privy Council have been enlarged to a fearful extent; an enormous increase of taxation is about to burden the people; government espionage in the shape of school inspectors will soon pervade every part of the country; those who form the national character are to be the creatures and dependants of the Privy Council; bribes, in the form of apprenticeship, gratuities, and pensions, are to place thousands and thousands in a state of civil, political and religious vassalage...'[38] During the debate that took place on the new minutes, Lord John Russell attempted to allay these fears. He assured the House that he did not think that an ex-pupil-teacher, when he was able to vote, would feel himself 'obliged to the Minister of the day...because he [had] received a grant from the Privy Council in consequence of a report of an inspector'.[39]

Familiarity with the scheme did not bring acceptance. In 1861 the Reverend Andrew Reed told a gathering of school managers that the Committee of the Privy Council on Education had needlessly incurred great expense by starting the pupil-teacher system. He congratulated his audience on having kept free of its meshes and having preferred to offer 'a good education —not too good—cheap, yet not too cheap, to the people'.[40] 'The government,' he continued, 'had enough to do, and required taxes enough for the civil list. . . . But when it undertook to regulate prices and markets, entered our homes, and relieved parents of their proper duty by educating the children...it was sure to do those things badly and extravagantly.'[41]

Harry Chester, the Assistant Secretary, expressed similar Whiggish sentiments in his evidence to the Newcastle Commissioners. 'The system of placing the education of the country under the control of a department of the political government appears to me,' he said, 'to be vicious in the extreme; and I do not believe that...the public will allow the [present] system to be extended, so as to cover the whole wants of the country with regard to education... Therefore, in any measure which I might suggest, for giving the Committee of Council greater power, I should propose to make it independent of the government for the time being.'[42]

However overdrawn these fears may seem, it has to be remembered that there were more than 15,000 pupil-teachers and 7,000 certificated teachers. These figures should be compared with the size of the civil service at this time. In 1851, it had been 17,815.[43] With a limited franchise and an open ballot still in existence, the fear persisted that the executive might gain undue political influence by increasing the number of government employees. Furthermore schoolmasters, who were accused of being conceited and ambitious, were regarded as dangerous fellows. Robert Lowe's speech of 13 February 1862 reflects all these prejudices. 'The great danger,' he told the House of Commons, 'is that the grant for education may become, instead of a grant for education, a grant to maintain the so called vested interests of those engaged in education... If Parliament does not set a limit to the evil, such a state of things will arise that the control of the educational system will pass out of the hands of the Privy Council and out of the House of Commons into the hands of the persons working that educational system... When this army of stipendiaries is created, if on the one hand the minister has a power over them, he gains an unconstitutional power; and if, on the other hand, these persons have more influence over him than he has over them, then there exists a dangerous organization for attacks on the Treasury.'[44]

Similarly, the introduction of the book grant had offended the canons of *laissez-faire* philosophy. This grant, doubtless because school managers took such little advantage of it, did not raise as big an outcry as did the pupil-teacher system. One objection, made in 1856 shortly before the Department extended its list, was that 'practically all the publishers of books on the Council list, have a most complete monopoly; quite as much so in fact, as if the government had published all the books on the list'. It was thus 'virtually impossible to get new books on so long as the system prevails of only having books that have already proved popular and acceptable'.[45] The most popular books were those published by the Irish Commissioners of Education.* As early as 1849, Messrs Longman and Messrs Murray had complained that this series was being sold in England below cost price. The Irish Commissioners denied this charge. The books were cheap,

---

* See p. 81.

they stated, not because they were subsidized, but because large contracts were placed that were open to public tender. In addition, a simple binding was specified. It is clear, though, that as some 1,000 books and 250 maps could be bought at nearly half the published price, the Department's policy substantially affected the free working of demand and supply in part of the book trade. Moreover, the Newcastle Commissioners had found that the grant was relatively expensive to administer and that the books 'left much to be desired'.* The administrative control of the third main grant was also unsatisfactory. The capitation grants 'were mere doles from the public purse, given on no principle except that of a certain rate of attendance at the schools'.[46]

Thus for a variety of reasons, the Department came under increasing attack as the 1850s progressed. As a result of this pressure, a Royal Commission was appointed to inquire into the whole field of public elementary education. After an exhaustive examination of the available evidence, the Commissioners paid a generous tribute to Kay-Shuttleworth's success in developing elementary education in England. His minutes had 'given a powerful stimulus to the building of schools, and had created a class of schoolmasters and pupil-teachers of a superior character to any previously known in this country'. Their days of usefulness, however, were numbered. Looking to the future they saw that if an administrative breakdown was to be averted, his system of grants had to be overhauled and simplified. 'On the other hand,' the Commissioners stated, 'we have exposed great and growing defects in its tendency to indefinite expense, in its inability to assist the poorer districts, in the partial inadequacy of its teaching, and in the complicated business which encumbers the central office of the Committee of Council; and these defects have led us to believe that any attempt to extend it unaltered into a national system would fail.'[47]

Strangely enough, although education had frequently been debated at great length during the 1850s, there was no full-scale debate on the Commissioners' findings. On 11 July 1861, the day on which the supply vote for education was taken that year, only Sir J. Pakington and the Rt. Hon. J. W. Henley, the leading

* See p. 80.

supporter and opponent of the Department respectively, spoke about the report. Henley, by drawing attention to one of the main problems posed by its publication, set the tone of the controversy of the next few years. He pointed out that the inspectors had stated that in 6,679 out of 7,500 schools reading was 'taught excellently, well, or fairly', while the figures for writing were even better, 6,782 schools out of 7,186.[48] These optimistic figures, Henley stated, were hard to reconcile with the findings of the Commissioners on the attainments of the children.

The Commission reported: 'Of the 1,549,312 children whose names are on the books of public elementary schools belonging to the religious denominations, only 19·3 per cent were in their twelfth year or upwards, and only that proportion, therefore, can be regarded as educated up to the standard suited to their stations.'[49] Elsewhere they estimated that two-thirds to three-quarters of the children left school without having obtained the modest minimum of education thought suitable to their humble social status. Such a child, they said, left school unable either to spell ordinary words correctly, write a letter to his mother that was legible and intelligible, if he had left home, or make out a common shop bill. Furthermore, he did not know the positions of the main countries of the world. Lastly, he was not sufficiently acquainted with the Scriptures to follow the allusions and arguments of a plain Saxon sermon, and to know his duties towards his maker and his fellow men.[50]

The sole response of the government to the publication of the report was to introduce the Revised Code, a step that sparked one of the major political storms of the century. The manner in which Lowe set about his task suggests that he had some idea of the strength of the opposition he would arouse. He presented the new code on the day that the House arose for the summer recess. The responsible ministers then departed, one to France, one to Switzerland, and another to Italy.[51] The government's attempt to avoid controversy failed. During the next few months the Department received over a thousand petitions and letters of protest.[52] In addition there were three lengthy and angry debates during the course of which the House of Commons twice forced Lowe to revise the Revised Code.

To some extent one feels that M.P.s, school managers, and the voluntary societies were taken unawares in the summer of 1861.

They need not have been. Lowe had clearly hinted at what was in his mind during the 1861 supply debate. 'We think,' he had told the House, 'that at present the capitation grant is not given on sufficiently stringent conditions. We think we ought to be satisfied not only that the children have attended a proper number of times...but that something has been done worthy of the attendance... We propose that an inspector shall examine the children in reading, writing, and arithmetic. If a child pass in the whole, the full capitation grant will be given...while if he fail in reading, writing, and arithmetic, no portion of the grant will be paid.'[53]

Furthermore the idea of payment by results was not new. Lowe did no more than extend a system that had been introduced by Kay-Shuttleworth in 1846.* Just as the Department, in the 1860s and later, largely determined the syllabus to be followed by school children, so had it already laid down the course of instruction for pupil-teachers and students in training colleges. In 1854, Canon Moseley's revision of the training college examination scheme had given the state as much control over the instruction of student teachers as it already possessed over the apprentices in the schools.† Even the extension of the method of payment by results to the children in the schools was not without precedent. Originally, the payment of the capitation grant had depended on the examination of the children. This part of the minute, however, had remained a dead letter. What was new about the Revised Code was that success in the basic subjects now constituted the main, though not the sole, determinant of the size of a school's grant. Similarly, it can be shown that the decision to concentrate on the three basic subjects was not entirely new. 'In all your examinations,' Lingen had told his inspectors in 1857, 'my Lords wish you to lay the greatest possible stress upon the ability of the children to read, write and work sums in such a manner as will really enable them to employ those attainments in the practical business of life. There is great reason to fear that school teachers are in the habit of often resting satisfied with a lower standard of proficiency in the reading, writing, and arithmetic, even of their best scholars, than would be tolerated in any handicraft or occupation by which, after leaving school, the same

* See pp. 93–4.
† See pp. 100–101.

children were to earn their living.'[54] The inspectors took note of this instruction. They gave much more attention in their subsequent reports to the state of the teaching of the 'three Rs'.

In the final analysis, the promulgation and enforcement of the Revised Code constituted a significant victory for the state in its struggle with the Churches for control over education. No longer was the state going to subsidize schools whose primary function was to rear the young in the principles of the Christian faith. This issue formed the basis of one of the chief complaints of the National Society. 'The Committee have directed their attention,' they informed Lowe, 'in the first instance to the most important subject of all, the religious education of the people… They must regretfully deprecate a system, the manifold tendency of which is to lead managers and teachers to think that the financial position of the school will be improved if less time be given to religious instruction, and more to the selected three subjects.'[55] The former inspector, John Allen, was even more outspoken. Quoting the terms of the *Instructions to Inspectors* of August 1840,* he wrote that it seemed to be monstrous that the Department that administered the public money should break faith with the public by encouraging intellectual instruction 'not subordinate to the regulation of the thoughts and habits of the children by the doctrines and precepts of revealed religion'.[56]

In contrast the Newcastle Commissioners, in their enunciation of what they considered to be an education that met the needs of the children of the labouring classes, had virtually reversed the earlier order of priorities. At the most, religious education was put on a par with the basic secular skills. Significantly it was the last in their list of *desiderata*. The Newcastle Commissioners wanted to provide a schooling that equipped children to meet 'the practical needs of life' in the England of the 1860s. The education provided by the Anglican church met the 'needs' of a pre-industrial society and economy.

By successfully introducing the Revised Code, Lowe had vindicated the state's right to make the content of elementary education meet the wider needs of contemporary society. He never said in so many words that this was part of his purpose. To have done so would have been tantamount to committing politi-

* See p. 37.

cal suicide. He did, however, make an oblique reference to the matter a few years later in a speech at Edinburgh. Primary education, or the education of the poor, he asserted, was the responsibility of the state. In it he declared, 'the state represents in the matter of education not the religious but the secular element'.[57] He went on to explain that the state, in return for the assistance it gave the schools, stipulated that a certain amount of secular instruction should be given. 'It is the duty of the state,' he added, 'above all things, to test and ascertain the nature of the education given.' In other words, the state had to see that public money was not wasted. In another respect he was more outspoken. He had no hesitation in betraying his impatience with the way in which the denominational system made public education unnecessarily expensive. He calculated that one third of the inspectorate could have been dispensed with by the introduction of nonsectarian inspection.[58] On another occasion he referred to the duplication of school building that the denominational system entailed. 'It was found,' he informed the House of Commons, 'that the liberality which made them [the schools] comprehensive was the truest economy, and that if they were built on exclusive principles the effect was greatly to increase the expenditure.'[59] Because the National Society refused to accept either the management or the conscience clauses, he had resorted to subterfuge. If there was a considerable Nonconformist population he struck a bargain with the Anglican incumbent. The clergyman agreed to ignore the National Society's term of union. Lowe, for his part, sanctioned a building grant.[60]

As well as being concerned over the possible subordination of religious instruction to the secular activities of the schools, managers were alarmed by the stringency of the terms on which the grants were to be offered in the future. Their fears, they naturally argued, did not imply that the schools were deficient in any way. On the contrary they attributed any shortcomings that the schools might possess to the disadvantages under which they worked. Their real complaint, though, was that the days of easily earned grants were over. Lowe had little sympathy with their protests. As he pointed out: 'If the inspectors are right, and ninety per cent of the schools are really taught, the language that might be expected...is "Your examination is superfluous; but if you think it right to put the country to the trouble and expense of an examination, we shall get more than we do at present. Our schools will bear any test".'[61]

During the discussions on the Revised Code, wider educational issues were neglected. Apart from their concern over the lesser emphasis that would be put on religious education, the National Society showed no anxiety about the effect that the new code might have on the daily work of the schools. Other petitioners showed a similar disregard. School managers were overwhelmingly concerned about the size of their grants and the place that religious education would enjoy in the syllabus. Only occasional reference was made to the fear that the Revised Code might stultify teaching methods.

If any subject should have been well taught, that subject should have been religious knowledge. Not only did it provide the *raison d'être* of many of the schools in the first place, but it was the one subject in which the certificated schoolmaster, firstly as a pupil-teacher and then as a training college student, had obtained a good grounding. Yet the general tenor of the inspectors' reports was that this subject was badly taught. When Bellairs was freed from the necessity of inspecting religious instruction after 1870, he welcomed the change with relief. 'I must confess that I feel thankful for this arrangement,' he wrote in his report at the end of the year. 'As a rule the religious examination of the children has been to me unsatisfactory, the children are sometimes presented as instructed in the whole of the Bible (in itself an absurdity)... I have never ventured, except in the extremest cases of neglect, to recommend the imposition of a fine, viz. a refusal of the whole annual grant.'[62] In the privacy of his diary, a few years earlier, another clerical inspector, W. H. Brookfield, had expressed his misgivings about the prospect of appearing before the Pakington Committee. 'We agreed', he wrote, 'that cross-examination might be awkward... as I did not believe in the religious instruction of the schools being anything more than instruction in sacred history, and that very inefficient.'[63]

Other Anglican inspectors were equally dismayed by what they saw. E. P. Arnold found that the syllabus was usually 'confined to Genesis and perhaps Exodus in the Old Testament, and to the early chapters in St Matthew's or St Luke's Gospel, or perhaps to one Gospel in the New Testament'.[64] F. Watkins found that lessons were restricted to 'the Creation, Flood, etc. ... and to the beginnings of these subjects [rather] than to the whole of them'.[65] A. F. Foster, an assistant commissioner to the Newcastle Commission, thought that undue attention was given to 'the exact number of kings that reigned in Israel, or the precise names of Jacob's sons'.[66] This charge was repeated by Lowe in the House of Commons who described 'a great deal of... religious instruction...[as] the mere burdening of the memory with the names of kings, dates, and geographical peculiarities of remote countries which, although necessary to the full and critical understanding of the Sacred writings, cannot be required for the religion of the poor'.[67] There seems little doubt that the charge made by J. J. Blandford, in 1851, still held good. The children were 'fairly well acquainted with the outline of Scripture history...and could prove points of doctrine, but when questioned as to their practical application and gearing upon everyday life and intercourse with each other, the inference, however obvious, could seldom be drawn'.[68]

A similar indictment can be made of the teaching of other subjects. J. D. Morell, for instance, wrote in his report for 1858: 'Of all subjects of elementary instruction, geography is the one of which the least good use is made in a great many of our primary schools...The number of times...I am obliged to hear the exact heights of certain mountains [and] the exact length of certain rivers...is something quite remarkable... These are points of information, mostly incorrect...that are quite unimportant in themselves.'[69] The Reverend W. W. Howard,* at the start of his career as an inspector, described his initial impressions to Watkins. 'I do not think,' he wrote, 'I can name a school where history is properly taught. Geography, in general, is a very meagre knowledge of England and the very outlines of Europe. Arithmetic is generally taught too mechanically...After arithmetic, I think, that the church catechism seems to be worst taught...Reading lessons are also very defective.'[70]

If the picture that has been outlined above is a fair one, there

---

* W. W. Howard was educated at King William's College, Isle of Man, and Sidney Sussex College, Cambridge (sixteenth wrangler, 1846; Fellow, 1849). He was assistant master at Repton School (1852), and H.M.I. (1855–91).

is little reason for believing that the introduction of the Revised Code brought a golden age of school teaching to a close. History, for instance, was probably taught in about one school in three.* Furthermore, the schoolmaster's training was being restricted more and more to a study of the basic subjects to the exclusion of any other. In many cases the so-called lessons in the 'extra' subjects were derived from passages in the reading books. When the subjects were taught in their own right, they were frequently little more than exercises in rote-learning. The temporary cessation of lessons that consisted mainly of learning the names of the capes and rivers of England and the regnal dates of English sovereigns was no great loss to anyone.

On the contrary, the inauguration of the Revised Code brought one great advantage. Since the size of the grant depended on the individual child's success in passing an examination, schoolmasters had to pay far more attention to each child in the school. One ingredient of the simultaneous lesson, given at times to the entire age-range found within a school, had been the simultaneous answer. One of the many disadvantages of this method of teaching was that the abler pupils carried the others. Hence it was difficult to spot those who were failing to understand a particular lesson. Even as late as 1858 and 1859, Brookfield and Cook respectively found it necessary to denounce this method of teaching.[71] Fearon and Bellairs found reading still being taught as a simultaneous lesson in the mid-1860s.[72]

Thus it seems that the need to satisfy the requirements of the Revised Code swept away a long-lingering legacy of the monitorial system. If this is so, the inauguration of the pupil-teacher system did not produce an immediate pedagogic revolution. The first apprentices probably differed little, except in age and in possessing slightly greater knowledge, from the monitors whom they replaced. After all, the masters for whom they worked had, in many instances, been trained in the 'method'. The old ideas lingered on until the inspector's examination of the *individual* child made earlier methods obsolete.†

In one respect the Revised Code was an expansionist and not a restrictionist measure. The Newcastle Commissioners,

* See Chapter 2, Table IV.
† On this issue, as on many others, it would be helpful if some informative diaries of ex-pupil-teachers and schoolmasters could be traced.

it will be remembered, had calculated that only 19·3 per cent of the 1,549,312 children whose names were on the registers of the denominational elementary day schools 'were in their twelfth year or upwards, and only that proportion, therefore, can be regarded as educated up to the standard suited to their stations.' They concluded: 'Much, therefore, still remains to be done to bring up the state of elementary education in England and Wales to the degree of usefulness which we all regard as attainable and desirable.'[73] Their estimate that 19·3 per cent (299,017) could be regarded as 'educated up to the standard of their stations' was wildly optimistic; 219,813 of the 555,502 children examined between 1 September 1863 and 31 August 1864 were over ten years of age. Yet 453,783 (81·6 per cent) were presented for examination below Standard IV.[74] In other words school managers did not allow them to take an examination requiring them to be able to read a short paragraph from a more advanced reading book used in the schools, write correctly a sentence dictated slowly from the same book, or complete a sum in compound rules, using money.[75] Only 58,233 children over the age of ten passed Standards IV to VI in 1864. By 1870, the number that had had an education minimally suited to the needs of their station had risen to 95,955.

These figures are not entirely reliable as school managers, anxious for their grants, presented children in as low a grade as possible. Although such tactics were probably most commonly adopted when the Revised Code was first introduced, it must not be thought that managers were able to practise them with impunity. The Department soon became aware of what was happening. School managers who were persistent offenders were liable to a fine. Although such a sanction was seldom invoked, its existence must have acted as a deterrent. A few years later, the 1868 Code* gave schools an incentive to obtain a fifth of all their passes in Standards IV to VI. For this reason the figures quoted for 1870 may reflect the performance of the children more accurately than do those for 1864. Lastly in areas where parents had a choice of school, the managers wanted to preserve the reputation of their institutions so as to be able to attract pupils. Working-class parents, wanting value for the money they spent

* See p. 217.

in fees, judged schools by the efficiency with which they gave a secular education.*

For their part the Newcastle Commissioners would only have regarded those children who had passed Standard VI† as fully prepared for their place in society. Yet the passes in reading, writing, and arithmetic, in 1864, it will be remembered, were as low as 3,523, 3,284 and 3,103 respectively. By 1870, the corresponding figures for the day schools in England and Wales had only reached 30,985, 27,289 and 22,839.[76] Thus the seemingly modest target of the Newcastle Commissioners was, in practice, far beyond the range of most working-class children at this time.

Furthermore, schools did not have to confine themselves to the basic subjects. 'What we fix,' Lowe said, 'is a *minimum* of education, not a *maximum*.‡ We propose to give no grant for the attendance of children at school unless they can read, write, and cipher; but we do not say they shall not learn more. We do not object to any amount of learning; the only question is how much of that knowledge we ought to pay for... It must not be forgotten that those for whom this system is designed are the children of persons who are not able to pay for the teaching. We do not propose,' he added in a passage that shows that Kay-Shuttleworth's concept of the function and purpose of elementary education still prevailed, 'to give these children an education that will raise them above their station and business in life.'[77] Twenty years later, Lowe reiterated the view that the Revised Code did not automatically exclude all other forms of instruction. 'My dear Lingen,' he wrote, 'As I understand the case, you and I viewed the three Rs not only or primarily as the exact amount of instruction which ought to be given, but as an amount of knowledge which could be ascertained thoroughly by examination, and upon which we could safely base the Parliamentary grant. It was more a financial than a literary preference. Had there been any other branch of useful knowledge, the possession of which could be ascertained with equal precision, there was nothing to prevent its admission. But there was not...'[78]

School managers, however, took the minimum of the examination schedule as their maximum. From their concern over the

* See p. 225.
† See p. 62.
‡ Original italics.

size of their annual grant flowed those evil consequences of the Revised Code that have been so frequently denounced. Children were presented in as low a grade as they thought politic. Often the entire work of the school was geared to the sole task of securing the largest number of passes possible in the basic subjects. To some extent the training colleges must share the blame for this state of affairs. Since the schoolmaster's training had been a matter of cram, he had not learnt any of the ways by which the teaching of reading, writing and arithmetic could be made exciting.* Hence the pedestrian methods that he already used were now concentrated on drilling the children in the three Rs. In 1865, for example, H.M.I. the Reverend C. J. Robinson reported that although 'the higher subjects of instruction... [had] never obtained in the schools which came under my observation that predominance which has been unduly charged upon them...the reading, writing, and arithmetic are, on the whole, less forward, are falling off in intelligence, in power to exercise the thoughts and draw out the mind, while the discipline loses in the competition with the urgent necessities of the examination schedule.'[79]

Publishers also joined in this conspiracy of restricting the syllabus. In the same report, Robinson quoted the following preface to a reading book. 'Although it contains but sixty-four pages, it comprises all that is necessary to enable the pupils to acquire the knowledge demanded by their Lordships' minutes; it need scarcely be said that any matter which is not absolutely required should for obvious reasons be omitted.'[80] Matthew Arnold, as befitted a professor of poetry, took particular exception to a poem entitled *My Native Land*. The two verses that are quoted show how restricted the vocabulary of some reading books became.

> She's not a dull or cold land,
> No she's a warm and bold land;
> Oh she's a true and old land,
>   This native land of mine.

> Oh she's a fresh and fair land
> Oh she's a true and rare land.
> Oh she's a rare and fair land,
>   This native land of mine.[81]

---

* Yet scattered through the inspectors' reports and the minutes of the Department there is a surprising amount of advice on lively teaching methods.

On the other hand many of the older books had been equally unsuitable. Schoolmasters had yet to learn that 'there was a golden mean equally remote from *Goody Two Shoes*, and from those appalling essays on the graminivorous quadrupeds and the monocotyledonous plants, which have so long bewildered the little readers of the Irish books'.[82]

Inevitably, the managers and masters examined the provisions of the code to see how they could maximize the grant-earning capacity of their schools. At times they showed a cupidity and ruthlessness that shocked the Department. 'We hope,' My Lords stated on one occasion, 'that not many cases occur like the two reported by Mr Warburton.' 'At a time when scarlatina was epidemic in a thickly populated district,' he stated, 'I had [some] children brought to be examined with their throats bandaged and skin peeling…one of whom had to be taken away during the examination.' At another school, he was asked to examine five who had been kept outside the schoolroom. He found the mother of one crying out of anxiety for the child she had brought from the sick-bed.[83]

Since no ages were prescribed for the various standards, school managers, at first, tried to have the children presented in as low a standard as possible. In extreme cases the whole school, at first, was examined in Standard I.[84] Lowe had anticipated this manœuvre. When he defended his original intention of examining by age, a provision he later had to abandon because of the school managers' opposition, he asked the House of Commons whether the ability of a boy aged eleven, about to leave school, who could read words of one syllable, make letters on a board, and count to twenty, was a result worth paying for.[85] The answer was clearly 'No'. What Lowe withdrew publicly in Parliament, he privately restored by administrative action. Inspectors were told in a circular letter, headed 'Not for publication', that 'If the lower classes of a school contain many children of advanced age, or if the higher classes are presented under low standards, this fact will demand the inspector's attention, and must appear in his report. If not satisfactorily explained, it will mark such "a fault of instruction" under Article 52A as requires the grant to be "reduced".'[86] Under the article that Lingen had cited, schools were liable to a loss of up to a half of their total grant.

As there was much inducement to falsify the ages of the children, it was never easy to enforce the regulation. Children under the age of six, in the infants' department, escaped the individual examination to which their elders were subjected. Children over the age of twelve, in the night school, could be examined year after year in the same grade, after 1868, and still earn a grant.[87] These practices were so common that H.M.I. S. N. Stokes asked the Department if he could inquire into a child's age. 'A child in appearance about ten,' he complained, 'may in the day school be represented as under six or in the night school as over twelve.'[88] Although Stokes was told to report those cases of suspected fraud he could not clear up on the spot, it was not always easy for an inspector to establish the age of a child. Not until 1874 did parents become liable to a penalty for failing to register the birth of a child.[89]

C. J. Robinson experienced similar difficulties. He found that 'it appeared to require great particularity, and to involve considerable trouble to arrive at the truth concerning the actual age of the scholars, especially when the parents professed to be uncertain as to the date of their children's birth'. Consequently the mistake of a year or two was by no means uncommon. In addition, when a minimum age was specified for admission to the infants' school, parents frequently overstated the age of their children.[90] At times, local custom added to the inspector's difficulties. The Reverend R. B. Girdlestone, curate in charge at Wordsley, near Stourbridge, Worcestershire, told the Select Committee of 1865 that 'A child says he is nine when he is eight. From a peculiar form of reckoning in our part of the country, everybody considers himself a year older than he is'.[91]

The Education Department condemned the illiberal interpretation that school managers and others gave to the provisions of the Revised Code. 'The Royal Commissioners,' they pointed out in their report for 1867, 'are often quoted to show the necessity for individual examination; but they insist in the very same passages...with equal emphasis, upon the necessity of retaining a liberal and intelligent inspection. There is room for other than mechanical inspection even within the limits of Article 48 [this article sets out the examination schedule]. It can only be by the express recommendation of an inspector that any school obtains its full grant while it produces nothing better than mechanical results, and if, after due warning, any school continues to do so, the reason must lie in the inspector's acting on only half of his instructions.'[92]

As the following table shows, the Department implemented the Revised Code with considerable leniency. In two important respects, inspectors were told to give the schools the benefit of

Table II DEDUCTIONS FROM THE GRANT PAID TO DAY SCHOOLS IN ENGLAND AND WALES, 1869–70

Gross grant	£579,860 0s. 7d.*
Penalties	
Article 51 (a) Unsatisfactory building	—
„ (b) Uncertificated teacher	£1,311 4s. 0d.
„ (c) No needlework taught	—
„ (d) Registers, accounts, etc. kept unsatisfactorily	—
„ (e) An objection of a gross kind	—
Article 52 (a) Deduction of one-tenth to one half of the grant earned for failures in instruction or discipline, failure to remedy (after one year's notice) defects in building, apparatus etc. that seriously interfere with the discipline of the school	£2,256 16s. 5d.
„ (b) Failure to maintain stipulated staff-pupil ratio	£3,027 10s. 0d.
„ (c) Deduction of excess of grant over:	
(1) Local subscriptions, school pence etc.	£5,135 15s. 1d.
(2) 15s. per pupil in average attendance	£87 16s. 1d.
„ (d) Adjustment of grant paid to a school that had endowed income	£5,429 10s. 9d.
Total deductions	£17,248 12s. 4d.
Net grant	£562,611 8s. 3d.

Source: *Report of the Committee*, P.P. 1871, XXII, p. 17.

* The Revised Code offered 4s. per scholar according to the average number in attendance. In addition, it gave 6s. 6d. for every infant who had made 200 attendances, provided the inspector was satisfied with the instruction given. Children, over the age of six, earned an additional 8s. for passing an examination in reading, writing and arithmetic. This sum was reduced by 2s. 8d. for each failure.

the doubt. They were instructed to pass children if 'reading is intelligible, though not quite good; dictation, legible, and rightly spelt in all common words, though the writing may need improvement, and less common words may be misspelt; arithmetic, right in method, and at least one sum free from error'. As regards fines under Article 52(a), inspectors were informed that 'My Lords do not wish this power to be exercised in any but serious cases'.[93]

The heaviest penalties were those imposed under Articles 52(c) and 52(d). This most affected the schools that had fared the best under the old regulations. Veneration for that great Victorian principle, self-help, had resulted in the channelling of government assistance into the areas that needed it least, those most able to help themselves. Thus, although the average annual grant, per pupil in average attendance, had been between 11s. 2d. and 11s. 6d. in 1860, there was much variation.[94] Lowe had found that one school received as much as £4 3s. 4d. a pupil and that another eleven had grants ranging between £1 7s. 6d. and 19s. 0d. a scholar.[95] Kay-Shuttleworth denied the possibility that local poverty hampered educational progress. 'When the word "destitute" is used,' he told the Newcastle Commissioners, 'I should rather substitute the word "apathetic", that is to say, destitute of the moral and intellectual sense necessary to induce them [the potential subscribers] to make the sacrifices necessary for education.'[96] Shortly afterwards, the Commissioners heard Temple endorse this view by describing the capitation grant as 'an illustration of both good and evil'. He explained: 'It introduces education where you would not otherwise have it, and it does also sanction the principle that if the proprietors will not do their duty, the Government will do it for them.'[97]

On the other hand, the Revised Code extended the benefits of inspection and an annual grant to some of those areas that had been previously neglected. This was done by the introduction of a fourth division of the certificate. This step, which diluted professional standards still further, allowed practising teachers, regardless of their age, to obtain government recognition and absorbed the former registered teacher into the ranks of the certificated. Former pupil-teachers, who now became eligible for a provisional certificate, were allowed to take charge of small rural schools.[98] These measures helped to increase the number of inspected schools, in England and Wales, from 5,538,* in 1861, to 6,367 in 1865.[99] Thus although the total grant paid for the *maintenance* of schools in England and Wales fell from £465,000 (approximately), in 1861, to £386,304, in 1865, it is difficult to generalize about the effects of the Revised Code on individual schools.

An examination of the grants earned by the first twenty-five schools in alphabetical order, inspected in the counties of Hertfordshire and Lancashire in 1865, yields the following results. Eleven Lancashire and three Hertfordshire schools earned more than in 1860. Four Lancashire and six Hertfordshire schools were recipients of grants in 1865 but not in 1860. The remainder, ten schools in the north-western county and sixteen in Hertfordshire, of which seven in the southern county had an endowed income, received less.[100] Two tentative suggestions can be put forward. Much of the loss in income fell on the longer established endowed schools. In contrast, parents in working-class industrialized areas valued the greater emphasis that was now placed on preparing their children for the ascertainable needs of a tangible world. Between 1862 and 1870, the number of children present on the day of the inspector's visit rose from 857,663† to 1,434,766. The extent to which the spread of elementary education was earlier hampered by the seemingly irrelevant concentration on religious studies, and working-class suspicions of the Established Church still remains to be explored.

The Table reproduced on p. 212 also shows that where a school's deficiencies could not be determined objectively, the penalties were either comparatively light or non-existent. If the criticisms that have been made of the quality of the teaching can be accepted at their face value, the fines imposed under Article 52(a), £2,256 16s. 5d., were inadequate. Similarly, it is impossible to reconcile the known existence of many other abuses with the failure to impose any penalty under Articles 51(d) and (e).

In some instances school managers had abdicated all responsibility for their schools by farming them out to the teachers who were left to make what they could out of the annual grant. The

* This figure includes Roman Catholic schools in Scotland.
† This figure includes attendances made by pupils in Roman Catholic schools in Scotland.

master at St Mary's National Society School, Preston, to the consternation of his nominal employers, made too much. His net profit was £130 a year. His successor was accordingly forced to share the profits with the managers who made him hand over £30 a year.[101]

In all such cases the account books had to be falsified. Article 52(c)§1 limited the grant to the amount of locally raised subscriptions and school fees. R. G. C. Hamilton, the accountant to the Education Department, examined the accounts of 200 schools in order to assess their accuracy. He found that 'In the majority of cases the totals given could not be arrived at by the addition of the details, nor could the balance at the close [of the year] be drawn either from the totals or from the details'. He also discovered evidence of deliberate fraud. Promised subscriptions were entered as though they had been received but were not called for unless they were wanted. This practice evaded the state's intention of limiting the grant to the amount of fees and subscriptions that had been raised locally.[102] Managers did not hasten to mend their ways. 'We are sorry to be obliged to add,' the Committee observed with pain a year later, 'that in more than one instance, the income of a school has been improperly (to use no harsher term) exaggerated in the returns.'[103]

Another badly kept record was the log-book. After 1862, teachers were required to maintain a school diary. Their occasional entries were intended to give the inspector a picture of the life of the school since his last visit. School managers had to enter a summary of the annual report together with details of any recommendations the inspector made concerning the running of the school. This procedure was designed to ensure some degree of continuity between one inspection and another. The intentions of the Department, unfortunately, were not always realized. The Committee complained in 1865 that 'the log-book is often ill and unintelligently kept by the teachers'.[104] By 1870 there may have been some improvement. H.M.I. the Reverend H. A. Pickard* found that many of the log-books were kept in a way that reflected very great credit on the teacher. One book, though, did not. 'Page after page contained..."ordinary

* H. A. Pickard was educated at Christ Church, Oxford (first class Lit. Hum. (moderated) 1853; second and fourth class Lit. Hum. Maths, 1855; Tutor 1857–64) and was H.M.I. (1864–97).

progress" or "usual lessons". At last...I saw an entry of more than one line..."April 1st, All Fools' Day. The boys made a fool of me".[105]

It is clear then that the Department never exercised its punitive powers to the full. In one sense the evils that have been attributed to the Revised Code were the result of the failure of the inspectorate to implement the new code fully. Bad teaching and harsh discipline could have been penalized. They seldom, if ever, were. The Department remained dependent, as it had done earlier, on the voluntary subscribers whose goodwill and generosity it could not afford to lose. Hence it had to accept what was virtually a perversion of its original intentions. The minimum became a maximum. The alternative would have been a 'strike' by the school managers. As it was, some managers did just that. They farmed out their schools.

The examiners, as did the inspectors, showed greater humanity than has customarily been attributed to them. According to Sir George Kekewich, 'the heavier the fines we imposed, the greater the credit we got from our superiors.' He has described how on one occasion, when he had recommended a deduction of two-tenths, Lingen not only increased this to five-tenths but suspended the teacher's certificate as well. 'That performance,' he alleged, 'was typical of the attitude of the Education Department towards the managers and teachers in schools in those days. The staff of distinguished scholars,' he averred, 'treated elementary education and elementary teachers with contempt.'[106]

These statements, made long after the event, cannot be reconciled with the available evidence. The total grant for 1869–70, for example, was cut by 3 per cent. Moreover, entries in the Secretary's minute book suggest that any move to treat the schools harshly came not from Lowe or the examiners but from H. A. Bruce, Lowe's successor. In July 1865, Lingen circulated a minute marked '*By order of Mr Bruce*'.* 'The examiners are expressly forbidden,' it stated, 'to make any exception whatever to the strict letter of the code, or of the supplementary rules, without previous reference to one of the assistant secretaries setting out the nature of the exception and the reason for it.' The examiners, far from treating the schools with contempt, signed a

* Lingen's underlining.

petition in which they all protested against this ruling. Lingen stood his ground, as he had to in the circumstances.[107]

He had been overruled by Bruce, only the year before. On that occasion, he had asked for a decision on the methods to be used for calculating the total grant. If, for example, a school had earned a grant of £60, less a fine of £10, and it had received only £40 in subscriptions and fees, should it be paid £40 or £30? Lingen's tendency in this, as well as in other cases he cited, was to interpret the regulations generously. 'Considering that…the reductions though a necessary are a very unpopular part of the code,' he minuted, 'I think that the more liberal view the better to take in each case.' Bruce disagreed. He laid down a stringent method of calculating the total grant in each case. He argued that if the school, in the example quoted, was paid £40 it would be immaterial if the inspector's report was good or bad.[108]

So far the administration of the Revised Code has been examined in broad terms. It now remains to see how it affected other aspects of school life. Such a discussion is complicated by two major factors. First, it is impossible to isolate the effect of the Revised Code on schools that formed part of a rapidly changing society and economy. Secondly, the Code itself did not remain static. The main changes can be summarized briefly. The original version did not allow any grants to schools in which the endowment exceeded 30s. per annum per child in average annual attendance. This regulation did not make any radical departure from previous practice. Kay-Shuttleworth had not allowed school managers to use endowed income as part of their contribution to a certificated master's salary.[109] In 1864 all schools with an endowed income had their grant reduced by the amount of their endowed income. Two years later, the reduction was suspended provided the yield of the grant and the endowment did not exceed 15s. per pupil. Further relaxations followed in 1868. An additional grant of 1s. 4d. per pass, up to a limit of £8, was offered to schools that had an improved staff-pupil ratio, achieved certain standards in the annual examination and taught a secular subject other than reading, writing and arithmetic. Schools were also encouraged to give more attention to the training of their boy apprentices. Grants of £5 and £10 were awarded to the schools if their apprentices obtained places in the colleges. A further sum of £5 or £8 was paid if their former pupils reached certain standards in the examinations held at the end of their first year at college.[110]

At first sight, it seems as if both the master and his pupil-teacher suffered as a result of the promulgation of the new code. The average salary of the certificated master, in Great Britain, rose from £90 in 1855 to £95 by 1861 and 1862. It then fell to £87 in 1865 and reached a new level of £96 at the end of the decade.[111] The drop in the mid-1860s is usually held to be a consequence of the introduction of the Revised Code. Yet there is evidence to suggest that the supply of teachers outstripped demand during the late 1850s and early 1860s. Moreover, the upward national trend of salaries during the year 1855–62 conceals local variations and movements together with the decline that occurred in the pay offered to certain newly-appointed teachers.* In some cases, it should be remembered, schoolmasters also received rent-free accommodation which was worth about £10 a year.

The provisions of the Revised Code itself provide a further complication. The minimum requirements of the teacher's certificate were lowered by the introduction of a fourth division for practising teachers. Candidates for this new grade had to answer 'plain and simple questions, specially noted for them…'.[112] Between 1862 and 1867, 1,448 acting teachers out of 1,896 candidates surmounted this particular obstacle. A further 346 pupil-teachers received provisional certificates; seventy-six of them obtained full certificates by 1867. If allowance is made for possible double-counting, 1,718 of the 12,837 certificated teachers employed in Great Britain had entered the profession by these means.[113] Such teachers naturally commanded smaller salaries than did their two-year trained colleagues. An analysis made of 3,251 masters, serving in schools receiving an annual grant in 1870, shows the extent to which professional standards had been diluted. Sixty-six per cent had trained for a minimum of two years, 17 per cent for one year; 14·7 per cent were untrained, and 2·3 per cent were provisionally certificated.[114] It is thus possible that the well-established two-year trained man, despite the fall in average earnings, held his own during the 1860s.

Compared with the rest of the community, however, he fell

* See pp. 104–5 and 143.

behind, for he failed to obtain his share of the country's growing wealth. If 1850 is taken as the base year, average money wages, not allowing for unemployment, rose from 100 to 116, in 1855, and to 133 by 1870. By that year, the price index was 113 and that for real wages 118.[115] Over the fifteen years 1855–70—the number of schoolmasters before 1855 is too small to provide reliable figures—the schoolmaster's salary had risen by only £6. Although 1855, a year that the Crimean War made one of high prices, is an unfortunate one with which to make a comparison, it seems clear that schoolmastering as a career was becoming increasingly unattractive. Hence boys and girls used apprenticeship more and more as a means of equipping themselves for the more prosperous world that lay outside the classroom. School managers could not, or would not, offer competitive wages. By 1867, the Department had become concerned over the fact that 'A considerable part of the apprenticeships never get beyond the third year.' 'The boys...are tempted with higher wages in other employments, and the managers are disposed to let them go as they become more expensive.'[116] Consequently, the 1,521 boy and 1,571 girl first-year apprentices of 1861 were whittled down to 508 male and 707 female college students by January 1866.

Admission to apprenticeship began to fall from the peak of 1859, the year in which schools were limited to four pupil-teachers each. By the end of 1864, the number of new entrants was down to 2,568, of whom 1,895 were first-year apprentices. Most of this fall had occurred before the Revised Code regulations were applied to all schools in England and Wales on 1 July 1863. The decline in admissions had coincided with a period of a rising wastage rate. Hence the total pupil-teacher labour force decreased by nearly a third from 16,277, in 1861, to 10,971, in 1866. The prompt offer of additional grants, in the minute of 20 February 1867, encouraged managers to keep their older children. Moreover, the Revised Code made it easier for older children to serve shortened articles. As a result of these changes, the loss had almost been made good by the end of 1869. There were 15,701 apprentices. Of the 4,557 new admissions, 4,031 had started in the first year of their articles.[117]

The overriding weakness of the Revised Code was that it increased the financial anxieties of the school managers. For the previous predictable earmarked grants there was substituted a general and unpredictable one. At the same time managers were given wide discretion over the spending of their money. As a result, teachers, pupil-teachers and children alike undoubtedly suffered. In making this arrangement, the Department had ignored the main lessons of nineteenth-century administrative experience. Where social progress had come, it had often come not because of, but despite the wishes of local communities.[118] It has also been argued that the poor suffered more at the hands of the workhouse officials, the employees of guardians anxious to keep down the poor rate, than at the hands of the Poor Law Commissioners whose attitude was comparatively humane.[119] Similarly, it can be argued that school children suffered more as the result of the tyranny of the schoolmaster, now the employee of managers anxious to keep subscriptions to a minimum, than of the Committee of the Privy Council on Education.

The introduction of the Revised Code, however, does not mark a great divide in the history of English elementary education. Robert Lowe and Sir James Kay-Shuttleworth had much in common. Both wanted to make effective use of the financial weapons of the state so that they might control the education of the children of the labouring poor. During a period of scarce resources, Kay-Shuttleworth had been concerned with building up, under state supervision, the means by which education was provided. Once much of this groundwork had been completed, Lowe was concerned with the end product, the nature of the education that was given. Much against his will, Kay-Shuttleworth had had to accept the subordination of a secular education to a religious one. He had also wanted an inspectorate that would have been an effective agency of central government control. Lowe attempted to make secular education at least as important as a religious one and to create a system of inspection that was administratively effective.

Neither had wanted to raise the children of the labouring poor above their station in life. Last, both saw the development of elementary education as a means of creating a barrier against revolutionary change. In 1832, the year of the first Reform Act, Kay-Shuttleworth had warned of the dangers that would arise 'if the higher classes were not willing to diffuse intelligence among the lower'. In 1867, the year of the second Reform Act, Lowe wrote 'We cannot suffer any large number of our citizens, now that they have obtained the right of influencing the destinies of the country, to remain uneducated. It was a great evil that we did so before—it was an evil and a reproach, a moral stigma upon us. But now it is a matter of self-preservation—it is a question of existence, even of the existence of our constitution, and upon those who shall obstruct or prevent such a measure passing, will rest a responsibility the heaviest that mortal man can possibly lie under.'[120]

In 1868, the Committee of the Privy Council on Education condemned the farmed-out schools in the following terms. 'It need scarcely be added that a voluntary system cannot take much credit for such schools which, in effect, have no disinterested person connected with them to check certificates and returns, and to see that there is a proper outlay on books, apparatus and assistant teachers.'[121] The Committee might well have extended their strictures to the voluntary system as a whole. The introduction of the new code had exposed the shortcomings of the existing schools. It had also demonstrated the inadequacy of a system based primarily on the generosity of local subscribers as a means of meeting the educational needs of the children of the labouring poor.

It has been fashionable to condemn the Department for having introduced the Revised Code at all. Yet the case for providing the majority of English children with a crash course in literacy and numeracy, in both their own interests and those of society as a whole, had become overwhelming by the early 1860s. Today the Revised Code is criticized for its narrowness. Yet when the school managers argued that their grants would be reduced they were saying, in effect, that the Department's requirements were too ambitious. Although one cannot condone all that they said and did, over one point it is possible to sympathize. A child's school career was a short one. Employers and parents alike expected children to start work at an early age. The Newcastle Commissioners thought that the 'attendance of most of the children who go to school at all is distributed with more or less regularity over about four years, between [the ages of] three and fifteen, and generally between six and twelve'.[122] Although this situation was unsatisfactory, the Commissioners were not prepared to recommend the introduction of compulsory school attendance. 'This state of affairs,' they admitted, 'leaves great room for improvement, but we do not think that it warrants very gloomy views or calls for extreme measures.' In these circumstances, they thought a realistic goal for the 63·7 per cent, who attended for 100 days and upwards over the course of four years, would be 'to learn to read and write without conscious difficulty, and to perform such arithmetical operations as occur in the ordinary business of life'.[123] Until the general level of wages rose, and it became both politically and economically possible to enforce full-time attendance, the curriculum of the school was bound to be a limited one. As it was, the syllabus and attendance requirements of the Revised Code were little more than a pious aspiration for many children.

Since the Department had little control over the inspectorate, it had little control over the expenditure of public money. Such a situation as this could not be tolerated at a time when the demand for education was growing. If universal education was to become a reality, a simpler and more effective financial control had to be devised. It is accordingly difficult to see how the administrative problems of the day could have been solved except by the introduction of some form of objective test. In the state's struggle for control over public education, the imposition of a predominantly secular syllabus in 1862 was an important prelude to the breaking, eight years later, of the monopoly previously enjoyed by the religious societies. Where Kay-Shuttleworth had failed, Lowe succeeded and Forster reaped the benefit.

Conclusion

1870 And After:

Plus ça change, plus c'est la même chose

SHERLOCK HOLMES: Look at those big, isolated clumps of buildings rising up above the slates, like brick islands in a lead-coloured sea.
DR WATSON: The Board Schools.
SHERLOCK HOLMES: Lighthouses, my boy! Beacons of the future! Capsules, with hundreds of bright little seeds in each, out of which will spring the wiser, better England of the future.

SIR ARTHUR CONAN DOYLE[1]

In 1802 Mrs Trimmer had argued that the national well-being depended on keeping some of the people in a state of ignorance. 'However desirable it may be to rescue the lower kinds of people from that deplorable state of ignorance in which the greatest part of them were for a long time suffered to remain,' she wrote, 'it cannot be right to train them *all** in a way which will most probably raise their ideas above the very lowest occupations of life, and disqualify them for those servile offices which must be fulfilled by some members of the community, and in which they may be equally happy with the highest, if they will do their duty.'[2] By 1870 the wheel had turned full circle. W. E. Forster, the Vice-President of the Committee of the Privy Council on Education, told the House of Commons: 'Upon the speedy provision of elementary education depends our industrial prosperity.'[3] He went on to explain why the government was introducing a bill to provide universal elementary education: 'It is no use trying to give technical education to our artisans without elementary education; uneducated labourers...are for the most part, unskilled labourers, and if we leave our work-folk any

---

* Mrs Trimmer's italics.

longer unskilled, notwithstanding their strong sinews and determined energy, they will become overmatched in the competition of the world.' Mindful of the extension of the franchise made three years before he continued: 'Upon this speedy provision [of education] depends also, I fully believe, the good, the safeguarding of our constitutional system...' Lastly he appealed to the policies of *real-politik* and racial supremacy: 'Upon this speedy provision of education depends also our political power. Civilized communities throughout the world are massing themselves together...; and if we are to hold our position among men of our own race or among the nations of the world we must make up for the smallness of our numbers by increasing the intellectual force of the individual.'

In grafting the new rate-assisted board schools on to the old stock of voluntary ones, a deliberate attempt was made to preserve as much of the old order as possible. 'There must be,' Forster declared, 'consistently with the attainment of our object, the least possible expenditure of public money, the utmost endeavour not to injure existing and efficient schools, and the most careful absence of all encouragement to parents to neglect their children.'[4]

Although the Anglican Church's political power was not as great in 1870 as it had been in the 1830s, the State's victory was far from complete. In 1833, the year of the first Treasury grant, the Church had successfully resisted a proposal to secularize some of its Irish revenue. In 1869 it protested in vain against its disestablishment in Ireland. Yet the provisions of the Elementary Education Act, 1870, gave the voluntary societies a new lease of life. Spurred on by the threat of the secular school boards, school managers rushed to apply for building grants before the deadline laid down in the Act, 31 December 1870. During the next seven years the societies found £1,290,716 to accommodate an extra 1,069,712 children in schools in England and Wales.[5] This should be compared with their achievement in the previous thirty-one years. Between 1839 and 1870 voluntary subscribers had produced £3,518,104 for seating 1,878,584 in annual grant schools.[6]

The great struggle that had been fought between Church and State has a curious air of unreality. It had been fought by a Church Militant that lacked an army. Although school managers attached much importance 'to the education of the children over whose parents they have influence, in the religious creed which they themselves profess', the consumers showed little brand preference. Parents were much more concerned with mundane considerations. They tended to judge a school 'by the efficiency with which such things as tend to the advancement in life of their children are taught in it, and by its general tone and influence'.[7] Similarly, the reform of the Church, obstructive at the episcopal level, had been beneficial at the parochial. As the nineteenth century advanced, non-residence receded and incumbents began to fulfil their pastoral duties with greater diligence. In many cases, one of their first activities was that of building a school for the children of their parishioners.

As a result of the diligence of countless incumbents, the Established Church had consolidated its position as a powerful pressure group whose interests successive governments could not ignore. The Elementary Education Act, 1876, by creating school attendance committees from the existing borough councils and Poor Law Unions, made it possible for non-school-board areas to enforce compulsory attendance. At the expense of administrative efficiency and educational progress, voluntary school managers were safeguarded from the competition they might have met from an extended school board system.[8] In 1889 the government had to retreat in face of the Bishop of London's attack on the proposal that voluntary schools, in common with board schools, should have ten square feet of floor space for each child.[9] A factor that helped to delay the introduction of free education until 1891 was the concern of the voluntary schools for the income they feared they would lose. The 1902 Education Act, which put the Church schools on the rates, can be interpreted as an attempt to halt their extinction. Judgement on these two issues, however, must be suspended until further research has been conducted. Finally, the Education Act, 1959, gave a 75 per cent grant to all aided schools—the name by which voluntary schools became known after the 1944 Education Act—'whether in existence or projected, to cater for children at existing primary schools'.[10]

The origins of other features of the educational system can be found in the nineteenth century. It may seem ironical that the National Union of Teachers celebrated its centenary year by holding the biggest strike of teachers in its history. Yet many of the causes of the profession's present discontents can be attributed to the influence of the past. The need to rely on the generosity of the charitable helped to depress the level of salaries before 1870. Although some of the school boards paid their staff well, the resources of many rural boards were scarcely adequate for the duties entrusted to them. The *ad hoc* nature of the boards, the limited area many of them covered, together with the holding of triennial elections, made their members highly 'rate-conscious'. Hence the salary bill, the chief item of recurrent expenditure, was always carefully scrutinized. Local authorities remain fully aware of the burden that teachers' salaries put on the rates.

The ease with which women could be recruited to the classroom also helped to hold down salary levels in the nineteenth century. There were few comparable opportunities for employment elsewhere. This state of affairs is to some extent true today. 'Women teachers in all types of schools, but particularly in grammar schools, have a higher social origin than men teachers. This undoubtedly reflects the greater alternatives open to men, and particularly to male graduates. Teaching still [the passage refers to 1968] offers more opportunity to the educated girl than most other careers open to her.'[11] A change may be coming, however. Nurses and teachers are showing a new militance. This may be the manifestation of an increase in the opportunities for prestigious employment outside the classroom and the hospital ward. The National Health Service and the schools may not be able to take the existence of this captive labour force for granted much longer.

Since the middle of the nineteenth century the state has played a major part in controlling the supply of and demand for teachers and has thereby influenced the level of their salaries. The state has been able to regulate the supply of teachers in two main ways. It has been the chief supplier of the provision made for their instruction and has manipulated the standards that it has been prepared to accept before granting teachers recognition. Central government policy has also determined changes in total demand. The relatively unsophisticated nature of the techniques used in the nineteenth century has been improved to such an extent that some of the best manpower forecasting in recent years has been on teacher needs.

A consideration of our current problems should lead us to

show some sympathy with the compilers of the *Newcastle Report* and with Robert Lowe, the initiator of the Revised Code. Today we are faced with the problem of financing an educational explosion at university level. Mid-Victorian England faced a similar problem at the elementary level. The sheer size of the task that faced the Education Department is often overlooked. In 1869 the estimated population of England and Wales was 21,869,607. With one person in every 7·2 of the population in the 'middle and upper classes'—the 'sociological' criteria adopted for this judgement were an ability and willingness to pay at least ninepence a week in school fees—18,745,378 fell 'within the class for whose benefit the Parliamentary grant is voted'. As it was a very young population, 21 per cent were within the age-range of three to twelve. At a time when there was accommodation for 1,824,306 children, there were 3,936,513 of school age.[12] By 1877 the figure had been revised upwards to 4,606,544. Already the provision of education was creating the demand for more. The later, higher estimate included those in their thirteenth year.[13]

By this time the demand for education had become self-generating. Many of those who now went to school were the children of artisans who had been members of the first generation to experience the economic benefits that even an indifferent elementary education could confer on the recipient. They wanted their own children to have a better chance in life. In response to this pressure, the school boards in the larger cities began to build higher elementary schools.

The nineteenth-century debate developed on lines that are familiar to us today. Could we afford to build the schools? Was it in the interests either of society as a whole or the children themselves that they should have such an elaborate, lengthy, and expensive education? The same questions, in a slightly different guise, are still being asked.

Populist pressures made an impact on elementary education in the half century before 1914, and after that on secondary education. Their force is now felt in the field of higher education. In the secondary schools, an élitist system of education based on the grammar school is gradually being replaced by a populist one centred on the comprehensive school. Despite the abandonment of the tripartite system—the grammar, technical and modern schools—the lessons of the past have not yet been learnt.

Educational institutions that perform different functions do not obtain parity of esteem in a society in which social status is largely a function of occupation.

In an attempt to combine timely concession to popular demand with the preservation of an élitist system, higher education has been divided into two sectors. Under what is known as the binary system, there are the theoretically autonomous universities and the publicly controlled Polytechnics and Colleges of Education. Yet the latter are subject to the vagaries and, at times, the prejudices of local authorities. Moreover, both are burdened with a legacy of the past. English society has traditionally held technological education in low esteem; the training colleges bear the social stigma of having once sought their students from the more trustworthy members of the working classes. The result of this arrangement has been that the hurdle of the 11 plus has been dismantled only to be re-erected further down the course at the 18 plus post.

In the light of these developments Lord Robbins asked the House of Lords: 'Why is it that we are now confronted with the prospects of an educational caste system more rigid and hierarchical than before?'[14] The answer is to be found in the way in which the recommendations made by the Committee on Higher Education, of which he was chairman, have been emasculated. The proposal that the Colleges of Education should be more closely integrated with the universities has not been implemented. Hence these institutions will continue to be burdened with the legacy of their nineteenth-century origins. One of their more critical ex-students, for instance, has recently written: 'It has always seemed to me very possible that perhaps the three-year college course was purpose designed to produce a semi-profession of docile, institution-respecting teachers.'[15] Lord Robbins has found in them, 'a sense of remoteness from the rest of the higher education system; a sense of gratitude if one takes an interest in them; a sense of student discipline often quite alien to what most academics would feel should be the atmosphere of an institution of higher education'.[16]

Similarly the Council for National Academic Awards was envisaged as a means of helping Regional Colleges to develop courses of degree standard so that they could move towards university status. Instead the introduction of the concept of the binary system has turned the C.N.A.A. into an instrument of divorce. In the long run, a policy of bifurcation seems doomed. If there is to be parity of esteem, the resources of the public sector must be built up so that they become comparable with those of the universities. We may well ask whether local authority control provides a suitable means by which this objective can be achieved. If it is achieved, can the maintenance of two separate administrative systems for what are theoretically comparable institutions of higher education be justified?

We are in danger of carrying into the last quarter of the twentieth century the socially stratified educational system of the nineteenth. As long as the binary system continues in its present form, the Secretary of State for Education and Science 'will not prevent most students with the necessary qualifications from first seeking entrance to the universities, traditional or techno-logical. If he wishes to force them into his sector, he will have to raise the requirements of the university sector and thus intensify the disparity of esteem which he professes...to wish to avoid'.[17]

The gradual abolition of a selective system of secondary education will give many previously under-privileged children a better chance in life. Along with many other factors, these new opportunities will increase the number who will regard higher education as a right. As with all the other social services, satisfy-ing such a demand is not a matter of whether we can afford it, it is a matter of reallocating resources. The binary system can be seen as a shortsighted administrative device to meet this demand 'on the cheap'. The children coming forward in the schools, many of whom will be the first in their families to have received a higher education, must not be fobbed off in this way. The ghosts of the nineteenth-century administrators who still haunt the corridors of power in Curzon Street must be finally laid to rest.

References

Chapter 1

1. TRIMMER, S., *The Sunday-School Catechist* (1788), p. 3.
2. BELL, A., *Elements of Tuition* (1813), Part II, p. 188.
3. HANSARD (Third Series), vol. 45, c. 5.
4. *Copy of Minutes and Regulations...reduced into the Form of a Code*, Articles 60 and 160, P.P. 1860, LIII, pp. 275–315.
5. *Report of the Committee*, P.P. 1861, XLIX, pp. x–xi.
6. *Papers Relating to the Reform of the Civil Service*, letter of Sir Stafford Northcote and Sir George Trevelyan to the Treasury, 10 April 1854, P.P. 1854–5, XX, p. 418 (420).
7. *Report on the Re-organization of the Civil Service*, P.P. 1854, XXVII, p. 9.
8. *Observer*, 15 September 1968.
9. Quoted by G. Sutherland in 'The Study of the History of Education', *History*, LIV (1969), pp. 49–59, from the collection of essays translated as *Education and Sociology* by Sherwood D. Fox (Glencoe, Illinois, 1956), p. 71.
10. STONE, L., 'Literacy and Education in England, 1640–1900', *Past and Present*, Number 42, February 1969, pp. 70 and 83.
11. THOMPSON, E. P., *The Making of the English Working Class* (Pelican Books, 1968), p. 12.
12. LANCASTER, J., *Outlines of a Plan for Educating Ten Thousand Poor Children* (1806), p. 41.
13. BELL, A., op. cit., Part II, pp. 191–2.
14. BINNS, H. B., *A Century of Education, 1808–1908* (1908), pp. 32–3; *Dictionary of National Biography*.
15. BELL, A., op. cit., Part II, pp. 302–3.
16. *H.M.I. the Reverend H. Moseley's Report*, P.P. 1846, XXXII, p. 368.

17. TRIMMER, S., *A Comparative View of the New Plan of Education promulgated by Mr Joseph Lancaster* (1805), pp. 8 and 20.

18. See the entry on Paulet (le chevalier) in *Biographie Universelle* (Paris and Leipzig).

19. MARSH, H., *The National Religion the Foundation of National Education* (1811), pp. 11–13, 19–20 and 41.

20. *Third Report from the Select Committee on the Education of the Lower Orders*, P.P. 1818, IV, pp. 56 and 58 (58 and 60).

21. ibid., W. Allen's evidence, p. 62 (64).

22. *Report from the Select Committee on the Education of the Lower Orders in the Metropolis*, P.P. 1816, IV, the Reverend T. T. Walmsley's evidence, p. 32.

23. BLOMFIELD, C. J., *Speech of the Lord Bishop of London on National Education on 28 May 1839 in Willis's Rooms* (1839), p. 10.

24. *Report from the Select Committee on the Education of the Poorer Classes*, P.P. 1838, VII, p. xi (167).

25. The condition of Berkhamsted Grammar School is described at greater length in the *Twenty-fifth Report of the Commissioners Appointed to Inquire Concerning Charities*, P.P. 1833, XVIII, pp. 289–303 and in the *Report from the Select Committee on Public Charities*, P.P. 1835, VII, pp. 631–760.

26. *Report from H.M.'s Commissioners for Inquiring into the Administration and Practical Operation of the Poor Laws*, P.P. 1834, XXVII, p. 205 (209).

27. HANSARD (Third Series), vol. 15, c. 760 and vol. 22, c. 850.

28. BRYANT, G. E. and BAKER, G. P. (eds.), *A Quaker Journal by William Lucas of Hitchin, 1804–61* (1934), vol. I, p. 163.

29. *The Times*, 19 November 1839.

30. HANSARD (Third Series), vol. 48, c. 593.

31. *Twenty-ninth Annual Report of the National Society* (1840), p. 1.

32. HANSARD (Third Series), vol. 48, c. 1235.

33. BLOMFIELD, C. J., op. cit., p. 6.

34. *Report from the Select Committee to Inquire into the Present State of Education of the People in England and Wales*, P.P. 1835, VII, Francis Place's evidence, Q. and A. 991.

35. HANSARD (Third Series), vol. 45, c. 288.

36. ibid., c. 309.
37. HOBSBAWM, E. J. and RUDÉ, G., *Captain Swing* (1969), p. 282.
38. HANSARD (Third Series), vol. 48, c. 298.
39. *Second Annual Report of the Poor Law Commissioners*, P.P. 1836, XXIX, A, Appendix B, 'Report of Dr J. P. Kay', pp. 149 and 163.
40. KAY-SHUTTLEWORTH, SIR J., *The Moral and Physical Condition of the Working Classes Employed in the Cotton Manufacture in Manchester* (1832), p. 72.
41. KAY-SHUTTLEWORTH, SIR J., 'Recent Measures for the Promotion of Education' (1839), reprinted in *Four Periods of Public Education* (1862), pp. 201–3 and 229–31.
42. *Report from the Select Committee on the Education of the Poorer Classes*, P.P. 1838, VII, Dr J. Kay's evidence, Q. and A. 121.
43. *Fourth Annual Report of the Poor Law Commissioners*, P.P. 1838, XXVIII, Appendix B (3), 'Report on the Training of Pauper Children', p. 146 (294).
44. *Twenty-eighth Annual Report of the National Society* (1839), p. 73 (footnote).
45. TUCKFIELD, H., *Letters to a Clergyman* (1840), pp. 15–16. Mrs Tuckfield was also the author of the previous quotation.
46. JONES, M. G., *The Charity School Movement in the Eighteenth Century* (Cambridge, 1938), p. 78.
47. *Quarterly Journal of Education*, I (1831), pp. 216–17.
48. GOLDSTROM, J. M., 'Richard Whateley and Political Economy in School Books, 1833–80', *Irish Historical Studies*, XV (1966). For a more detailed study, see the same author's Ph.D. thesis, 'The Changing Social Content of Elementary Education as reflected in school books in use in England, 1800–1870' (University of Birmingham, 1968).
49. *Report from the Select Committee to Inquire into the Present State of Education of the People in England and Wales*, P.P. 1835, VII, H. Dunn's evidence, Qs. and As. 83–4.
50. *Thirty-third Annual Report of the National Society* (1844), p. 1.
51. *Thirty-second Annual Report of the National Society* (1843), p. 2.

52. *Thirty-fourth Annual Report of the National Society* (1845), pp. 5 and 22.

53. BINNS, H. B., op. cit., pp. 81–2, 103 and 114; *Hansard* (Third Series), vol. 45, c. 279.

54. *Fifth Annual Report of the National Society* (1816), pp. 10–11.

55. *Twentieth Annual Report of the National Society* (1831), p. 13; *Twenty-first Annual Report of the National Society* (1832), p. 10.

56. *Report from the Select Committee on the State of Education*, P.P. 1834, IX, H. Dunn's evidence, Qs. and As. 344–8.

57. Minute Book of the General Committee of the National Society, vol. III, folio 283, 23 April 1834; folio 342, 4 March 1835; folios 422 and 430, 13 April 1836; folio 448, 2 November 1836. Folio 506, 5 July 1837, states that the postal concession was renewed on the accession of Queen Victoria.

58. *Twenty-second Annual Report of the National Society* (1833), p. 12.

59. *Treasury Minute*, 30 August 1833, P.P. 1839, XLII, p. 527.

60. Minute Book of…the National Society, vol. III, folio 305, 11 July 1834.

61. ibid., vol. IV, folio 72, 7 November 1838.

62. WIGRAM, J. C., *Practical Hints on the Formation and Management of Sunday Schools* (1833), p. 43.

63. CRAIK, H., *The State in its Relation to Education* (1884), p. 15.

64. Minute Book of…the National Society, vol. IV, folio 55, 18 July 1838.

65. *Report from the Select Committee on the Education of the Poorer Classes*, P.P. 1838, VII, the Reverend J. C. Wigram's evidence, Qs. and As. 725–33.

66. HANSARD (Third Series), vol. 45, c. 275.

67. SINCLAIR, J. (ed.), *Correspondence of the National Society with the Lords of the Treasury and with the Committee of Council on Education* (1839), pp. 5–17 (*passim*).

68. *Report from the Select Committee on the Education of the Poorer Classes*, P.P. 1838, VII, p. x (166).

69. HANSARD (Third Series), vol. 45, c. 293–7.

70. *Papers on Education*, P.P. 1839, XLI, p. 255.

71. *Copy of an Order in Council appointing a Committee of Council*, P.P. 1839, XLI, p. 265.

72. *Minute of 11 April 1839*, P.P. 1839, XLI, p. 259.

73. *Minute of 3 June 1839*, P.P. 1839, XLI, p. 263.

74. Minute Book of...the National Society, vol. IV, folios 175–6, 12 July 1839.

75. ibid., folios 192–3, 16 October 1839.

76. ibid., folios 202–9, 22 October 1839.

77. SINCLAIR, J. (ed.), op. cit., pp. 25–6.

78. Minute Book of...the National Society, vol. IV, folio 211, 30 October 1839; folio 252, 29 April 1840; folio 253, 20 May 1840.

79. ibid., folios 264–5, 22 June 1840.

80. *Extract from the Minutes of the Committee of Council on Education*, 15 July 1840, P.P. 1840, XL, pp. 386–7.

81. *Instructions to Inspectors*, 8 August 1840, P.P. 1841, XX, pp. 1–5 (99–104).

Chapter 2

1. *Report of the Royal Commission on the State of Popular Education in England and Wales (Newcastle Report)*, P.P. 1861, XXI, A, p. 230.

2. ibid., p. 241.

3. *H.M.I. M. Arnold's Report*, P.P. 1854–5, XLII, p. 620.

4. GRIER, R. M., *William Allen* (1889), pp. 46, 65 and 80.

5. EDMONDS, E. L. and O. P., *I Was There, the Memoirs of H. S. Tremenheere* (Eton, Windsor, 1965), pp. 127–8.

6. *The Times*, 11 December 1839.

7. ibid., 7 November 1839.

8. SINCLAIR, J. (ed.), *Correspondence of the National Society etc.*, p. 13.

9. Minute Book of the Committee of the Privy Council on Education, 1839–41, P.R.O., Ed. 9/1, folio 46, 29 November 1839.

10. TAYLOR, SIR H., *The Statesman* (Cambridge, 1927 edn.), pp. 127–8.

11. Minute Book of the Committee etc., folio 72, letter of 18 December 1839.

12. ibid., folio 314, 5 February 1841.

13. *Report from the Select Committee on Miscellaneous Expenditure*, P.P. 1847–8, XVIII, A, p. xxv (25).

14. *Minute of 25 July 1850*, P.P. 1851, XLIV, p. xi (11).

15. *Report from the Committee of Inquiry: Privy Council Office*, P.P. 1854, XXVII, p. 237 (269).

16. *Minute of 19 May 1863*, P.P. 1864, XLV, pp. ix–xi (9–11).

17. *Return of the Number, Names, and Salaries of the Inspectors*, P.P. 1875, XLII, pp. 28–33 (212–17).

18. *Instructions to Inspectors*, 8 August 1840, P.P. 1841, XX, p. 1 (99).

19. HANSARD (Third Series), vol. 189, c. 356.

20. DENISON, G. A., *Church Education. The present state of the Management Clause Question* (1849), Appendix B; see also his obituary notice, *The Times*, 23 March 1896.

21. *Newcastle Report*, P.P. 1861, XXI, F, the Reverend W. J. Unwin's evidence, Q. and A. 2137.

22. ibid., Qs. and As. 2142 and 2304.

23. *H.M.I. the Reverend J. J. Blandford's Report*, P.P. 1857, (session II), XXXIII, p. 369 (377).

24. *Second Report from the Select Committee on the Constitution of the Committee of Council on Education* (cited hereafter as first and second Pakington Reports), P.P. 1866, VII, the Reverend J. P. Norris's evidence, Q. and A. 1924.

25. CHESTER, H., *Hints on the Building and Management of Schools* (1860), pp. 4–5.

26. *First Pakington Report*, P.P. 1865, VI, Lowe's evidence, Qs. and As. 284–8, 812.

27. Minute Book of the Sub-Committee of the Hertfordshire Board of Education, Hockerill College, Bishop's Stortford, Herts.

28. *Educational Times*, IX (1850), pp. 189–90.

29. *The Correspondence between the National Society and the Committee of the Privy Council on Education* is printed in P.P. 1849, XLII, pp. 87–130.

30. *Revised Code*, Article 12, P.P. 1871, LV, p. 5 (307).

31. HANSARD (Third Series), vol. 4, c. 978.

32. *The Correspondence between the British and Foreign School Society and the Department* is printed in P.P. 1843, XL, pp. 593–669.

33. *H. S. Tremenheere's Report on South Wales*, P.P. 1840, XL, pp. 208–18 (614–24).

34. ibid., p. 212 (618).

35. *H. S. Tremenheere's Report on Norfolk etc.* can be found at P.P. 1842, XXXIII, pp. 192–213 (306–27).

36. MACDONAGH, O., *A Pattern of Government Growth* (1961), p. 322.

37. *H.M.I. the Reverend J. Allen's Report*, P.P. 1841, XX, p. 52 (150).

38. *Allen's Report*, P.P. 1842, XXXIII, p. 265 (379).

39. *Allen's Report*, P.P. 1846, XXXII, pp. 1 and 8 (211 and 218).

40. *H.M.I. the Reverend F. Watkins's Report*, P.P. 1845, XXXV, p. 117 (455).

41. *Minute of 22 November 1843*, P.P. 1844, XXXVIII, p. 219.

42. *Minute of 25 August 1846*, P.P. 1847, XLV, p. 1 (11).

43. *Circular Letter to H.M.I.s*, 26 July 1849, P.P. 1850, XLIII, pp. xxx–xxxii (270–2).

44. *Watkins's Report*, P.P. 1851, XLIV, p. 119 (523).

45. *H.M.I. the Reverend E. D. Tinling's Report*, P.P. 1851, XLIV, p. 197 (601).

46. *H.M.I. J. Fletcher's Report*, P.P. 1851, XLIV, p. 553 (957).

47. *H.M.I. the Reverend H. W. Bellairs's Report*, P.P. 1851, XLIV, p. 59 (463).

48. *Letter of Instructions*, 15 October 1850, P.P. 1851, XLIV, pp. xiv–xvi.

49. *Newcastle Report*, P.P. 1861, XXI, F, T. W. M. Marshall's evidence, Qs. and As. 1274–6.

50. *Report of the Committee of Inquiry: Privy Council Office*, P.P. 1854, XXVII, p. 238 (270).

51. *Report of the Committee*, P.P. 1861, XLIX, Appendix I, p. 3 (31).

52. *First Pakington Report*, P.P. 1865, VI (Lowe's evidence), Q. and A. 634.

53. *Correspondence Relating to the Dismissal of Mr Morell*, P.P. 1864, XLIV, p. 15 (543).

54. ibid., Morell's letter to Lingen, February 1863, p. 33 (561).

55. MORELL, J. R., *The Case of Mr Morell* (Privately printed, 1864). British Museum catalogue number B.M. 1419 k46 (6).

56. ibid., p. 10.
57. *Correspondence Relating to...Mr Morell*, P.P. 1864, XLIV, Lingen's letter to Morell, 13 February 1864, p. 35 (563).
58. Copies of Letters selected from old Letter Books, 1847–58. Typescript copies in the library of the Department of Education and Science and in the Public Record Office at Ed. 9/12, folio 296, 31 January 1853.
59. ibid., folio 308, 17 September 1853.
60. *Newcastle Report*, P.P. 1861, XXI, A, p. 230.
61. ibid., P.P. 1861, XXI, F, Lingen's evidence, Qs. and As. 426–7.
62. ibid., P.P. 1861, XXI, F, the Reverend F. C. Cook's evidence, Q. and A. 859.
63. ibid., P.P. 1861, XXI, A, pp. 230–1.
64. ROBERTS, D., *The Victorian Foundations of the British Welfare State* (New Haven, 1960) pp. 119–20.
65. *Return of...Inspectors etc.*, P.P. 1875, XLII, pp. 185 *et seq.*
66. *Newcastle Report*, P.P. 1861, XXI, D, M. Arnold's Report on Popular Education in France, Holland, and the French Cantons of Switzerland, p. 72.
67. ibid., P.P. 1861, XXI, F, Cook's evidence, Q. and A. 947.
68. *The Times*, 13 September 1854.
69. Copies of Letters etc., P.R.O., Ed, 9/12, folio 306, 30 May 1853.
70. *H.M.I. the Reverend W. H. Brookfield's Report*, P.P. 1854–5, XLII, p. 502.
71. *Brookfield's Report*, P.P. 1857–8, XLV, p. 395.
72. *Newcastle Report*, P.P. 1861, XXI, A, p. 236.
73. ibid., p. 237.
74. ibid.
75. *Report of the Committee*, P.P. 1865, XLII, p. 9 (103).
76. *Watkins's Report*, P.P. 1854–5, XLII, p. 445.
77. *Newcastle Report*, P.P. 1861, XXI, A, p. 68.
78. *Reports of the Reverends E. P. Arnold and Watkins*, P.P. 1870, XXII, pp. 53 and 258.
79. *Instructions to Inspectors*, 8 May 1871, P.P. 1871, XXII, p. cxxxvii.
80. *H.M.I. the Reverend D. J. Stewart's Report*, P.P. 1871, XXII, pp. 206–7.

81. *First Pakington Report*, P.P. 1865, VI, C. B. Adderley's evidence, Q. and A. 968; Lowe's evidence, Q. and A. 1923.
82. SNEYD-KYNNERSLEY, E. M., *H.M.I.* (1908), pp. 72 and 151.
83. *First Pakington Report*, P.P. 1865, VI, E. Carleton Tufnell's evidence, Q .and A. 1159; the Reverend W. J. Kennedy's evidence, Qs. and As. 2520–2; J. D. Morell's evidence, 3084–5.
84. ARMYTAGE, W. H. G., 'A. J. Mundella as Vice-President of the Privy Council, and the Schools Question, 1880–5', *English Historical Review*, LXIII (1948).

Chapter 3

1. *Second Report from the Select Committee on the Education of the Lower Orders*, P.P. 1818, IV, the Reverend T. T. Walmsley's written evidence, p. 18.
2. *Moseley's Report*, P.P. 1847, XLV, p. 94 (104).
3. *Cook's Report*, P.P. 1857–8, XLV, p. 243.
4. *Report of the Committee*, P.P. 1863, XLVII, p. 1 (50).
5. *Minute of 22 November 1843*, P.P. 1844, XXXVIII, p. 219.
6. *Journal of Education*, II (1844), p. 337.
7. *Minutes of 2 April 1853; 14 July 1855; 4 May 1859; 21 January 1860*. The terms of the grants are summarized in P.P. 1898, XXIV, Special Reports on Education, pp. 503 *et seq.*; in addition P.P. 1854–5, XLI, pp. 1–128 (191–353), contains all the minutes published between 1839 and 1855. This list is continued in P.P. 1857–8, XLVI, pp. 1–14 (151–64), in which the then extant minutes are summarized. The 1860 Code is in P.P. 1860, LIII, pp. 273 *et seq.*
8. *Fourth Annual Report of the Poor Law Commissioners*, P.P. 1838, XXVIII, Appendix B (3), 'Report on the Training of Pauper Children', pp. 140–1 (288–9).
9. For the dispute over Kempthorne's fee, see Minute Book of the Committee of the Privy Council on Education, 1839–41, P.R.O., Ed. 9/1, folio 281, 9 November 1840.
   For the plans of schools, see *Minutes of the Committee*, P.P. 1840, XL, pp. 218 (624) *et seq.*
10. *Newcastle Report*, P.P. 1861, XXI, F, Chester's evidence, Qs. and As. 670–2.

11. CHESTER, H., *Hints on the Building and Management of Schools* (1860), pp. 13–14.
12. *Newcastle Report*, P.P. 1861, XXI, F, Chester's evidence, Q. and A. 676.
13. ibid., Lingen's evidence, Q. and A. 129.
14. *Circular Letter to H.M.I.s*, 14 January 1854; *Letter from the Board of Health*, 8 February 1854, P.P. 1854, LI, pp. 51–3.
15. Minute Book of the Secretary of the Committee of the Privy Council on Education, September 1848–October 1871, P.R.O., Ed. 9/4, folio 46, 13 May 1856.
16. *Newcastle Report*, P.P. 1861, XXI, F, Chester's evidence, Q. and A. 685.
17. *H.M.I. the Reverend C. J. Robinson's Report*, P.P. 1866, XXVII, p. 167 (349).
18. *Stewart's Report*, P.P. 1857 (session II), XXXIII, pp. 429–30 (437–8).
19. *Newcastle Report*, P.P. 1861, XXI, B, A. F. Foster's Report, p. 364.
20. *Watkins's Report*, P.P. 1846, XXXII, p. 283 (493).
21. *Moseley's Report*, P.P. 1850, XLIII, p. 30 (660).
22. *H.M.I. the Reverend M. Mitchell's Report*, P.P. 1857 (session II), p. 343 (351).
23. *H.M.I. the Reverend E. P. Arnold's Report*, P.P. 1864, XLV, p. 19 (99).
24. *The Times*, 19 June 1860.
25. *Educational Times*, II (1849), p. 191.
26. *Report of the Inter-Departmental Committee on Physical Deterioration*, P.P. 1904, XXXII, the Hon. Mrs Lyttleton's evidence, Q. and A. 5456.
27. *Report of the Inter-Departmental Committee on Medical Inspection and Feeding of Children attending Public Elementary Schools*, P.P. 1906, XLVII, Dr J. Kerr's written evidence, p. 237 (401).
28. CHESTER, H., *Hints etc.*, pp. 20–9.
29. *School and the Teacher*, II (1855), pp. 18 and 74; *Educational Guardian*, I (1859), pp. 29 and 53.
30. *Circular Letters to H.M.I.s*, 5 May 1859, P.P. 1859, XXI, A, p. xvii.
31. CHESTER, H., *Hints etc.*, p. 22.

32. Minute Book of the Secretary etc., P.R.O., Ed. 9/4, folio 100, May 1864.

33. *Moseley's Report*, P.P. 1846, XXXII, p. 150 (360).

34. WIGRAM, J. C., *Elementary Arithmetic* (1832), p. 51.

35. COMMISSIONERS OF NATIONAL EDUCATION IN IRELAND, *Second Reading Book for the Use in Schools* (Dublin, 1865), p. 62.

36. Copies of Letters etc., P.R.O., Ed. 9/12, folio 11, 28 July 1847.

37. *Minute of 18 December 1847*; *Schedule of Lesson Books*, P.P. 1847–8, L, pp. x–xx.

38. *Minutes of the Committee*, P.P. 1851, XLIV, p. lxxiv; *Minute of 21 February 1853*.

39. TILLEARD, J., *On Elementary School Books* (1860), p. 2.

40. *Newcastle Report*, P.P. 1861, XXI, A, pp. 350–1.

41. ibid., P.P. 1861, XXI, B, A. F. Foster's Report, p. 339.

42. For these and other examples, see TILLEARD, J., op. cit.; *English Journal of Education*, VIII (1854), pp. 365–72 and IX (1855), pp. 45–53.

43. DAWES, R., *Remarks Occasioned by the Present Crusade against the Educational Plans of the Committee of Council on Education* (1850), pp. 9 and 37.

44. TILLEARD, J., op. cit., p. 4.

45. *Newcastle Report*, P.P. 1861, XXI, F, Lingen's evidence, Q. and A. 134.

46. *Stewart's Report*, P.P. 1857 (session II), XXXIII, p. 446 (454).

47. *Minute of 29 April 1854*.

48. HANSARD (Third Series), vol. 165, c. 203.

49. *Newcastle Report*, P.P. 1861, XXI, F, Lingen's evidence, Q. and A. 425.

50. *Minute of 17 July 1857*.

51. *School and Teacher*, IV (1857), pp. 103 and 122.

52. *Minute of 26 January 1856*; *Report of the Committee*, P.P. 1861, XLIX, p. xxiv.

Chapter 4

1. *Cook's Report*, P.P. 1847–8, L, p. 26 (194).

2. *Cook's Report*, P.P. 1846, XXXII, p. 63 (273).

3. *English Journal of Education*, XV (1861), p. 238.

4. *Extract from the Minutes of the British and Foreign School Society*, 9 August 1839, P.P. 1843, XL, p. 1 (593).

5. *Fourth Annual Report of the Poor Law Commissioners*, P.P. 1838, XXVIII, Appendix B (3), 'Report on the Training of Pauper Children', p. 152 (300).

6. SMITH, F., *The Life and Work of Sir James Kay-Shuttleworth* (1923), pp. 35–121.

7. *Twenty-seventh Annual Report of the National Society* (1838), p. 23.

8. ibid., p. 24.

9. *Twenty-eighth Annual Report of the National Society* (1839), p. 43.

10. *Report from the Select Committee on the State of Education*, P.P. 1834, IX, the Reverend J. C. Wigram's evidence, Q. and A. 784.

11. Anon, 'Schools for the Industrious Classes', *Central Society of Education Papers* (1838), pp. 359–60.

12. *Report from the Select Committee appointed to Inquire into the State of Education of the People in England and Wales*, P.P. 1835, VII, Francis Place's evidence, Q. and A. 836.

13. BURGESS, H. J., *Enterprise in Education* (1958), pp. 49–50.

14. *Fourth Annual Report of the National Society* (1815), p. 10. *Fifth Annual Report of the National Society* (1816), p. 21.

15. *Fourth Annual Report of the National Society* (1815), p. 11. *Fifth Annual Report of the National Society* (1816), pp. 12–13.

16. *J. D. Morell's Report*, P.P. 1859, XXI, A, p. 146.

17. BURGESS, H. J., op. cit., p. 95.

18. *Allen's Report*, P.P. 1846, XXXII, p. 62 (272).

19. *Reports of the British and Foreign School Society*, Thirty-sixth (1841), pp. 7–8; Thirty-ninth (1844), p. 8; Fortieth (1845), p. 4; Forty-first (1846), p. 3.

20. *Thirty-third Annual Report of the National Society* (1844), p. 21.

21. *Thirty-fourth Annual Report of the National Society* (1845), p. 20.

22. ibid., p. 22.

23. *Thirty-third Annual Report of the National Society* (1844), p. 4.

Thirty-fourth Annual Report of the National Society (1845), p. 2.

24. *Report of the Departmental Committee on the Pupil-Teacher System*, P.P. 1898, XXVI, p. 2 (344).

25. SMITH, F., op. cit., p. 170.

26. ibid.

27. *Newcastle Report*, P.P. 1861, XXI, F, Kay-Shuttleworth's evidence, Qs. and As. 2345 and 2347.

28. *Thirty-sixth Annual Report of the National Society* (1847), pp. 1, 5 and 44.

29. For convenient location of the Departmental minutes, see reference 7, Chapter 3.

30. *Circular Letter to H.M.I.s*, 25 November 1848, P.P. 1849, XLII, pp. 108-9 (194-5).

31. *Minute of 4 May 1859.*

32. *Kay-Shuttleworth's Letter to the British Schoolmasters' Association*, 11 March 1847, P.P. 1847, XLV, p. 10 (29).

33. *Thirty-sixth Annual Report of the National Society* (1847), p. 38.

34. *Minute of 10 December 1851.*

35. *Minute of 25 July 1850.*

36. *Minute of 20 August 1853.*

37. *Moseley's Report*, P.P. 1854, LI, pp. 421 and 424.

38. *Minute of 12 May 1852.*

39. *Minute of 23 July 1852.*

40. *Newcastle Report*, P.P. 1861, XXI, A, p. 638.

41. *Minute of 20 August 1853.*

42. *Minute of 6 August 1851; Minute of 10 December 1851.*

43. *Minute of 20 August 1853.*

44. *Minutes of 28 June 1854 and 14 July 1855.*

45. *Minute of 29 April 1854.*

46. *Newcastle Report*, P.P. 1861, XXI, A, p. 165.

47. *Minute of 2 June 1856.*

48. *Newcastle Report*, P.P. 1861, XXI, F, Lingen's evidence, Q. and A. 270.

49. *Moseley's Letter to the Lord President of the Council*, 2 May 1854, P.P. 1854-5, XLII, p. 15.

50. *Circular Letter from the Education Department*, 22 January 1857, P.P. 1857 (session II), XXXIII, p. 7 (15).

51. *Newcastle Report*, P.P. 1861, XXI, A, p. 121.

52. *H.M.I. the Reverend B. J. Cowie's Report*, P.P. 1863, XLVII, p. 204 (262).

53. *Newcastle Report*, P.P. 1861, XXI, A, pp. 143–4.

54. *Report of the Schools' Inquiry Commission (Taunton Report)*, P.P. 1867–8, XXVIII, A, p. 613.

55. *Minute of 26 July 1858*.

56. *Cowie's Report*, P.P. 1862, XLII, p. 275 (331).

57. *Circular Letter to Principals of Training Colleges etc.*, 15 November 1854, P.P. 1854–5, XLII, p. 32; *Minute of 24 April 1851*.

58. *Minute of 20 August 1853*.

59. *Minute of 1 March 1855*.

60. *Circular Letter to Principals of Training Colleges etc.*, P.P. 1856, XLVII, p. 33 (41).

61. *Minute of 4 May 1859*.

62. *Minute of 21 January 1860*.

63. *Report of the Committee*, P.P. 1859, XXI, A, pp. xxx–xxxiii.

64. *Newcastle Report*, P.P. 1861, XXI, A, p. 165.

65. *Bellairs's Report*, P.P. 1860, LIV, p. 28.

66. *H.M.I. the Reverend J. P. Norris's Report*, P.P. 1863, XLVII, pp. 51–2 (109–10).

67. *Kennedy's Report*, P.P. 1862, XLII, p. 69.

68. *Watkins's Report*, P.P. 1864, XLV, p. 165 (245).

69. *Newcastle Report*, P.P. 1861, XXI, A, p. 165.

70. ibid., pp. 671 and 676.

71. ibid., p. 638.

72. *Taunton Report*, P.P. 1867–8, XXVIII, C, J. Robson's evidence, Qs. and As. 8, 13, 27, 49 and 50.

73. ANON., *Fifty Years of Progress in Education, A Review of the Work of the College of Preceptors, 1846–96* (1896), pp. 4–9.

74. *Educational Times*, II (1850), p. 87.

75. *English Journal of Education*, XV (1861), p. 239.

Chapter 5

1. GRIER, W., *William Allen* (1889), letter from Allen to Shuttleworth, 15 September 1843, p. 114.

2. *H.M.I. the Reverend B. M. Cowie's Report*, P.P. 1863, XLVII, p. 231 (289).

3. *Moseley's Report*, P.P. 1851, XLIV, p. 35 (279).

4. Quoted by Lord John Russell, HANSARD (Third Series), vol. 45, c. 131.

5. HANSARD (Third Series), vol. 24, c. 131.

6. *Second Annual Report of the Poor Law Commissioners*, P.P. 1836, XXIX, A, 'Report on the Administration, under the Poor Law Amendment Act, in Suffolk and Norfolk', p. 185.

7. ibid., p. 148.

8. *Fourth Annual Report of the Poor Law Commissioners*, P.P. 1838, XXVIII, Appendix B (3), 'Report on the Training of Pauper Children', p. 140.

9. ibid., p. 141.

10. Quoted by SMITH, F., op. cit., p. 87.

11. HANSARD (Third Series), vol. 24, c. 127.

12. ibid., c. 130.

13. The *Return* is printed at P.P. 1857–8, XLVI, pp. 1–5 (261–5).

14. *Copy of Minutes and Regulations...reduced into the Form of a Code*, P.P. 1860, LIII, p. 5 (279).

15. *Article 4 of the Revised Code*, P.P. 1862, XLI, p. 5 (119).

16. *Report of the Committee*, P.P. 1865, XLII, pp. xxi–xxii (footnote).

17. *Report from the Select Committee on Arts and Manufactures*, P.P. 1835, V, p. iii (377).

18. TYLECOTE, M., *The Mechanics' Institutes of Lancashire and Yorkshire before 1851* (Manchester, 1957), Chapters II and VIII, *passim*.

19. *Taunton Report*, P.P. 1867–8, XXVIII, A, pp. 15–16.

20. *Report from the Select Committee on the State of Education*, P.P. 1834, IX,

  Qs. and As. 1075–6 J. T. Crossley, a master in a British and Foreign School.

      1318–9 W. F. Lloyd, secretary of the Sunday School Union.

      1596–8 H. Althans, secretary of the East London Auxiliary Sunday School Union.

      2547 Bishop of London.

21. *Moseley's Report*, P.P. 1851, XLIV, p. 38 (282).
22. *Cook's Report*, P.P. 1847–8, L, p. 31.
23. *Allen's Report*, P.P. 1846, XXXII, pp. 8–61 (218–71).
24. KAY-SHUTTLEWORTH, SIR J. and TUFNELL, E. CARLETON, 'Report on the Training School at Battersea', *Reports on the Training of Pauper Children* (1841), p. 248.
25. KAY-SHUTTLEWORTH, SIR J., *Four Periods of Public Education* (1862), p. 399.
26. *Newcastle Report*, P.P. 1861, XXI, A, pp. 110–11.
27. See reference 24.
28. KAY-SHUTTLEWORTH, SIR J. and TUFNELL, E. CARLETON, op. cit., p. 214.
29. *Allen's Report*, P.P. 1843, XL, p. 83 (301).
30. ibid.
31. *Newcastle Report*, P.P. 1861, XXI, D, the Reverend H. G. Robinson's statement, p. 408.
32. Quoted by MARSH, P. T., *The Victorian Church in Decline* (1969), p. 67 from DENISON, G. A., *The Tempter's Cup* (Oxford and London, 1875), p. 50.
33. The Timetable is printed in *Allen's Report*, P.P. 1843, XL, pp. 78–9 (296–7).
34. *Cowie's Report*, P.P. 1863, XLVII, p. 205 (263).
35. ROBINS, S., *The Church Schoolmaster* (1850), p. 10.
36. *Cook's Report*, P.P. 1846, XXXII, p. 99 (309).
37. *Circular Letter to H.M.I.s*, 12 March 1849, P.P. 1849, XLII, pp. 110–11 (196–7).
38. *Minute of 21 December 1846*.
39. *Cook's Report*, P.P. 1847–8, L, pp. 31–2 (199–200).
40. ibid., p. 31 (199).
41. *Moseley's Report*, P.P. 1850, XLIII, p. 21 (651).
42. *Mitchell's Report*, P.P. 1850, XLIII, p. 316 (946).
43. *Report of the Committee*, P.P. 1867, XXII, p. xix (19).
44. *Circular Letter*, 18 February 1851, P.P. 1851, XLIV, p. lxxxix.
45. THOMPSON, F. M. L., *English Landed Society in the Nineteenth Century* (1963), p. 194.
46. *Return of Wages published between 1830 and 1886*, P.P. 1887, LXXXIX, *passim*.
47. *Report of the Committee*, P.P. 1870, p. lxxxii.
48. *Report of the Committee*, P.P. 1873, XXIV, p. ccv.

49. *Cook's Report*, P.P. 1854, XLII, pp. 13–14.

50. *Pupil-Teacher*, II (1859), pp. 81–3.

51. *Circular Letter Addressed to Schoolmasters*, undated, P.P. 1847–8, L, p. lxii (112).

52. *Watkins's Report*, P.P. 1852–3, LXXX, pp. 147 and 150.

53. *Watkins's Report*, P.P. 1851, XLIV, p. 124.

54. *Moseley's Report*, P.P. 1850, XLIII, p. 23 (653).

55. *Newcastle Report*, P.P. 1861, XXI, A, p. 638.

56. *Moseley's Report*, P.P. 1851, XLIV, p. 17 (421).

57. *H.M.I. the Reverend W. H. Brookfield's Report*, P.P. 1851, XLIV, p. 380 (784).

58. *Kennedy's Report*, P.P. 1851, XLIV, p. 440 (848).

59. *Tinling's Report*, P.P. 1852–3, LXXX, p. 237.

60. Copies of Letters etc., P.R.O., Ed. 9/12, folio 15, 3 August 1847; folio 73, 10 April 1848; folio 299, 2 February 1853.

61. ibid., folio 180, 7 August 1849.

62. Minute Book of the Secretary etc., P.R.O., Ed. 9/4, folio 9, 11 June 1851.

63. *Minute of 20 August 1853*. The first examinations were held in 1854 (para. 13).

64. *Minutes of the Committee*, P.P. 1854–5, XLII, p. 13.

65. *Circular Letter to H.M.I.s*, 8 March 1854, P.P. 1854, XLII, p. 84.

66. Minute Book of the Secretary etc., P.R.O., Ed. 9/4, folio 11, 9 July 1851.

67. ibid., folio 17, 13 February 1852.

68. ibid., folio 17, 21 February 1852.

69. ibid., folio 17, 23 February 1852.

70. ibid., folio 57, 24 June 1858.

71. ibid., folio 59, 4 December 1858.

72. BALL, N., *Her Majesty's Inspectorate, 1839–49* (Edinburgh and London), p. 74.

73. WOOD, SIR H. T., *A History of the Royal Society of Arts* (1913), pp. 426–8.

74. ACLAND, SIR T. D., *Some Account of the Origin and Objects of the New Oxford Examinations* (1858), p. 112.

75. *Watkins's Report*, P.P. 1850, XLIII, p. 146 (776).

76. *Mitchell's Report*, P.P. 1850, XLIII, p. 322 (952).

77. Copies of Letters etc., P.R.O., Ed. 9/12, folio 176, 19 July 1849.

78. *Circular Letter to H.M.I.s*, December 1853, P.P. 1854, LI, p. 59.

79. Copies of Letters etc., P.R.O., Ed. 9/12, folio 327, 6 December 1854.

80. *Letter of Instructions to H.M.I.s*, 5 December 1856, P.P. 1857 (session II), XXXIII, p. 38 (46).

81. The correspondence is printed at P.P. 1852, XXXIX, pp. 119–24 (455–60).

82. *School and the Teacher*, VI (1859), pp. 166–7.

83. Copies of Letters etc., P.R.O., Ed. 9/12, folio 185, 18 August 1849.

84. *Circular Letter to H.M.I.s*, 16 December 1852, P.P. 1852–3, LXXIX, p. 65.

85. *National Society Monthly Paper* (1850), p. 240.

86. Copies of Letters etc., P.R.O., Ed. 9/12, folio 371, 11 August 1848.

87. *Newcastle Report*, P.P. 1861, XXI, A, pp. 103–4.

88. *Circular Letter to H.M.I.s*, 15 June 1855, P.P. 1856, XLVII, p. 15.

89. *Circular Letter to H.M.I.s*, 16 October 1852, P.P. 1852–3, LXXIX, p. 65.

90. *Stewart's Report*, P.P. 1857 (session II), XXXIII, p. 452 (461).

91. *Cook's Reports*, P.P. 1852, XL, p. 42 (672); P.P. 1856, XLVII, pp. 222–3 (230–1). For the trials and tribulations of a pupil-teacher after the turn of the century, see MACKERNESS, E. D. (ed.), *Journals of George Sturt*, 2 vols (Cambridge, 1967), vol. I, pp. 338; 354–7 and 359.

92. *Circular Letter to H.M.I.s*, 14 March 1857, P.P. 1857 (session II), p. 35 (43).

93. *National Society Monthly Paper* (1850), p. 239.

94. *Report of Her Majesty's Commissioners appointed to inquire into the Revenues and Management of certain Colleges and Schools, and the Studies pursued and Instruction given therein (Clarendon Report)*, P.P. 1864, XX, pp. 23–4 (33–4).

95. *Second Report of Her Majesty's Civil Service Commissioners*, P.P. 1857 (session II), III, pp. iii–vi, 16 (75–8, 108).

96. ibid., p. ix (81).

97. BURNS, W. L., *The Age of Equipoise* (1963), pp. 172–3.

98. *Newcastle Report*, P.P. 1861, XXI, A, p. 107.

99. *Cook's Report*, P.P. 1845, XXXV, p. 87 (425).

100. *Watkins's Report*, P.P. 1854, LII, p. 160.

101. *Stewart's Report*, P.P. 1854, LII, p. 581.

102. *Blandford's Report*, P.P. 1854, LII, p. 352.

103. *Kennedy's Report*, P.P. 1854, LII, p. 352.

104. *Stewart's Report*, P.P. 1854–5, XLII, p. 574.

105. *Watkins's Report*, P.P. 1857–8, XLV, p. 293.

106. *Watkins's Report*, P.P. 1857 (session II), XXXIII, p. 296 (304).

107. *Stewart's Report*, P.P. 1854–5, XLII, p. 570.

108. *Watkins's Report*, P.P. 1854–5, XLII, p. 436.
  Further information on the educational standards required of railway clerks can be found in KINGSFORD, P. W., 'Railway Labour, 1830–70', Ph.D. thesis (University of London, 1951).

109. *Stewart's Report*, P.P. 1857 (session II), XXXIII, p. 432 (440).

110. *Newcastle Report*, P.P. 1861, XXI, D, the Reverend H. G. Robinson's statement, p. 396.

111. *Newcastle Report*, P.P. 1861, XXI, A, p. 162.

112. ibid., p. 129.

113. *Newcastle Report*, P.P. 1861, XXI, D, Robinson's statement, p. 396.

114. ibid., p. 404.

115. ibid., p. 413.

116. RUNCIMAN, J., *Schools and Scholars* (1887), p. 154.

117. ibid., p. 137.

118. ibid., p. 141.

119. *Newcastle Report*, P.P. 1861, XXI, A, p. 135.

120. ibid., p. 136.

121. *Newcastle Report*, P.P. 1861, XXI, D, Robinson's statement, pp. 404–5.

122. ibid., p. 408.

123. *Newcastle Report*, P.P. 1861, XXI, F, Cook's evidence, Q. and A. 905.

124. *Newcastle Report*, P.P. 1861, XXI, A, p. 163.

125. BLAKE, R., *Disraeli* (1966), p. 555.

126. HANSARD (Third Series), vol. 164, c. 723–4.

127. *Pupil-Teacher*, IV (1861), p. 169.

128. ibid., pp. 192–3.
129. HANSARD (Third Series), vol. 165, c. 211.
130. *Newcastle Report*, P.P. 1861, XXI, B, Foster's Report, p. 362.
131. PUDNEY, T. S., *The Thomas Cook Story* (1953), p. 53–7; PIMLOTT, J. A. R., *The Englishman's Holiday* (1947), pp. 192–3.
132. WOOD, E. M., *The Polytechnic and Quintin Hogg* (1932), pp. 152–3.
133. *Watkins's Report*, P.P. 1854, LII, p. 158.
134. *Newcastle Report*, P.P. 1861, XXI, B, the Reverend J. Fraser's Report, p. 95.
135. *Newcastle Report*, P.P. 1861, XXI, A, p. 161.
136. *Taunton Report*, P.P. 1867–8, XXVIII, A, pp. 234–5.
137. ibid., pp. 15–16.
138. HANSARD (Third Series), vol. 91, c. 1058.
139. Quoted in *Newcastle Report*, P.P. 1861, XXI, A, p. 117 from his celebrated speech to the House of Commons on 19 April 1847 printed in HANSARD (Third Series), vol. 91, c. 1006–26. The passage occurs in c. 1016–17.
140. *Newcastle Report*, P.P. 1861, XXI, A, p. 133.
141. ibid., p. 155.
142. TROPP, A., *The School Teachers* (1957), pp. 103–10.
143. *Newcastle Report*, P.P. 1861, XXI, A, p. 160.
144. *Final Report of the Royal Commission appointed to Inquire into the Elementary Education Acts (England and Wales) (Cross Report)*, P.P. 1888, XXXV, p. 72.

Chapter 6

1. CLOUGH, A. H., *Dipsychus*, II, ii.
2. MOZLEY, J. R., *In Memoriam F. C. Hodgson* (1921), p. 4.
3. KEKEWICH, SIR G. W., *The Education Department and After* (1920), p. 21.
4. *Report from the Select Committee on Civil Service Appointments*, P.P. 1860, IX, Major G. Graham's evidence, Q. and A. 2591.
5. ibid., Q. and A. 2594.
6. HANSARD (Third Series), vol. 27, c. 1294 *et seq.*, vol. 29, c. 222–3.

7. Minute Book of the Committee of the Privy Council on Education, April 1839 to March 1841, P.R.O., Ed. 9/1.
8. *Order in Council*, 5 April 1852, P.P. 1852, XXXIX, p. 40 (376).
9. *Order in Council*, 28 February 1855, P.P. 1854-5, XLII, p. 113.
10. Debate of 16 March 1855 reported in HANSARD (Third Series), vol. 137, c. 640 *et seq.*
11. 19 and 20 Vic. c. 116.
12. HANSARD (Third Series), vol. 175, c. 373-4.
13. *Second Pakington Report*, P.P. 1866, VII, p. ix (123).
14. ibid.
15. *First Pakington Report*, P.P. 1865, VI, Granville's evidence, Q. and A. 1882.
16. ibid., Q. and A. 1887.
17. ibid., Lingen's evidence, Qs. and As. 56, 60, 361-5.
18. ibid., Salisbury's evidence, Q. and A. 1318 and 1345.
19. ibid., Adderley's evidence, Qs. and As. 963-6.
20. ibid., Lingen's evidence, Qs. and As. 65, 66 and 72.
21. ibid., Q. and A. 117.
22. ibid., Qs. and As. 58, 71-3.
23. ibid., Lowe's evidence, Qs. and As. 763-807, especially 763, 765-7 and 804-7.
24. ibid., Russell's evidence, Q. and A. 2890.
25. ibid., Granville's evidence, Qs. and As. 1902-5.
26. *Second Pakington Report*, P.P. 1866, VII, p. x (124).
27. *Newcastle Report*, P.P. 1861, XXI, F, Kay-Shuttleworth's evidence, Q. and A. 3008.
28. *First Pakington Report*, P.P. 1865, VI, Lingen's evidence, Qs. and As. 39-40.
29. *Report from the Select Committee on Education (Inspectors' Reports)*, P.P. 1864, IX, Lowe's evidence, Qs. and As. 706-7.
   See also FINER, S. E., 'The Individual Responsibility of Ministers', *Public Administration*, vol. XXXIV (1956). The whole question of the development of the concept of ministerial responsibility requires far more detailed analysis than is possible in this particular context.
30. *First Pakington Report*, P.P. 1865, VI, Lowe's evidence, Qs. and As. 620-1.

31. ibid., Bruce's evidence, Q. and A. 830.
32. ibid., Qs. and As. 827–8.
33. ibid., Granville's evidence, Q. and A. 1872.
34. ibid., Q. and A. 1873.
35. *Newcastle Report*, P.P. 1861, XXI, F, Chester's evidence, Q. and A. 716.
36. *First Pakington Report*, P.P. 1865, VI, Lingen's evidence, Qs. and As. 380–5, 523–9.
37. ibid., Qs. and As. 508–9.
38. ibid., Qs. and As. 50–5.
39. ibid., Granville's evidence, Qs. and As. 2309–11.
40. ibid., Salisbury's evidence, Q. and A. 1326.
41. ibid., Granville's evidence, Q. and A. 2462.
42. ibid., Salisbury's evidence, Q. and A. 1390.
43. BALL, N., op. cit., pp. 43–4.
44. '"Statesmen in Disguise": Reflexions on the History of the Neutrality of the Civil Service', *Historical Journal*, II (1959).
45. For a wider discussion of this subject, see WILLSON, F. M. G., 'Ministries and Boards: Some Aspects of Administrative Development since 1832', *Public Administration*, XXXIII (1955).
46. For a case study of this process, see PROUTY, R., *The Transformation of the Board of Trade, 1830–55* (1957).
47. *Report from the Select Committee on Miscellaneous Expenditure*, P.P. 1847–8, XVIII, A, p. xvi.
48. ibid., Greville's evidence, Q. and A. 3185.
49. Out Letter Book of the Privy Council Office, P.R.O., P.C. 7/6, folio 66, 8 August 1840.
50. *Report from the Select Committee on Miscellaneous Expenditure*, P.P. 1847–8, XVIII, B, p. 101 (107).
51. Minute Book of the Committee etc., P.R.O., Ed. 9/1, folios 278–9, 6 August 1840.
52. HURT, J. S., 'Harry Chester', *Journal of the Royal Society of Arts*, CXVI (January to March 1968) *passim*.
53. See reference 51.
54. ibid., folio 286, 9 November 1840.
55. ibid., folio 288, 9 November 1840.
56. *Newcastle Report*, P.P. 1861, XXI, F, Kay-Shuttleworth's evidence, Q. and A. 2444.

57. Quoted by SMITH, F., op. cit., p. 215.
58. COHEN, E. W., *The Growth of the Civil Service, 1780–1939* (1941), p. 86.
59. SMITH, F., op. cit., p. 219.
60. Lingen's *Report* is printed in P.P. 1847, XXVII, A.
61. Minute Book of the Secretary etc., P.R.O., Ed. 9/4, folio 153, 17 February 1865.
62. ibid., folio 172, 25 July 1865.
63. ibid., folio 229, 16 July 1867.
64. KEKEWICH, SIR G., op. cit., pp. 15–16.
65. *Report and Papers Relating to the Re-organization of the Civil Service*, P.P. 1854–5, XX, pp. 105–7
66. Minute Book of the Secretary etc., P.R.O., Ed. 9/4, folio 55, 5 March 1858; folio 69, 17 February 1860; folio 98, 28 April 1863; folio 260, 29 October 1868.
67. *Newcastle Report*, P.P. 1861, XXI, F, Kay-Shuttleworth's evidence, Q. and A. 6128.
68. *Reports of the Committees of Inquiry into Public Offices, and Papers connected therewith*, P.P. 1854, XXVII, p. 223 (225).
69. *Report from the Select Committee on Civil Service Appointments*, P.P. 1860, IX, Appendix V, pp. 362–412 (398–412) *passim*.
70. *Report of the Civil Service Inquiry Commission* (*Playfair Report*), P.P. 1875, XXIII, Cumin's evidence, Q. and A. 5418.
71. KEIR, SIR D. L., *The Constitutional History of Modern Britain, 1485–1937* (Third edition, 1948), p. 418.
72. *Civil Estimates for 1849–50*, P.P. 1849, XXXI, p. 3 (377).
73. *Civil Estimates for 1853–4*, P.P. 1853–4, LVIII, p. 3 (411).
74. *Reports of the Committees of Inquiry into Public Offices*, P.P. 1854, XXVII, Treasury Minute of 29 November 1853, p. 243 (275).
75. *Report from the Select Committee on Civil Service Writers*, P.P. 1871, XI, Lingen's evidence, Q. and A. 5.
76. *Report from the Select Committee on Civil Service Appointments*, P.P. 1860, IX, Chester's evidence, Q. and A. 4044.
77. ibid., p. xxii.
78. ibid., evidence from J. G. Maitland and H. Mann, secretary

and assistant secretary to the Civil Service Commission, Qs. and As. 46–8.

79. ibid., Q. and A. 44.
80. ibid., Chester's evidence, Q. and A. 4004.
81. HURT, J. S., op. cit.
82. Typescript copies of correspondence between the Education Department and the Treasury, P.R.O., Ed. 23/71, letter of 2 February 1857.
83. *Report from the Select Committee on Civil Service Super-annuation*, P.P. 1856, IX, 'Annual Expenditure of a married clerk, compiled by Mr Hammack of the Statistical Department, Registrar-General's Office, from information that can be relied upon', p. 451 (471).
84. Typescript copies of correspondence etc., P.R.O., Ed. 23/71, letters of 20 March 1867 and 20 August 1867.
85. ibid., letters of 28 December 1868 and 5 January 1870.
86. *Report from the Select Committee on Civil Service Appointments*, P.P. 1860, IX, Lingen's evidence, Q. and A. 3178.
87. ibid., Chester's evidence, Q. and A. 4044.
88. Quoted by MUSGROVE, F., 'Middle Class Education and Employment in the Nineteenth Century', *Economic History Review*, XII (1959).
89. KEKEWICH, SIR G., op. cit., pp. 8–9.
90. ibid., p. 9.
91. *Playfair Report*, P.P. 1875, XXIII, Appendix C (48), 'Case of the clerks of the Education Department', pp. 326–8 (360–2).
92. ibid., evidence from H. J. Gibbs and A. Bakewell, Q. and A. 5301.
93. ibid., Cumin's evidence, Q. and A. 5406.
94. ibid., Qs. and As. 5415–16.
95. ibid., Q. and A. 5432.
96. *Reports of the Committees of Inquiry into Public Offices*, P.P. 1854, XXVII, pp. 230–1 (262–3).
97. ibid., p. 234 (266).
98. ibid., p. 232 (264).
99. *Report and Papers Relating to the Re-organization of the Civil Service*, P.P. 1854–5, XX, pp. 105–7.
100. QUILLER-COUCH, SIR A., *Memoir of A. J. Butler* (1917), p. 88.

101. KEKEWICH, SIR G. W., op. cit., p. 5.
102. *Return of Persons in Public Offices*, P.P. 1862, XXXI, pp. 10–11.
103. *Return of the Number, Names, and Salaries of the Inspectors ...in Departments of the Civil Service*, P.P. 1871, XXXVII, pp. 20–5 (264–9).
104. *Report of the Royal Commission on the State of the University and Colleges of Oxford*, P.P. 1852, XXII, p. 61 (89).
105. ibid., p. 62 (90).
106. HANSARD (Third Series), vol. 232, c. 593.
107. *Report of the Royal Commission on the State of the University and Colleges of Oxford*, P.P. 1852, XXII, p. 149 (177).
108. *Report of the Royal Commission on the State of the University and Colleges of Cambridge*, P.P. 1852–3, XLIV, p. 156 (164).
109. ibid, p. 148 (156).
110. *Report of the Royal Commission on the State of the University and Colleges of Oxford*, P.P. 1852, XXII, p. 33 (61).
111. MALLET, C. E., *A History of the University of Oxford*, 3 vols (1924–7), vol. III, p. 287.
112. HUGHES, E., 'Civil Service Reform, 1853–5', *Public Administration*, XXXII (1954).
113. HANSARD (Third Series), vol. 174, c. 1187.
114. MUSGROVE, F., op. cit.
115. *The Times*, 17 March 1969.
116. Crockford's *Clerical Directories* (various editions).
117. *Report from the Select Committee on Education, Science, and Art (Administration)*, P.P. 1884, XIII, Sandford's evidence, Qs. and As. 238, 240 and 331.
118. BIRKENHEAD, S., *Illustrious Friends* (1965), pp. 113–18.
119. MEYRICK, F., *Memoirs of Life at Oxford and Elsewhere* (1905), pp. 83–4.
120. KEKEWICH, SIR G., op. cit., p. 5.
121. SNEYD-KYNNERSLEY, E. M., *H.M.I.* (1910), p. 58.
122. TUFNELL, E. B., *The Family of Tufnell* (1924), p. 8.
123. For Balliol men, see ELLIOTT, SIR I. D'O., *The Balliol College Register, 1833–1933* (1934); for old Rugbeians, see SOLLY, G. A., *The Rugby School Register* (1933).
124. WARD, W. R., *Victorian Oxford* (1955), pp. 130–5, 187, 243 and 280–1.

125. SANDFORD, E. G. (ed.), *Memoirs of Archbishop Temple* (1906), vol. II, p. 489.
126. LEVY, G., *A. H. Clough* (1938), p. 52.
127. LOWRY, H. F., *The Letters of M. Arnold to A. H. Clough* (Oxford, 1932), pp. 118 and 122.
128. PALGRAVE, G. F., *F. T. Palgrave* (1899), pp. 33, 41, 44 and 56.
129. BROOKFIELD, F. M. (ed.), *Brookfield's Sermons with a biographical sketch by Lord Lytton* (1875), *passim*.
130. *Rules, Regulations and Lists of Members of the Athenaeum Club* (1860, 1881), *passim*.
131. *Newcastle Report*, P.P. 1861, XXI, F, Cook's evidence, Qs. and As. 907–9.
132. ibid., Q. and A. 909.
133. Minute Book of the General Committee of the National Society, vol. V, folio 85, 9 November 1848.
134. LILLEY, A. L., *Sir Joshua Fitch* (1906), pp. 22–3.
135. ADAMS, F., *History of the Elementary School Contest in England* (1882), pp. 114–15.
136. *The Civil Service, Report of the Committee, 1866–8, Chairman: Lord Fulton* (cmnd 3638), p. 9.
137. *Minute of 19 May 1863*, P.P. 1864, XLV, pp. x–xi.

Chapter 7

1. HANSARD (Third Series), vol. 160, c. 1293.
2. *Bellairs's Report*, P.P. 1865, XLII, p. 14 (108).
3. *H.M.I. the Reverend J. Gordon's Report*, P.P. 1867, XXII, p. 304 (440).
4. *Civil Estimates for 1860–1*, P.P., 1860 XLIII, pp. 1–7 (43–9). The balance of the education vote was made up by a number of other items, the largest of these were 'Public Education, Ireland, £270,722' and 'British Museum £100,850'.
5. *Thirteenth Annual Report of the Poor Law Board*, P.P. 1861, XXVIII, p. 9.
6. *Civil Estimates for 1860–1*, P.P. 1860, XLIII, p. 18 (60).
7. HANSARD (Third Series), vol. 155, c. 341–2.
8. ibid., c. 342.

9. ibid., c. 342–3.
10. ibid., c. 343.
11. *Report from the Select Committee on Miscellaneous Expenditure*, P.P. 1860, IX, p. ii (474).
12. ibid., Laing's evidence, Qs. and As. 79–80; Table VI, pp. 212–13 (696–7).
13. ibid., Laing's evidence, Qs. and As. 155–7.
14. ibid., Qs. and As. 159–65 and 173.
15. *Third Report from the Select Committee on Civil Services Expenditure*, P.P. 1873, VII, evidence of R. E. Welby, a principal clerk to the Treasury, Q. and A. 241.
16. *Minute of 26 January 1856*.
17. *Minute of 20 January 1858*; for the work of the Science and Art Department see, DUKE, C., 'The Department of Science and Art: policies and administration to 1864', (Ph.D. thesis, University of London, 1966).
18. *Minute of 26 July 1858*.
19. Minute Book of the Secretary etc., P.R.O., Ed. 9/4, folio 70, 12 June 1860.
20. ibid., folio 71, 5 May 1860.
21. HANSARD (Third Series), vol. 164, c. 720.
22. *Newcastle Report*, P.P. 1861, XXI, B, Fraser's Report, pp. 73–4.
23. HANSARD (Third Series), vol. 160, c. 1293.
24. ibid., vol. 166, c. 180–81.
25. Minute Book of the Secretary etc., P.R.O., Ed. 9/4, folio 6, 9 June 1851.
26. Copies of Letters etc., P.R.O., Ed. 9/12, folio 333, 3 January 1855.
27. *Cook's Report*, P.P. 1850, XLIII, p. 42 (672).
28. *Watkins's Report*, P.P. 1850, XLIII, p. 137 (767).
29. *Kennedy's Report*, P.P. 1850, XLIV, p. 185 (189).
30. *Minute of 21 December 1846*.
31. *Watkins's Report*, P.P. 1854, LII, pp. 160–61.
32. Copies of Letters etc., P.R.O., Ed. 9/12, folio 55, 14 February 1848.
33. *The Code of 1860, s. 124*, P.P. 1860, LIII, p. 18 (292).
34. *Newcastle Report*, P.P. 1861, XXI, A, p. 172.
35. *Report of the Committee*, P.P. 1864, XLV, p. xviii.
36. *Newcastle Report*, P.P. 1861, XXI, A, p. 83.

37. ibid., p. 652.
38. PARSONS, B., *The Unconstitutional Character of the Government Plan of Education proposed by the Marquis of Lansdowne* (1847), p. 10.
39. HANSARD (Third Series), vol. 91, c. 974.
40. REED, A., *The Educational Dilemma : or results of the grants of public money for education in England* (1861), pp. 7, 8 and 13.
41. ibid., p. 23.
42. *Newcastle Report*, P.P. 1861, XXI, F, Chester's evidence, Q. and A. 713.
    Chester expressed similar views in his pamphlet, *The Proper Limits of the State's Interference in Education* (1861).
43. *Census of Great Britain, 1851*, P.P. 1852–3, LXXXVIII, A, 'Population Tables, II Ages...of the People', p. cccxlix.
44. HANSARD (Third Series), vol. 165, c. 211.
45. *School and the Teacher*, III (1856), p. 21.
46. HANSARD (Third Series), vol. 155, c. 331.
47. *Newcastle Report*, P.P. 1861, XXI, A, pp. 542–3.
48. HANSARD (Third Series), vol. 164, c. 716.
49. *Newcastle Report*, P.P. 1861, XXI, A, p. 294.
50. ibid., p. 243.
51. HANSARD (Third Series), vol. 165, c. 1139.
52. *Copies of all Memorials and letters...on the Subject of the Revised Code*, P.P. 1862, XLI, pp. 189 *et seq.*
53. HANSARD (Third Series), vol. 164, c. 734.
54. *Circular Letter to H.M.I.s*, 30 September 1857, P.P. 1857–8, XLV, p. 25.
55. *Copies of all Memorials etc.*, P.P. 1862, XLI, pp. 68–72 (256–60).
56. *The Times*, 11 July 1861.
57. LOWE, R., *Primary and Classical Education, An Address* (Edinburgh, 1867), p. 4.
58. HANSARD (Third Series), vol. 155, c. 319.
59. ibid., vol. 160, c. 1296.
60. ibid., vol. 164, c. 731–2.
61. ibid., vol. 165, c. 204.
62. *Bellairs's Report*, P.P. 1871, XXII, p. 24.
63. BROOKFIELD, F. M. (ed.), op. cit., p. xxv.
64. *E. P. Arnold's Report*, P.P. 1864, XLV, p. 27 (107).

65. *Watkins's Report*, P.P. 1864, LXV p. 169 (249).
66. *Newcastle Report*, P.P. 1861, XXI, B, Foster's Report, p. 343.
67. HANSARD (Third Series), vol. 165, c. 224.
68. *Blandford's Report*, P.P. 1851, XLIV, pp. 327–8 (731–2).
69. *J. D. Morell's Report*, P.P. 1859, XXI, A, p. 144.
70. *Watkins's Report*, P.P. 1857 (session II), XXXIII, p. 304.
71. *Brookfield's Report*, P.P. 1857–8, XLV, pp. 391–4; *Cook's Report*, P.P. 1859, XXI, A, pp. 22–3.
72. *H.M.I. the Reverend D. R. Fearon's Report*, P.P. 1865, XLII, p. 66 (160); *Bellairs's Report*, P.P. 1865, XLII, p. 17 (111).
73. *Newcastle Report*, P.P. 1861, XXI, A, pp. 294–5.
74. *Report of the Committee*, P.P. 1865, XLII, p. xxiv.
75. *The Revised Code, 1862, Article 48*, P.P. 1862, XLI, p. 9 (175).
76. *Report of the Committee*, P.P. 1871, XXII, p. 11.
77. HANSARD (Third Series), vol. 165, c. 237.
78. MARTIN, A. P., *Life and Letters of the Rt Hon. Robert Lowe, Viscount Sherbroke*, 2 vols (1893), vol. II, letter of 17 March 1882, p. 217.
79. *H.M.I. the Reverend C. J. Robinson's Report*, P.P. 1866, XXVII, p. 166 (348).
80. ibid., p. 172 (354).
81. *M. Arnold's Report*, P.P. 1867–8, XXV, p. 300.
82. *H.M.I. J. Fitch's Report*, P.P. 1865, XLIII, p. 168 (262).
83. *Report of the Committee*, P.P. 1866, XXVII, p. xvi (132).
84. *First Pakington Report*, P.P. 1865, VI, Lingen's evidence, Q. and A. 237; the Reverend W. Lea's evidence, diocesan inspector for Worcestershire, Q. and A. 2146.
85. HANSARD (Third Series), vol. 165, c. 239.
86. Minute Book of the Secretary etc., P.R.O., Ed. 9/4, folio 90, 12 January 1863.
87. *The Revised Code, 1869, Articles 40(b)2, 43, 46^2*, P.P. 1868–9, XX, pp. liii–liv.
88. Minute Book of the Secretary etc., P.R.O., Ed. 9/4, folio 104, 15 August 1863.
89. 37 and 38 Vic. c. 88, s. 39.
90. *C. J. Robinson's Report*, P.P. 1867–8, XXV, p. 220.

91. *First Pakington Report*, P.P. 1865, VI, the Reverend R. B. Girdlestone's evidence, Q. and A. 3275.

92. *Report of the Committee*, P.P. 1867–8, XXV, p. xxxv.

93. *Instructions to Inspectors*, September 1862, P.P. 1863, XLVII, pp. xvii *et seq.*, paras. 11 and 20.

94. *Newcastle Report*, P.P. 1861, XXI, A, p. 67.

95. HANSARD (Third Series), vol. 165, c. 207.

96. *Newcastle Report*, P.P. 1861, XXI, F, Kay-Shuttleworth's evidence, Q. and A. 2370.

97. ibid., the Reverend F. Temple's evidence, Q. and A. 2490.

98. *The Revised Code, 1862, Articles 67, 90, 132 and 133*, P.P. 1862, XLI, pp. 1–22 (167–88).

99. *Reports of the Committee*, P.P. 1862, XLII, Appendix I, p. 3 (59); P.P. 1866, XXVII, Appendix I, p. 183.

100. Details of the annual grants for 1860 are printed in P.P. 1863, XLVI, pp. 423 *et seq.*, those for 1865 are at P.P. 1866, XXVII, pp. 495 (677) *et seq.*, a list of schools in receipt of endowed income with particulars thereof for 1862 and 1863 is at P.P. 1864, XLIV, pp. 429 *et seq.*

101. *First Pakington Report*, P.P. 1865, VI, Kennedy's evidence, Qs. and As. 2604–5.

102. *Report of the Committee*, P.P. 1867, XXII, pp. xxxi and xliii.

103. *Report of the Committee*, P.P. 1868–9, XX, p. xxxvi.

104. *Report of the Committee*, P.P. 1866, XXVII, p. xv (131).

105. *H.M.I. the Reverend H. A. Pickard's Report*, P.P. 1871, XXII, pp. 143–4.

106. KEKEWICH, SIR G. W., op. cit., pp. 10–11.

107. Minute Book of the Secretary etc., P.R.O., Ed. 9/4, folios 168–9, 5 July 1865.

108. ibid., folio 139, 1 June 1864.

109. *Minute of 21 December 1846.*

110. *Special Reports on Educational Subjects*, P.P. 1898, XXIV, 'The Revised Code of 1862', p. 521.

111. ibid., 'Average Salaries of Teachers, certificated and uncertificated in Great Britain', p. 542.

112. *A Statement of the Examination to be passed by Acting Teachers in order to obtain a Certificate*, P.P. 1863, XLVI, p. 637.

113. *Report of the Committee*, P.P. 1867–8, XXV, p. xvi.

114. *Report of the Committee*, P.P. 1870, XXII, pp. xx–xxi.
115. MITCHELL, R. B. and DEANE, P., *Abstract of British Historical Statistics* (Cambridge, 1862), p. 343.
116. *Report of the Committee*, P.P. 1870, XXII, p. lxxxii.
117. *Report of the Committee*, P.P. 1870, XXII, p. lxxxii; *The Revised Code, 1862, Article 8lf, marginal note 8*, P.P. 1862, XLI, p. 12 (178).
118. For the part played by government departments in the innovation of social services in the Macclesfield area, see ROBERTS, D., *The Victorian Foundations of the British Welfare State* (New Haven 1960), pp. 310–15.
119. ROBERTS, D., 'How Cruel was the Victorian Poor Law?', *Historical Journal*, VI (1963).
120. LOWE, R., op. cit., p. 9.
121. *Report of the Committee*, P.P. 1868–9, XX, p. xxxvi.
122. *Newcastle Report*, P.P. 1861, XXI, A, p. 172.
123. ibid., p. 174.

Conclusion

1. DOYLE, SIR A. C., 'The Naval Treaty', *Memoirs of Sherlock Holmes* (1926 edn.), p. 208.
2. TRIMMER, S., *Reflections upon the Education of Children in Charity Schools* (1802), p. 7.
3. HANSARD (Third Series), vol. 199, c. 465–6.
4. ibid., c. 443.
5. *Report of the Committee*, P.P. 1878, XXVIII, pp. ix–x.
6. *Report of the Committee*, P.P. 1871, XXII, pp. ix and clxiv.
7. *Newcastle Report*, P.P. 1861, XXI, A, p. 34.
8. BLAKE, R., *Disraeli* (1966), p. 554; SMITH, P., *Disraelian Conservatism and Social Reform* (1967), p. 249.
9. HANSARD (Third Series), vol. 335, c. 1686.
10. CRUICKSHANK, M., *Church and State in English Education, 1870 to the present day* (1963), pp. 173–4.
11. BANKS, O., *The Sociology of Education* (1968), p. 139.
12. *Report of the Committee*, P.P. 1870, XXII, p. xiv.
13. *Report of the Committee*, P.P. 1878, XXVIII, p. xv (footnote).

14. HANSARD (Fifth Series, House of Lords), vol. 270, c. 1262.
15. TINKHAM, L., 'Learning One's Lesson', *Student Power* (Penguin Books, 1969), p. 94.
16. HANSARD (Fifth Series, House of Lords), vol. 270, c. 1253.
17. ibid., c. 1261.

Bibliography

Although this bibliography is not exhaustive, it includes all the sources, published and unpublished, to which reference has been made in the body of the book.

I Unpublished Material

At the Public Records Office
Education Department Papers
At the National Society, Westminster
Minute Books of the General Committee
At Hockerill College, Bishop's Stortford, Hertfordshire
Hockerill College General Register, 1852–73
Minute Book of various committees, 1847–60

II Official Publications

(*a*) The Voluntary Societies
British and Foreign School Society Annual Reports
National Society Annual Reports
National Society Monthly Paper
(*b*) Parliamentary Papers
(i) *Minutes of the Committee of the Privy Council on Education, 1839–58.*
Reports of the Committee of the Privy Council on Education, 1859 et seq.
(ii) *Reports of Royal Commissions, Select Committees, etc.*
1816 IV *Report from the Select Committee on the Education of the Lower Orders in the Metropolis.*
1818 IV *Second Report from the Select Committee on the Education of the Lower Orders.*
1818 *IV Third Report.*

1833 XVIII *Twenty-fifth Report of the Commissioners Appointed to Inquire Concerning Charities.*

1834 IX *Report from the Select Committee on the State of Education.*

XXVII *Report from Her Majesty's Commissioners for Inquiry into the Administration and Practical Operation of the Poor Laws.*

1835 V *Report from the Select Committee on Arts and Manufactures.*

VII *Report from the Select Committee on Public Charities.*

Report from the Select Committee appointed to Inquire into the Present State of the Education of the People in England and Wales.

1836 XXIX, A, *Second Annual Report of the Poor Law Commissioners.*

1838 VII *Report from the Select Committee on the Education of the Poorer Classes.*

XXVIII *Fourth Annual Report of the Poor Law Commissioners.*

1847–8 XVIII, A, *Report from the Select Committee on Miscellaneous Expenditure.*

1852 XXII *Report of the Royal Commission on the University of Oxford.*

1852–3 XLIV *Report of the Royal Commission on the University of Cambridge.*

1854 XXVII *Report on the Organization of the Permanent Civil Service.*

Reports of Committees of Inquiry into Public Offices, and Papers connected therewith.

1854–5 XX *Report and Papers Relating to the Reorganization of the Civil Service.*

1856 IX *Report from the Select Committee on Civil Service Superannuation.*

1857 (session II) III *Second Report of Her Majesty's Civil Service Commissioners.*

1860 IX *Report from the Select Committee on Miscellaneous Expenditure.*

Report from the Select Committee on Civil Service Appointments.

1861 XXI, A–F, *Report of the Royal Commission on the State of Popular Education in England and Wales (The Newcastle Report).*

1861 XXVIII *Thirteenth Annual Report of the Poor Law Board.*

1864 IX *Report from the Select Committee on Education (Inspectors' Returns).*

　XX *Report of Her Majesty's Commissioners appointed to inquire into the Revenues and Management of certain Colleges and Schools, and the Studies pursued and instruction given therein (The Clarendon Report).*

1865 VI *First Report from the Select Committee on the Constitution of the Committee of Council on Education (The Pakington Committee).*

1866 VII *Second Report from the Pakington Committee.*

1867–8 XXVIII, A, *Report of the Royal Commission on Schools not comprised within Her Majesty's two recent Commissions on Popular Education and Public Schools (The Taunton Report).*

1871 XI *Report from the Select Committee on Civil Service Writers.*

1873 VII *Third Report from the Select Committee on Civil Services Expenditure.*

1875 XXIII *Report of the Civil Service Inquiry Commission (The Playfair Report).*

1884 XIII *Report from the Select Committee on Education, Science and Art (Administration).*

1888 XXXV *Final Report of the Royal Commission appointed to Inquire into the Elementary Education Acts (England and Wales) (The Cross Report).*

1898 XXIV *Special Reports on Educational Subjects.*

　XXVI *Report of the Departmental Committee on the Pupil-Teacher System.*

1904 XXXII *Report of the Inter-Departmental Committee on Physical Deterioration.*

1906 XLVII *Report of the Inter-Departmental Committee on Medical Inspection and Feeding of Children attending Public Elementary Schools.*

Cmnd 3638 *The Civil Service, Report of the Committee, 1966–8,* Chairman: Lord Fulton.

(iii) *Miscellaneous Papers, Returns, etc.*

1839 XLI *Papers on Education.*

1841 XX *Instructions to Inspectors of Schools.*

1852–3 LXXXVIII, A, *Census of Great Britain, 1851, Population Tables.*

1860 LIII *Copy of Minutes and Regulations of the Committee of the Privy Council on Education, reduced into the Form of a Code.*
1862 XXXI *Return of Persons in Public Offices.*
    XLI *Copies of all Memorials and Letters...on the Subject of the Revised Code.*
1864 XLIV *Endowed Schools receiving Grants from Government in the years 1862 and 1863.*
Correspondence Relating to the Dismissal of Mr J. R. Morell.
1870 XLI *Return of Number, Salaries, and General Duties of Inspectors, etc.*
1871 XXXVII *Return of the Number, Names, and Salaries of the*
  and   *Inspectors...in Departments of the Civil Service.*
1875 XLII
1887 LXXXIX *Return of Wages published between 1830 and 1886.*
(iv) *Civil Estimates*
1849 XXXI *Civil Estimates for 1849–50.*
1853–4 LVIII *Civil Estimates for 1853–4.*
1860 XLIII *Civil Estimates for 1860–61.*

III Newspapers and Periodicals

Educational Guardian
Educational Times
English Journal of Education
Journal of Education
Journal of the Royal Society of Arts
Observer
Pupil-Teacher
Quarterly Journal of Education
School and the Teacher
The Times

IV Works of Reference

Athenaeum Club, *Rules, Regulations, Lists of Members.*
Bibliographie Universelle.
F. Boase, *Modern English Biography* (Truro, 1892–1921).
Burke's *Landed Gentry.*
Burke's *Peerage, Baronetage and Knightage.*

Crockford's *Clerical Directory*.
Dictionary of National Biography.
Hansard (Parliamentary Debates).
Mitchell, R. B. and Deane, P., *Abstract of British Historical Statistics* (Cambridge, 1962).
Public General Acts.

Considerable use has also been made of the registers of admission to the universities, the colleges of the universities, and the leading public schools.

V Contemporary Works

ACLAND, SIR T. D., *Some Account of the Origin and Objects of the New Oxford Examinations* (1858).

ANON., *Fifty Years of Progress in Education, A Review of the Work of the College of Preceptors, 1846–96* (1896).

'Schools for the Industrious Classes', *Central Society of Education Papers* (1838).

BELL, A., *Elements of Tuition*, 2 vols (1813–15).

BLOMFIELD, C. J., *Speech of the Lord Bishop of London on National Education on 28 May 1839 in Willis's Rooms* (1839).

CHESTER, H., *Education and Advancement for the Working Classes* (1863).

Hints on the Building and Management of Schools (1860).

The Proper Limits of the State's Interference in Education (1861).

COMMISSIONERS OF NATIONAL EDUCATION IN IRELAND, *Fifth Book of Lessons for the Use of Schools* (Dublin, 1865).

DAWES, R., *Remarks Occasioned by the Present Crusade against the Educational Plans of the Committee of Council on Education* (1850).

DENISON, G. A., *Church Education. The present state of the Management Clause Question* (1849).

H.M.S.O., *Correspondence of Messrs Longmans and John Murray with Lord John Russell* (Dublin, 1851).

KAY-SHUTTLEWORTH, SIR J., *Four Periods of Public Education* (1862).

The Moral and Physical Condition of the Working Classes Employed in the Cotton Manufacture in Manchester (1832).

KAY-SHUTTLEWORTH, SIR J. and TUFNELL, E. CARLETON, *Reports on the Training of Pauper Children* (1841).

LANCASTER, J., *Outlines of a plan for educating ten thousand poor children* (1806).

LOWE, R., *Primary and Classical Education, An Address* (Edinburgh, 1867).

MARSH, H., *The National Religion the Foundation of National Education* (1811).

MORELL, J. R., *The Case of J. R. Morell* (1864).

PARSONS, B., *The Unconstitutional Character of the Government Plan of Education proposed by the Marquis of Lansdowne* (1847).

REED, A., *The Educational Dilemma : or results of the grants of public money for education in England* (1861).

ROBINS, S., *The Church Schoolmaster* (1850).

RUNCIMAN, J., *Schools and Scholars* (1887).

SINCLAIR, J. (ed.), *Correspondence of the National Society with the Lords of the Treasury and with the Committee of Council on Education* (1839).

TILLEARD, J., *On Elementary School Books* (1860).

TRIMMER, S., *A Comparative View of the New Plan of Education promulgated by Mr Joseph Lancaster* (1805).
Reflections upon the Education of Children in Charity Schools (1802).
The Sunday-School Catechist (1788).

TUCKFIELD, H., *Letters to a Clergyman* (1840).

WIGRAM, J. C., *Elementary Arithmetic* (1832).
Practical Hints on the Formation and Management of Sunday Schools (1833).

VI Later Secondary Works

(i) *Books*

ADAMS, F., *History of the Elementary School Contest in England* (1882).

BAGWELL, P. S., *The Railway Clearing House in the British Economy, 1842–1942* (1968).

BALL, N., *Her Majesty's Inspectorate, 1839–49* (Edinburgh and London, 1963).

BANKS, O., *The Sociology of Education* (1968).

BELLOT, H. H., *University College, London* (1929).

BINNS, H. B., *A Century of Education, 1808–1908* (1908).

BIRKENHEAD, S., *Illustrious Friends* (1965).

BLAKE, R., *Disraeli* (1966).

BROOKFIELD, F. M. (ed.), *Brookfield's Sermons with a Biographical Sketch by Lord Lytton* (1875).

BRYANT, G. E. and BAKER, G. P. (eds.), *Lucas of Hitchin (1804–61)*, 2 vols (1934–5).

BURGESS, H., *Enterprise in Education* (1958).

BURNS, W. L., *The Age of Equipoise* (1963).

CLARKE, A. K., *History of the Cheltenham Ladies' College* (1953).

COCKBURN, A. and BLACKBURN, R. (eds.), *Student Power* (1968).

COHEN, E. W., *The Growth of the Civil Service, 1780–1939* (1941).

CRAIK, H., *The State in its Relation to Education* (1884).

CRUICKSHANK, M., *Church and State in English Education* (1963).

EDMONDS, E. L. and O. P., *I Was There, the Memoirs of H. S. Tremenheere* (Eton, Windsor, 1965).

FIDDES, E., *Chapters in the History of Owen's College and of Manchester University* (Manchester, 1937).

GRIER, R. M., *William Allen* (1889).

HOBSBAWM, E. J. and RUDÉ, G., *Captain Swing* (1969).

JONES, M. G., *The Charity School Movement in the Eighteenth Century* (Cambridge, 1938).

KEIR, SIR D. L., *The Constitutional History of Modern Britain, 1485–1937* (1938).

KEKEWICH, SIR G., *The Education Department and After* (1920).

LEVY, G., *A. H. Clough* (1938).

LILLEY, A. L., *Sir Joshua Fitch* (1906).

LOVELL, A. L., *The Government of England*, 2 vols (New York, 1908).

LOWRY, H. F., *The Letters of M. Arnold to A. H. Clough* (Oxford, 1932).

MACDONAGH, O., *A Pattern of Government Growth* (1961).

MALLET, C. E., *A History of the University of Oxford*, 3 vols (1924–7).

MARSH, P. T., *The Victorian Church in Decline* (1969).

MARTIN, A. P., *Life and Letters of the Rt Hon. Robert Lowe, Viscount Sherbroke*, 2 vols (1893).

MEYRICK, F., *Memoirs of Life at Oxford and Elsewhere* (1905).

MOZLEY, J. R., *In Memoriam, F. C. Hodgson* (1921).

PALGRAVE, G. F., *F. T. Palgrave* (1899).

PIMLOTT, J. A. R., *The Englishman's Holiday* (1947).

PROUTY, R., *The Transformation of the Board of Trade, 1830–55* (1957).

PUDNEY, T. S., *The Thomas Cook Story* (1953).

QUILLER-COUCH, SIR A., *Memoir of A. J. Butler* (1917).

SANDFORD, E. G. (ed.), *Memoirs of Archbishop Temple*, 2 vols (1906).

SMITH, F., *The Life and Work of Sir James Kay-Shuttleworth* (1923).

SMITH, P., *Disraelian Conservatism and Social Reform* (1967).

SNEYD-KYNNERSLEY, E. M., *H.M.I.* (1908).

TAYLOR, SIR H., *The Statesman* (1836). Reprinted with an introduction by H. J. Laski (Cambridge, 1927).

THOMPSON, E. P., *The Making of the English Working Class* (1963).

THOMPSON, F. M. L., *English Landed Society in the Nineteenth Century* (1963).

TODD, A., *On Parliamentary Government in England: its origin, development and practical operation*, 2 vols (1867–9).

TROPP, A., *The School Teachers* (1957).

TUFNELL, E. B., *The Family of Tufnell* (1924).

TYLECOTE, M., *The Mechanics' Institutes of Lancashire and Yorkshire before 1851* (Manchester, 1957).

WARD, W. R., *Victorian Oxford* (1965).

WATSON, D. F., *Professional Solidarity among the Teachers of England* (New York, 1927).

WEST, E. G., *Education and the State* (1965).

WOOD, E. M., *The Polytechnic and Quintin Hogg* (1932).

WOOD, SIR H. T., *A History of the Royal Society of Arts* (1913).

(ii) *Articles*

ARMYTAGE, W. H. C., 'A. J. Mundella as Vice-President of the Privy Council, and the Schools Question, 1880–5', *English Historical Review*, LXIII (1948).

CLARK, G. KITSON, '"Statesmen in Disguise": Reflexions on the History of the Neutrality of the Civil Service', *Historical Journal*, II (1959).

CROMWELL, V., 'Interpretations of Nineteenth Century Administrations: An Analysis', *Victorian Studies*, IX (1966).

FINER, S. E., 'The Individual Responsibility of Ministers', *Public Administration*, XXXIV (1956).

GOLDSTROM, J. M., 'Richard Whateley and Political Economy in School Books, 1833–80', *Irish Historical Studies*, XV (1966).

HUGHES, E., 'Civil Service Reform, 1853–5', *Public Administration*, XXXII (1954).

HURT, J. S., 'Harry Chester', *Journal of the Royal Society of Arts*, CXVI (1968).

MACDONAGH, O., 'The Nineteenth Century Revolution in Government: A Reappraisal', *Historical Journal*, I (1958).

MUSGROVE, F., 'Middle-Class Education and Employment in the Nineteenth Century', *Economic History Review*, XII (1959).

PARRIS, H., 'The Nineteenth Century Revolution in Government: A Reappraisal Reappraised', *Historical Journal*, III (1960).

PERKIN, H. J., 'Middle-Class Education and Employment in the Nineteenth Century: A Critical Note', *Economic History Review*, XIV (1961).

ROBERTS, D., 'How Cruel was the Victorian Poor Law?', *Historical Journal*, VI (1963).

STONE, L., 'Literacy and Education in England, 1640–1900,' *Past and Present* (Number 42, February 1969).

SUTHERLAND, G., 'The Study of the History of Education', *History*, LIV (1969).

WEST, E. G., 'Education, A Framework for Choice', in BEALES, A. C. F., *et al.*, *Papers on Historical, Economic and Administrative Aspects of Choice in Education and its Finance* (1967).

WILLSON, F. M. G., 'Ministries and Boards: Some Aspects of Administrative Development since 1832', *Public Administration*, XXXIII (1955).

(iii) *Theses*

DUKE, C., 'The Department of Science and Arts: Policies and Administration to 1864', (Ph.D. thesis, University of London, 1966).

GOLDSTROM, J. M., 'The Changing Social Content of Elementary Education as reflected in school books in use in England, 1800–70', (Ph.D. thesis, University of Birmingham, 1968).

HURT, J. S., 'The Development of Elementary Education in the Nineteenth Century; the roles of the Committee of the Privy Council on Education and the Hertfordshire Gentry', (Ph.D. thesis, University of London, 1968).

JOHNSON, J. R. B., 'The Education Department 1839–64: a study in Social Policy and the Growth of Government', (Ph.D. thesis, University of Cambridge, 1968).

KINGSFORD, P. W., 'Railway Labour, 1830–70', (Ph.D. thesis, University of London, 1951).

Index

Index

Moseley, Rev. H. (H.M.I.)
  career 68 n.
  classroom conditions 68
    quotn 2, 75–6
  teacher training 97,
    100–101, 110 quotn 3,
    117, 126, 201
Mundella, A. J. biog. 67 n.
  Revised Code (1883) 67

National Society
  founded 16–17
  subscriptions to 25–7
  postal privileges 25–6
  relations with Education
    Department 28–38, 41,
    92–4, 159–60, 202
  training of teachers 87,
    88–91, 95
  Revised Code 202–4
  see also 18, 47, 50
National Union of (Elementary) Teachers 145,
  225–6
Newcastle Commissioners,
  Report of
  inspectorate 39 quotn 2,
    57, 59, 61, 62, 83–4
  school buildings 72–3, 75
  pupil-teachers 92, 135
  assistant teachers 97
  teacher training 101–2,
    104–5, 107–9, 119,
    138–40
  status of teachers 140–41,
    143–4, 145–6
  payment by results 155
  Kay-Shuttleworth 160,
    199

school attendance 195–6,
  200, 207, 221–2
Nicholls, Rev. A. B. 131
Norris, Rev. J. P. (H.M.I.)
  career 47 n. 3
  school managers 47
  school inspection 59, 63 n.
    2
  supply of teachers 104–5
  Athenaeum Club 182
Northcote, Sir S. 12, 180,
  187–8

Otter, Dr W. 33, 40
Oxford Movement 18, 45
Oxford University
  examinations 129, 133, 175
  Education Department
    172–82
  Balliol College 175, 177,
    181–2
  Oriel College 175
  Fellowships 175–6, 178–9
  cost at 177
  see also 43

Pakington, Sir J. career 149 n.
  2; 150, 186 quotn 1,
  199
Palgrave, F. T. examiner
  176, 178, 182, 183
Patronage, see Civil Service
  and Education Dept.
Peel, Sir R. 21, 91–2, 178
Pickard, Rev. H. A. (H.M.I.)
  career 215 n.
  log-books 215–16
Place, F. career 20 n.
  on secular education 20
  on monitorial schools 89